JACK NICHOLSON

JACK
NICHOLSON

FACE TO FACE

Robert David Crane
and
Christopher Fryer

M EVANS AND COMPANY INC   NEW YORK NY 10017

M. Evans and Company titles are distributed in
the United States by the J. B. Lippincott Company,
East Washington Square, Philadelphia, Pa. 19105;
and in Canada by McClelland & Stewart Ltd.,
25 Hollinger Road, Toronto M4B 3G2, Ontario

Library of Congress Cataloging in Publication Data

Crane, Robert David.
  Jack Nicholson, face to face.
  Includes index.
    1. Nicholson, Jack. I. Fryer, Christopher, joint author.
PN2287.N5C7   791.43′028′0924   74-31265
ISBN 0-87131-175-5
ISBN 0-87131-176-3 pbk.

To Barbara and David Fryer
and Patrick Morrow
—C.F.

To My Father
—R.D.C.

one

INTERVIEWS

two

COMMENTARY
with Christopher Fryer and Robert David Crane

three

FILMOGRAPHY
—Casts, Credits, and Synopses for Jack Nicholson's films

four

ACKNOWLEDGMENTS

INDEX

one

INTERVIEWS

JACK NICHOLSON

The varied and highly successful film career of Jack Nicholson began in 1958 with *The Cry Baby Killer*. Before that, the native of Neptune, New Jersey, bounced around studios, doing odd jobs and occasional television shows, such as *Divorce Court* and *Matinee Theatre*. After doing *The Cry Baby Killer*, Nicholson was featured in a series of psycho-exploitation films with titles like *Little Shop of Horrors, Too Soon To Love, The Terror,* and *The Wild Ride*. In the latter film, Nicholson first became acquainted with Monte Hellman, who was a significant influence behind Nicholson's venture into film production. Together, in 1964, they did back-to-back films in the Philippines, *Back Door To Hell* and *Flight To Fury,* Nicholson scripting the latter. Then in 1965 they co-produced two low-budget Westerns, *The Shooting* and Nicholson's screenplay entitled *Ride In The Whirlwind,* both of which Nicholson co-starred in. Although these films didn't catapult Nicholson into stardom, they supplied him with a good store of film-making knowledge and added a few significant credits.

In 1967 Nicholson teamed up with director Richard Rush and cinematographer Laszlo Kovacs to do an A.I.P. classic, *Hell's Angels On Wheels,* in which Nicholson played a disillusioned gas-station attendant who tries to find nirvana atop a Harley-Davidson 1000. In this film, we get our first look at the Nicholson anti-heroic, soul-searching loner in quest for the real America. It is Nicholson's schizophrenic ability to be aloof and concerned at the same time that gives his character an unapproachable level of brilliance. Then, in 1968, Rush and Kovacs again called on Nicholson to star in the Dick Clark Production of *Psych-Out*.

The team that worked so successfully in *Easy Rider* came together for the first time in *The Trip*. In *The Trip,* scripted by Jack Nicholson and starring Peter Fonda and Dennis Hopper, Nicholson's own experiences with LSD are realized in a not too successful way on the screen, despite that fact that Peter Fonda called it the most beautiful script he had ever read. Nicholson's writing efforts also took a beating in the ill-fated experimental 1968 production of *Head,* starring The Monkees rock group, directed by Bob Rafelson, and co-produced by Rafelson and Nicholson.

In the nick of time came the chance to fill in for a fellow actor in another low-budget bike film, called *Easy Rider*. Needless to say, the film was an astounding success and a revolution in film, and netted Nicholson his first Academy Award nomination.

In an attempt to salvage an otherwise ludicrous film, a part for Jack Nicholson was written into *On A Clear Day You Can See Forever,* in hopes of attracting the youth market. It didn't work, partially because of the writing and partially because of Nicholson's uninspired performance. His powerful personage, his formula of honesty and virtuosity, are out of place in this dreary, commonplace musical.

Adrien Joyce's profound profile of a disenchanted intellectual offered Nicholson one of his best roles to date, and captured for him a second Academy Award nomination for his role of Bobby Dupea in *Five Easy Pieces*.

Nicholson's directorial debut, *Drive, He Said,* which he co-scripted and co-produced, is a film about alienation. It is so complex that after one viewing of the film the audience is alienated from it. This raises an interesting problem. Is the film successful because we, the audience, don't give a damn at the end, or is it a failure because we don't give a damn at the end? Even though the film failed at the box office, the chances are that it will someday be viewed as a very important work.

Following *Drive, He Said,* Nicholson gave a brilliant performance in Mike Nichols' *Carnal Knowledge,* in which he played a man in search of the perfect female, oftentimes measured in terms of curves here and inches there. The film deals with frustration and male ideologies, and as a result, Nicholson became a kind of symbol for male chauvinism. Despite the fact that there is little nudity in the film, the subject matter and frank language caused the film to be banned in parts of the country, and it wasn't until recently that the Georgia Supreme Court ruled the film was not obscene.

Nicholson also did a standout cameo in Henry Jaglom's film, *A Safe Place*. This sometimes uneven film had Nicholson in a role where he seemed most like himself, probably due to the fact that that is what Jaglom had in mind and consequently had no script for Nicholson.

Then, after more than a year's absence from the

screen, Jack reappeared in *The King of Marvin Gardens*, Bob Rafelson's first film since *Five Easy Pieces*. This offbeat film brought Jack back to his birth state, but in the strange environment of Atlantic City, New Jersey, during the bleakness of winter. Though the film received mostly favorable reviews, it was very flat at the box office and closed without much of a run. Some critics knocked Nicholson for his subdued portrayal of David Staebler, but the part showed not only his remarkable versatility but a bit of daring as well.

After being off the screen for almost another year, Nicholson emerged as a lifer in the Navy in Hal Ashby's *The Last Detail*. His brawling, cursing, hard-nosed portrayal of Billy "Bad Ass" Buddusky brought him his third Academy Award nomination. Nicholson did receive the Best Actor Award at the 1974 Cannes Film Festival for *The Last Detail*, although he lost the Oscar to Jack Lemmon.

Another facet of Nicholson's talent was unveiled in Roman Polanski's *Chinatown*, in which he played a Bogartesque private eye opposite Faye Dunaway. This high-tension murder mystery was hailed by many critics as the best American film of 1974. Along with *Last Detail, Chinatown* firmly re-established Nicholson as a major box-office attraction as well as bringing rave reviews from most major critics for his performance as J. J. Gittes.

Nicholson went on to star with *Last Tango in Paris*'s Maria Schneider in Antonioni's *The Passenger*, Michelangelo's first American film since *Zabriskie Point*. The story centers on a reporter who assumes the identity of somebody else, but is really struggling with his own identity.

Though he had only a cameo role, Nicholson made his on-screen singing debut in Ken Russell's *Tommy*, the film version of The Who's rock opera. He did sing a song in *On a Clear Day*, but it was cut from the finished film. Rounding out his 1974 schedule were appearances opposite Warren Beatty in the Mike Nichols' comedy, *Fortune*, and in Milos Forman's version of Ken Kesey's novel, *One Flew Over the Cuckoo's Nest*.

Our first interview with Jack Nicholson took place at Nicholson's hilltop house off Mulholland Drive. We were cordially greeted by Nicholson, who was wearing a blue bathrobe with a bat pin on the lapel. Our conversation was held informally in his living room, which overlooks a redwood-decked pool and Coldwater Canyon below. The walls of the living room are adorned with memorabilia from his movies, a poster in Japanese advertising *The Terror*, and a large photograph of an oil field reminiscent of the locale of *Five Easy Pieces*, among others. His large bookshelf is representative of his neo-intellectualism and research of movie roles, bearing such titles as *The Psychedelic Experience* and *Napoleon*.

After clearing the room of the friends and people who are constantly dropping in, we settled into his brown suede sofa for our two-hour talk.

In doing research on Jack Nicholson and his films, one issue that seemed to be clouded over was the editing of *Easy Rider*, which played an important part in the success of the film. We decided to clear up this issue immediately.

Question: Who edited *Easy Rider*?

Nicholson: The editing was all supervised by a combination of Dennis Hopper and his financial people, Bert Schneider and Bob Rafelson. I worked on some of it, but it was all under their supervision. What I did was more like literary editing. In other words, I didn't go back into the film or anything like that. They offered me an opportunity to edit the section of the film that I was in—again, all was subject to Dennis' feelings. Also, from the time I came in through to the end, I had an editorial position about it. I put the "trip" sequence in, which everyone hates so much. I put it together out of the film they had. Within my editing, of course, were things that other people had solved already. You know, mine was just a repositioning and refining; more of a polish job than an editing job.

Question: Having been connected with films from all angles, which aspect of film-making do you like best?

Nicholson: Well, because I've done all these things I can't come to any real conclusions about that. I first produced about six or seven years ago, so I was twenty-seven, and the problems for a twenty-seven-year-old producer in Hollywood are enormous. I mean a producer in Hollywood doesn't go out and rent trucks at U-Haul, and go down and pick the wardrobe at Western Costume. I was originally drawn to films by a creative drive, so I really did almost any film. I'm not much involved in what the credits are. When I'm *involved* in a film I'll do whatever they want me to, and if I'm producing I'll do whatever I can. I mean, acting is where I started so I feel most comfortable in that role. I've only been a failure as a director, so I'd like to get back into that and make use of the experience that I've had. It's also the most expressive part of film-making. I don't like the fact that if you're going to author, write, and oversee a film, it takes a minimum of a year. That's a lot to give to a film. I mean, it was a lot for me to give to *Drive, He Said,* particularly since not a lot of people went to see it.

Question: Why do you think *Drive, He Said* failed at the box office?

Nicholson: Everyone analyzes these things. I don't know. What I do, just to keep myself creatively sharp, is to say, "Well, it was a perfectly satisfactory film to me." I mean, I honestly feel, based on the way I do things, that I did the best that I could do with it, which is all you can ask of yourself. That that apparently wasn't good enough is the way people get bogged down in rationalizations. Most people say, "Well, it's simply ahead of its time," or "the subject matter was already dead." [Despite the fact that it was reviewed as the only film on its subject that was fairly honest, that didn't help it.] People say, "So what? Who gives a shit about what the college kids are doing?" Even the college kids, they were interested in Dick Powell and Ruby Keeler and so on by that time.

Question: Back at the time of your Westerns, *Ride the Whirlwind* and *The Shooting,* Roger Corman turned down a project of yours. What was that project?

Nicholson: It was a very down, dry, Antonioni, British naturalist-influenced look at the malaise of Hollywood. Something that Roger wouldn't really be interested in producing, but he did recognize that it was pretty good writing; it *was* at that time. All I knew about writing was how to write scenes that you would act well. It read well.

Question: But it took more than two days to shoot.

Nicholson: Right.

Question: Do you have plans to do that project you showed to Corman?

Nicholson: No. God, I wrote that—it must be getting close to ten years old now.

Question: How did you shoot *Little Shop of Horrors* in two days?

Nicholson: The interiors only. In other words, there are a lot of exteriors in the film involving one character, and all of that was done in post-production. The two days' shooting was all rehearsed and the sets were prelit; they were all on one sound stage. There were about six sets. All we had to do was go over and plug it in, set up the camera, and shoot it.

Question: Did working with Mike Nichols on *Carnal Knowledge* give you any insights into your own work as a director?

Nicholson: Yes. He's a very precise director. The environment he creates on the set, the pace he shoots at, where he places his concerns, his own temperament related to the moment to moment experience of directing, the kind of dialogue he gives to his characters—all of those things. He's very specific about it. There are a lot of things that he does that are worthwhile for anyone to adapt. It won't ultimately affect the contour of your product, but it'll affect the efficiency you get it together with.

Question: Do you have a favorite film of yours, so far?

Nicholson: No. I'll tell you; early on when I first got started in movies, I think because you haven't made many, most of your thinking about it is very theoretical. That was because of where I was functioning, in low-budget films and horror movies that everyone else hated, including my best friends. I had a conversation with a guy I lived with for a while, another actor, and he frankly admitted, even though he was in classes with me, that he never thought I'd be a good actor because of all these horror pictures. Because of that, sort of protectively, I started thinking of my own work as a body of work, and then because I had the idea, I noticed that a lot of other people did, too. That sort of reinforced it, and that's the way I feel about it.

There are a lot of projects where I think I might just pluck characters out of the situations that I left them in in several movies and as a writing exercise take them and let them see how they feel about one another. For instance, the way it comes out is all for your own creative seeds. The way I relate to inside things is, I don't relate them to the audience. It's an inwardly energizing thing for me that gets my particular insight and feelings about a character going.

I used an actor in *Drive, He Said* who is really a director, who has done two movies, one of them the Western and the other one *Drive, He Said.* At the last minute I changed the name of his character to the name of the character he had played in the other movie. Because he was a one-scene character, for my own point of view, I just assumed this was the man's grandson. Because he was the only survivor of the Western, the film I wrote. All of the characters are killed during the course of the film. All of the outlaws are hung; the two guys who are in the *Les Misérables* situation are killed, one immediately and the other during the chase. The leading character does get away. The outlaw, the part this guy played, is the look-out man who falls asleep, and the posse just rides off, and that's the last you see of him in the film. That's the kind of way I relate to film as a body of work.

Question: Can you explain the ending of *The Shooting*?

Nicholson: People, especially early in their careers, before they get into a very practical thing about their work, where they become purely film people and less literate as they go along, hope that their films become more literate. For instance, Dennis Hopper borrows from his understanding of art history in his movie forms. I mean all of the anti-art of the Dada painting period is what he's into. I mean there's nothing unique about it except in films it's unique, but it's all borrowed from this other medium. The philosophy of exposing your own work, or saying that it's shit or whatever.

In this case, Carol Eastman [Adrien Joyce] was using a more poetic technique where you were using one image, the falling effect at the end was really an attempt to, like a tuning fork, reattune those impulses that you got from watching the Jack Ruby piece of footage, which at the time this was written was a very strong piece of footage. The whole thing was a brother chasing a brother. Carol was trying to translate the experience of writing poetry, where you write well to the side of an issue, and hope that the film touched the corresponding realities; but it's very high-blown, you can never talk to a major studio about it. But in terms of where we were at at the time it was very logical. I mean everyone understood what impressionistic poetry was, and parallel writings and all of these things that are really literature and that you don't get to bring up in film discussions.

In this case, it was the brother catching the brother, and it was a sort of a revealing of the existentialist character of the hunter. I always seem to put in a couple of lines in everything Carol does. She hates to write thematically summating scenes. The character Warren [Oates] plays is accused by the girl in the film. She says, "What's all this shit? What are you giving me all this moralistic stuff for? You're out here. You're helping me track. What's all that?" And he tries to take the rationale of the hunter, and her point of view is: "But every hunter knows that the reason for a hunt

is the kill. So whatever you think you're doing here, by tracking your own brother—that's your function. You're leading someone to a kill; there's no cop out to it." That was sort of the thematic center of the movie.

Question: How close to you are the characters that you portray? Are they an extension of yourself?

Nicholson: Well, I work very personally. Their life and their behavior are extensions of my behavior. There are always differences between the characters and myself. I always try to translate them into what I consider to be a positive philosophy for that character. In other words, I try to feel what they're doing is what they think is the right thing, and is what is motivating their life force, and so on. In that way, it's an extension of my thinking, but it's separate. You know, I feel it's their thinking, and so in that way I'm separate.

An interesting phenomenon is that sometimes, because—this has only happened in the last three films, and never in any of my other work—you play a character that creates such a large impression abroad that you're suddenly dealing with the feedback from the character you played and it will change your life after it's done. You see what I mean? I suppose I'm a symbol for male chauvinism at this time because of *Carnal Knowledge*. That's not an area that I've ever been particularly into. I've always had very good relationships with women, but because the new women I meet have this super image of me, I'm in the dialogue whether I want to be or not. In that way, they move closer to you after you're done with them.

Question: So in that respect, has being a movie star affected your relationships with people you're close to?

Nicholson: Absolutely. It's impossible to be a movie star and not have all of your relationships affected. All of them.

Question: Do you think it has affected your acting?

Nicholson: It has affected the rhythm in my acting. I don't do as much as I used to.

Question: How careful were you in choosing scripts after *Easy Rider*?

Nicholson: I've only accepted one job since *Easy Rider* that I wasn't already committed to do, so for all the offers that you get after becoming a known actor, that's pretty selective. It's based on the fact that you can only do so much work, and I've really done as much or more work than any-

14

Nicholson and a high-class call girl played by Rita Moreno in a scene from Carnal Knowledge

body around. I've never been able to afford to be selective before this, so now I am, and I'm affected by it.

Question: We understand that Stanley Kubrick approached you about doing Napoleon.

Nicholson: We had some talks about it. I was very excited about it, and still would be, but at this point I've been involved with him and it for so long that it's moved into the realm of semi-daydream. I don't think it's ever going to come together, knowing how directors are, whims and

fancies and all. It would be good. I have a counterplan if he doesn't use me. I'll just make a better movie.

Question: Would you like to work with him?

Nicholson: Oh, yes. I said that kiddingly, of course. He's gotten me interested in the character. I've done research on it, and all that kind of stuff, and I'd like to use that material sometime.

Question: Is the character you play in *The King of Marvin Gardens* the antithesis of your previous roles?

15

Bruce Dern (l.) and Nicholson in The King of Marvin Gardens

Nicholson: This character is sort of what I call a one-roomer. He's Kafkaesque. He lives alone. He's a radio monologist. He's an intellectual, and he's been institutionalized. He has a brother who's very colorful; he is not. He's involved strongly in the absurdities of life. He's not really in with society, he's like a bystander. He's very laid back. Most of his thinking and verbosity relate to his work and not to his life. He's a watching character in life.

Question: Was your script for *The Trip* based mostly on your own experiences with LSD?

Nicholson: Mostly. And what was going on in my life at the time. I felt that it would be good, I always shoot for well-rounded, unbiased views of a subject. That a film doesn't have a "one thing"

that you can say about it makes it hard to sell. That's the reason why I don't like to work with producers that say, "Wow, here's the film that . . ." Although I never felt that the film was going to be one-hundred per cent brilliant, or really cover it or anything like that, I felt that my being in it with Roger [Corman], between the two of us would make it a more well-rounded film than if he had made it alone or with someone who didn't have as much experience with the drug as I did.

Question: Have you acted while under the influence of drugs?

Nicholson: Yeah, I've acted stoned.

Question: Does it help or hinder your performance?

Nicholson: For the most part it's not a help.

16

For one thing, being stoned takes a lot of your energy away, and that's difficult. The only thing I can really say being stoned has helped me with creatively is writing. It relaxes you, and makes you a little more content to be in a room all by yourself. It's easier to entertain yourself mentally. It produces a lot of shit, too. Most writers have more trouble writing than coming up with quality stuff.

Question: How much of a script ever makes it to the screen?

Nicholson: Well, with *The Trip* it was a particularly small amount that made it. I knew that what they wanted to do was to show the interior mind of fantasy, which is wrong for the movies. It's like the exact thing you don't want to do when you put a novel on the screen, unless the fantasy has a scenario of its own. The images are much too specific to go as fantasy images, so I did that part of it with subliminal cuts, or very fast cuts, and not a lot of them at once, so that you almost couldn't see them. That was the technique that I thought

would be wise to use. Even though I went to the trouble of specifying the content of each image.

The idea of the whole script was seeing the objective camera-eye experience of the guy actually on the trip when he's got the orange. He can't believe it. Or seeing an actor when he's regressed to where he's three years old, and talking that way or not, but seeing the objective experiences by juxtaposing the little flashes as a key to what might be going on. That was really the balance of my script. They blew up all of the fantasy images and minimized the juxtapositions greatly by doing so. So in that case, while all the words are said, but maybe sixty per cent of the images make it to the screen, I feel the big idea of the script is completely left out.

Question: Why did you do *On A Clear Day You Can See Forever*?

Nicholson: Primarily for the bread. At that time I needed it, and I used it for what I needed it for. I'm glad I did it. It didn't hurt me much. It was a good experience. I would never do anything

Barbra Streisand discusses her love life with step brother (Nicholson) in On a Clear Day You Can See Forever.

totally for the bread. My character in that film could have been good. The subject of that film could have been ESP. My character had a very good philosophy. He was the girl's former step-brother who sort of loved her from that relationship and hears that she's going to get married, and comes to wish her well. And at the same time, to see what the real situation is, and should that relationship not be what it appears to be, he would offer himself as an alternative. It's not an uninteresting character; it's just sort of aside from the film. The part was added; it wasn't in the original script. They added it, I should have known, to try and get a young audience and blah, blah, blah. It wasn't well understood by the people who wrote it. I couldn't even be as helpful as I can be sometimes. My suggestions were almost incomprehensible. I was supposedly playing a rich hippie. They asked me to cut my hair for the part. Ways of dressing, and stuff like that, they didn't really understand. I don't mind failing at jobs, it takes some of the pressure off.

Question: Do you feel you've reached a plateau?

Nicholson: I've reached a plateau, but I've never been that much in love with my own work. I still even have a certain desperation of wanting to get beyond it, and into where I'm doing it the way I think I can. I don't have very strong limitations because of the kind of worker that I am.

Question: But you sound as though you want the "bubble" to burst. Do you want to get back to the basics?

Nicholson: No. Hmmm, the basics. I don't want to get back to anything. I want to go on. I want to open it up.

Question: Do you feel you've reached a plateau with the "Jack Nicholson anti-hero" role?

Nicholson: I think it's easy to group things as anti-heroic. But you could put all American films under that. I think the films that I've done show a lot of diversity, and more than most actors ever get to show. Most of the characters are very, very different. When you really look at it, they're tremendously different. The overall themes of the pictures you can group as anti-heroism, but you can say that about every other picture made in those years, or in the last ten years since *Angry Young Men.* I don't vibrate too strongly to that kind of character.

I think the most impressive thing about me, unbeknownst to most people, is that I've done twenty to twenty-five films, and none of the characters are alike. That's a lot of characters to have played already. Even the two Westerns I did, which were filmed back to back, had characters that were totally different. You could easily categorize them if you wanted, but in reality they're totally different. I feel I function well and properly in that area. That's not an area I'm concerned about. It's other things, you know, like styles rather than the thematic content of the characters, that I'd like to open up.

Question: Do you think that your characters in *Carnal Knowledge, Five Easy Pieces,* and *Easy Rider* represent the hero of the seventies?

Nicholson: Well, I think that's where it has been. None of these characters covers a lot of people. I mean they do cover a lot of people, but they don't cover everyone. They're specific characters, but many people identify with them totally. Some would only identify with one out of the three, and others all three. I think heroes are bailing out the boat today, trying to get it so that it'll go. I think it's a very difficult transitional period. I think that people are overloaded now, not only with information, but with philosophical interpretations of that information. Coupled with that is the fact that most human beings are in a striving situation where their mind is not really quiet. They have some reason, if it's only a girl, a job, a car, or a trip, a piece of merchandise, a piece of work, or something, that is futurized. Coupled with that is the fact that most people that I talk to, you can find a counterargument to what they believe most deeply in their souls that's as effective as what they have, and give them sources for it that are readily available to them. So I think that people are suspended. They don't really know, nor, maybe, should they know. I think the person that could be considered heroic is someone who's trying to keep his own humanity vital, and trying, as I say, to bail out the boat and keep the thing ready to go if it's called upon. I don't know of anybody who's strongly in action at this moment, who I would consider to be a true heroic figure.

Question: Who were your heroes?

Nicholson: Early on, I would say Brando was a big hero of mine as a worker, something he's never let me down in, I might add. Whatever it is that makes him continue to grow. Castro was a hero of mine. I like Galbraith, Dylan. I haven't had lots of heroes. Joe DiMaggio, when I was a kid. Some friends of mine have always seemed heroic to me. Women that I've lived with have given me a lot in that area; things they go through.

Question: Do you or have you ever believed in the Method style of acting?

Nicholson: Yeah, I went to the Studio.

Question: Do you find that that helped you at all?

Nicholson: I agree with Strasberg's definition: anything that works; that's the Method. That's what he says, that's what he's always said. Everything else you've read has been a misunderstanding by whoever happened to be writing a bad interview on it. He has certain techniques related to certain problems for people who are trying to expand their thinking into a larger communications area. They should be trying to find out what's specific about them. That's the central idea. If it works; that's the Method.

Question: Do you place any value on the Oscar at all?

Nicholson: Personally, I feel that the fact that I didn't get nominated [for *Carnal Knowledge*] probably cost me a couple of hundred thousand dollars. If that's value, yes.

Question: Why do you think *Carnal Knowledge* was overlooked in the Oscar race, except for Ann-Margret?

Nicholson: A combination of things. I think a lot of people hated the movie, and when people hear that they think it's because it's a bad movie. And in the conglomeration that goes on during any kind of an election, it's mainly what you hear and not what you think. Many of the people don't even see all the movies. A lot of people are voting for friends; a lot of people are doing a lot of things. But the movie's a negative comment, and a fairly good one. Certainly honest, related to the artists, Mike Nichols and Jules Feiffer, who put together the concepts. Pretty well executed, I think. People resent Mike's success very strongly. Some people do. That hurts the movies. People will get tired of seeing you get nominated. No one is particularly upset that I didn't get nominated for an Oscar, even people that think that I should have been. They don't go, "Ah, what a disaster this is." A certain part of them says, "That's good, he's been getting too much attention, anyway."

Question: Would you like to win one?

Nicholson: I wish I had already won one. The only thing that's tough about it is going up to accept it. In other words, everything else is just like a real nice party. It's nice if your peer group singles you out.

Question: Do you think that being outspoken, like Peter or Jane Fonda for instance, hinders your career in the film industry?

Nicholson: Well, you can't do a hundred jobs a year, so you may alienate fifty people, but there might be eight or nine people who might give you jobs because you're outspoken. I don't think it helps or hinders you in that way. I think as an artist your public statements are best made in the work. That's my own feeling, but that's because I care a lot about the work. I'm not a public figure as such.

Question: Do you feel that Peter Fonda has grown into a puppet figure for the youth culture?

Nicholson: My feeling about Peter is that he doesn't have that much weight to where he's sweeping people's minds. When he touches upon something they agree with, obviously they say, "I agree with Peter Fonda about that," but I don't know if Peter has the kind of strong rhetoric that really changes someone's mind, or way of thinking.

Question: There's been a lot of conjecture about the similarities between *Five Easy Pieces* and *Some Came Running*. Do you know if Carol Eastman was influenced at all by *Some Came Running*?

Nicholson: Yes. I know she was not. Well, then, can it also be derivative of *Sweet Bird of Youth* or *You Can't Go Home Again*? You can go on forever.

Questions: Do you see a lot of films?

Nicholson: Yes. I see as many as I can. It's my entire social life, almost. I like to do other stuff. This year I've been skiing in Switzerland, visiting friends in the Bahamas in the sun. All of these things I enjoy doing. During none of these do I see movies. But when I'm in L.A.—in New York I don't see movies—in New York I see movies there that you never see here. They're the movies that get to the Los Feliz theater five years later, that you can see first-run in New York. The noncommercial, more serious, European films by nonstar directors. That's what I see when I go to New York. But in L.A. that's about all the social movement there is, unless you guys can tell me if there's something else happening.

Question: How much has the L.A. culture affected your life?

Nicholson: I've been living here over half my life, and I'm very into it. I like it here. I see L.A. win people over who totally hate it when they first come here. There's no other city that you can compare it to. That's one of the charming things about it.

Question: If you were not associated with film-making, what would you like to be doing?

Nicholson: Well, I don't know a lot about other jobs. If I were not working at what I would like to be working at, I suppose I'd rather not be working at all. I guess the situation would create its own action. I think in terms of writing, or something like that. Being a lawyer might be interesting, but only at a serious level. I think that I have enough grace of person that if I were forced to be the complete public servant, cleaning the toilets, it wouldn't destroy my life, or my ego, or any of that. But it's not something that I would choose to do.

Question: Do you think you could survive if you were to lose your house, or your car, et cetera?

Nicholson: Yeah, I think I'm very well set up in that way. You say, lose the house. I bought this house before I had much bread, knowing that if I lost it totally overnight, that it was the action of doing it where the positive thing was, not the ownership of it. In other words, once you buy a house you're no longer in that problem, "Shall I rent it, shall I buy it? Is it grim to own a house? Am I a political reactionary?" You're out of it, because the act is over. You sit there and enjoy your house, or you don't. That's the positive part of that action. As you see, a lot of people here are enjoying the house.

I like sleeping on the floor. It wouldn't bother me at all. I could even deal with public disgrace or vilification. None of that would bother me, because I've done it all already.

Question: Do you ever find yourself mentally and emotionally through with a part before you ever start shooting?

Nicholson: No, I almost always grow with it during the filming. One of the things that was wrong with my work in low-budget film-making was that you always shot them in two weeks. I've noticed that my own rhythm in a movie that's shooting eight to twelve weeks, which is average, I'm really not to the character for the first week and a half. I've got it, and I know where I want it to go in my mind, and so on. I don't have this diamond-hard gem carved out, but I've got all the impulses. You tend to overcharacterize when you first step into a part. You tend to show it. You know, this guy's got a limp or he doesn't like dogs. Where once you've done it for a while, you know the actor's thinking about it all day long, you get with it much more. In a two-week picture all you've done is that early stage of overshowing a character.

Question: What did you think of *A Safe Place*?

Nicholson: I think it's a good movie in a lot of ways, and not a good movie in a lot of other ways. Something that I'm in is hard for me to have a qualitative judgment about. The movie has been cut down. A large portion of the audience finds the movie tedious and pretentious, so the impulse is always to make something like that shorter. I liked the movie when it was longer. Did you ever see any of the early Warhol pictures, like *Sleep?* This is just a social phenomenon seeing a movie. There comes a moment when you get beyond that a little bit. I think this movie's rhythm got beyond that. I don't think the movie was improved in editing. The first time I saw the movie I liked it best.

I really resent critics—because all the critics that have rapped Dennis Hopper's movie, Henry Jaglom's movie, my movie, and a few others, while extolling all these others and making them into blockbusters, are now, six months later, saying, after they have created the commercial groove, "This tendency to imitate all movies, where are the new movies coming from, blah, blah, blah?" Well, they're destroying them. Obviously anybody, just by concidence who's a new film-maker at this age, my age, Henry's age, Dennis' age, even if he's never read him, is being influenced by McLuhan. You only get one major communications figure every decade, and McLuhan is it. What does he say? Nonlinear configuration, fragmentary blah, blah, blah. Well, they're pissed off because they're from the linear tradition, and they want their critical bias to be universal. No critical bias is ever universal, and now they're complaining, but they're offering no encouragement.

My film, *Drive, He Said,* has been censored a lot, for frontal nudity and simple language, so I've had a lot of talks with censors. My point ultimately gets to be, "Yes, yes, I understand that you're trying to protect the unsuspecting public from rampant immorality, but where is your positive responsibility to an artist?" I have affidavits from Arthur Schlesinger, Jr., and an entire psychiatric conference. When we got the rating change from an X to an R, everyone agrees that the movie is not immoral, and the movie should be seen by young people, blah, blah, blah. But, "Hey, it's too tough, and other films will creep in under, you know what I mean." But my point is, where is your responsibility to the creative artist who's honestly trying to deal with the problems that are causing the difficulties? I'm not trying to exploit them. There's not one ounce of pandering in that movie.

I don't try to make myself attractive to young people. It's a movie that's actually critical of young people, while accepting their momentary values.

Well, you asked me about Henry's movie. I could destroy the movie; I could tell you everything about it that doesn't work. I could tell you why it doesn't work, because I know him so well. He's an old friend of mine, who almost everyone else I know has trouble with. He's a *provocateur;* he loves it that they hate his movie. But he's still back there, he's still in postnatal *tristesse.* He can't get out of New York. He's still trying to pump the movie over. I mean, that happens to you. I felt it. I haven't been able to get anything off. I can't write. I'm fucking confused. I've never wanted to be an incredibly popular artist, in that way, but my feeling always was that if you did a piece of quality it would have some kind of quality response. In fact, I suppose I've gotten my just deserts in that area. The movie *Drive, He Said* was talked about more than the average complete failure.

I'm not a huckster. I don't go into a financier and say, "Hey, I'm gonna give you this and . . . so give me the million," and then I go fuck him over in the street. If I'm going to make a movie with somebody's money, I'm going to include their point of view, and try to get their money back, anyhow. Or if I don't present that, I'm going to say, "Look, you'll lose some money, are you interested in making a statement," and they'll say, "No," and I'll go someplace else. I'm confused in that area. I honestly don't know what the movie said to people. The movie is, in its own way, a very avant-garde movie. It's very fragmentary; it's got a tough point of view. If it were any other subject, that's what they would say about *Drive, He Said.* That's what they say about Henry's movie. That's what they say about Dennis' movie, *The Last Movie,* but they resent all these movies on those grounds. That's fair, we all have other weaknesses in our work. I'm very oblique, oblique as an actor. I go the hard way every time. I don't say this is a good thing. It's a disguise in its own way. It's like a guy who knows that he's good-looking, and is constantly making himself not good-looking by dressing weird, and being grimmed out all the time.

I originally think of these things as, "Who gives a shit what they say in the papers?" After you've read two hundred reviews—I've got one critic that I pay attention to, and he happens to not know too much about acting. He does like me a lot.

Question: Who is that?

Nicholson: Stanley Kauffmann. I mean, he does know a lot about actors, but he has this certain thing—for instance, he didn't like Marlon in *The Godfather.* He gives great reasons, all of which, to me, are things that I think are good about actors. But as far as his context, and what he says about the film, I read him and I pay attention to him.

So, my first reaction of these guys is, "Who cares?" They'll write this, they'll write that, and so on. But in reality it affects these people; I know how it affects me. But that's not what criticism is intended to be. I think a certain portion of criticism should be for educating the audience to the product. In other words, if they just have a little idea about what they're supposed to be looking for, they'll enjoy it more.

Question: Are there any current social problems that you would change if you could?

Nicholson: I don't know what I'd do about it, or how to change it—but the concept of public honesty. I'm just curious about what the race would be like if our deceptions were less easy to pull off. Just from working in the movies and seeing the guys out in the streets saying, "Ah, that guy's a bum. He's a son of a bitch." And here's a guy that's doing his job, he's a little lame, but he's better than the guy calling him a bum.

We've built up an incredible matrix of communications capacity, but we keep communicating the same things over and over again. I always wonder what would happen with a really well-informed public. I mean, here's the reasons, here's the philosophy, here's the moves.

Question: You said in an article that you have to attack the audience and their values. Why?

Nicholson: Because it's good for them, I think. I don't think you should attack the good things and say, "Eat your children," or anything like that, although very valid artists have said that. It's part of the overall energy of the piece that you provoke, that you restir the values, so that it doesn't become something that's in the mental world. It should be more fluid and not so concrete. It's hard to keep up with the changing realities of the day. There are certain endless values that we don't really have, but have always existed.

Also, I think it's good for the person making something to have this point of view, because if you don't feel that way you wind up pandering to the audience. I find that the worst that can be done. There are subtle ones, though. Say, *The God-father,* for instance, for in a time of chaos and a time where there are ninety Presidential candidates, and no centralization, what do people want, but a nice little God figure, a father figure, to take care of them. I know that everyone in the world thinks that somewhere there are twelve gray-haired men in an oak-paneled room who sit down and decide the affairs of humanity. It doesn't exist. It's about as nonexistent as a gray-haired God sitting on an alabaster throne. But I think that everyone believes that "they" are getting together this week. In that way I think that *The Godfather* tends to pander to that aspect.

Question: Do you consider the audience when you write or act in a film?

Nicholson: Yes. I take a relatively classical position, in other words, the fact that *Drive, He Said* in ten years will be shown around, and people will say, "Hey, why didn't I see that before?"

doesn't mean a lot to me. Because I classically do work for the moment. It's not fair to make a movie for ten years from now.

I'm very eclectic in style. I'm not one who says, "You must shoot at eye level, no dollies, you must always move when you're moving." So when I think about a movie I think about styles, which ones to use or not to use, new ones, or where to try and force it open. I never, as an actor, consider the audience.

Question: Do you get embarrassed when you look at your previous work?

Nicholson: Sure. I haven't done anything that I thought was perfect. Or even close to it. You see stuff, and you're just doing bad stuff. It's embarrassing because you couldn't do much better, because you didn't want to. Whenever that moment came, it was "action, go," and you just weren't up to it.

Question: Do you have a favorite film of yours?

Nicholson giving instructions to a young actor in his directorial debut, Drive, He Said

Nicholson: I don't have a big favorite. I like them all. I like them according to what they've done for me. I feel I've been very consistent. I've always been trying to function to the best of my abilities according to the development of my abilities at that time, and so in that way I don't have a favorite film. I like the Westerns a lot, because of what they meant to me, starring, producing, the kind of honesty they had. I liked the last three films that we talked about [*Easy Rider, Five Easy Pieces, Carnal Knowledge*]. A better standard applied to them, more time taken, less obstacles to overcome in the work. All three of those films are all good. Out of them all, I would say that philosophically I'm most attuned to the character in *Five Easy Pieces*. I have a little bit different feeling about things that *Carnal Knowledge* puts forward. I see it differently. In other words, there is a third male character that's not represented in that movie, if you're just trying to peel archetypes down. It tends to pose as a superstructural movie. I wish there were things in there that were not in there, but there's nothing in it that I don't like.

Question: Do you like the ending to *Five Easy Pieces*?

Nicholson: Yes. It had lots of endings. Bob [Rafelson] likes to work with lots of endings. He doesn't like to know the ending while he's shooting it. He likes to feel like something's going to happen. He usually ends up shooting the ending that he had, but he's constantly weird at night. He bores you to death.

Question: Does your character come to any resolution at the end?

Nicholson: Yes. Leave his present situation.

Question: Where is he headed?

Nicholson: Canada. He'll pick up some job there, just like he left someplace and picked up the job at the oil fields.

Question: Do you like to be recognized?

Nicholson: I have the most control over that of any celebrity I've known. I really am a very changeable-looking person. I like being recognized. I love it in New York, because they're really into that. They recognize you everywhere. Even I can't hide out much in New York. It's nice; there are a lot of lines in New York.

Question: Do you feel that people approach you as Jack Nicholson, movie star, rather than Jack Nicholson, person?

Nicholson: That's true, but at the same time, everyone approaches everyone with an erroneous image of what it is they're approaching. People have as complicated a way of approaching A as they do B, so it really doesn't make that much difference. I mean, obviously a lot of people take a lot of effort showing you that they're not going to relate to you.

Question: Do you always tell the truth?

Nicholson: No. I always try to.

Question: When do you find that you can't?

Nicholson: Well, number one, if it involves the confidence of another person. That's a problem I haven't had for some while. But in a relationship when you're with a chick and you ball somebody else, it's hard to tell the truth in that situation. I've tried it. I find that's the general area of most people's dishonesty. Some people can't even be honest about what they think at a given moment, because they think it will down them socially. But I always tell the truth in that situation. I sort of relish it. I've cleared a few rooms in my day.

I can be rude; and I don't admire the quality at all. Then I have this horrible tendency, after I've been rude, to say, "What did I do?"

Question: What qualities don't you like in people?

Nicholson: I don't like the head ushers of the world. Officious people. People whose office in life keeps them out of touch with reality.

Question: Do you like working?

Nicholson: Yes, I do like working. I wanted to go right back to work after I finished *The King of Marvin Gardens*, but there wasn't anything around that I could do.

Question: What do you do in your spare time?

Nicholson: I lay around and read, I run every day, play a little tennis, see films. Eat light.

Roger Corman

One of the necessary stops for a young actor or director in Hollywood has been to work on a Roger Corman project. Jack Nicholson, of course, is the most famous alumnus of Corman films, having appeared in *Little Shop of Horrors, The Raven,* and *The Terror* among others, and having written *The Trip.* Writer-director Francis Ford Coppola (*The Godfather, Patton, The Great Gatsby*) wrote and directed his first feature-length film, *Dementia 13,* under Corman's supervision in 1963. Peter Bogdanovich (*The Last Picture Show, What's Up, Doc?*) worked as an assistant to Corman on *Wild Angels,* and later was given a chance to write and direct his first film, *Targets,* starring Boris Karloff in 1968.

Roger Corman started his own career in 1954 as the author of *Highway Dragnet.* By the late fifties and early sixties he was producing and directing films like *House of Usher, The Pit and the Pendulum, Premature Burial, The Man With the X-Ray Eyes,* and *The Raven.* By the mid-sixties he was into producing and directing motor-psycho-acid films like *Wild Angels* and *The Trip,* occasionally interrupted by a *St. Valentine's Day Massacre,* or, much later, *Boxcar Bertha.* The amount of Corman productions greatly decreased toward the end of the sixties and the early seventies. He was clearly evaluating what he had accomplished and what new direction he would take. At the end of 1972 came the announcement that Roger Corman and his New World Distribution Company would be releasing Ingmar Bergman's latest film, *Cries and Whispers.* Corman, at this time, has also arranged the distribution of Federico Fellini's newest film, *Amarcord,* his first since *Fellini's Roma.*

Roger Corman in his New World Productions office

After a few phone calls between Roger Corman and ourselves, the interview was scheduled to be conducted at his penthouse offices on the Sunset Strip in Hollywood.

Upon arriving, we waited in his outer office, admiring the French film posters decorating his walls and checking grosses of current films in his show-business magazines.

As we were ushered into his spacious, but simple office, we were informed that he was in the middle of negotiations on a project (possibly Bergman's film) and that he was sorry that he could only offer us limited time for an interview.

Question: Can you tell us how you first discovered Jack Nicholson?

Roger Corman: As a director I enrolled in an acting class of Jeff Corey's, feeling I wanted to know a little bit more about acting. I wasn't trying to be an actor, but just to add to my working background as a director, and Jack was in the class and I was very much impressed by his work. So Jack and I became friends, and we worked together in a number of films. This was about ten or twelve years ago.

Question: How many films has Jack done for you?

Corman: I don't even remember because some of them were very small. For instance, there was a picture I shot in two days, called *The Little Shop of Horrors,* in which he played—and he was really great in it—a masochist in a dentist's office. The whole scene was shot in an hour, maybe two hours. Other pictures he played the lead in, so including everything he was in, maybe ten or twelve pictures.

Question: We understand that Jack was supposed to get the lead in *St. Valentine's Day Massacre,* but turned it down for a smaller role.

Corman: He wasn't supposed to get the lead; he was supposed to get one of the leads. What it amounts to is the various members of the gang were going to be killed. He could have had one of those roles, which were not co-starring roles but featured roles. Each one had one basic vignette, and then the death. They were good sequences; Bruce Dern played one of them, and Bruce is doing well now. I tried to choose really good actors for each one of them, and build a little section of the picture around them. And Jack, who needed some money at the time, preferred to play a driver who had something like one or two lines in the picture, but because of the break in the schedule the driver had to be in certain places, and therefore worked a longer period of time and made more money. I don't blame him, I can well understand that.

Question: What kind of director-actor relationship did you have with Jack?

Corman: I would say a very good relationship, because Jack and I were friends and I had a sincere appreciation of his work as an actor, and I think we always got along well. As a matter of fact, there was one picture I shot called *The Terror,* where he and Boris Karloff played the two leads. Now what happened was I was shooting the picture for AIP, and there were some very big sets from a horror picture called *The Raven,* so I decided to make a movie. I had very little money, and all I could do was go on those sets for two days. Jack came in and we shot for those two days. All I had was a script for those two days, and then I shut down. That portion of the film was union, and the rest of the picture was made nonunion, and since I'm personally signed with the unions I couldn't direct. I had various friends of mine directing the rest of the picture, and Jack would appear every now and then whenever we needed him. Francis Coppola, who directed *The Godfather,* directed three or four days on the film, and then he got a deal with Seven Arts and signed with them. Then Monte Hellman, who directed *Two-Lane Blacktop* and a few pictures, came in and directed Jack for a few days. And then Jack Hale and Dennis Jacob each directed for a day, and finally at the end of it there was still one day left to finish, and by that time I'd run out of friends of mine who were

directors who'd come around for a day, and Jack said, "Well, I'm as good as these guys; I'll direct it." So Jack directed himself the final day of shooting, and we put the picture together, and the story line was not completely logical, because each director had a different interpretation as to what we were doing, but the net result is that the picture was really quite successful for a slightly disjointed story and multiple-directing styles.

One of the things that made the picture go, despite a constantly changing plot line—and the plot line did change from time to time with the different directors—was that Jack as an actor was able to bring a certain continuity to his work and hold it together under very difficult circumstances.

Question: Is there any one thing that you can say Jack learned from working with you?

Corman: I think he probably gained more of a sense of what production is like than most actors do, because I shoot fairly inexpensively, on low budgets, and quickly. And Jack understood what my problems and what the problems of the company were, because I was a young director and he was a young actor, and we had various young actors and writers, and everyone knew each other and we would discuss the problems. So as a result of working that way he's learned much more about the technical aspects of motion pictures, working behind the camera as well as in front, than most actors, and I think it's helped him. I wouldn't overstate it. It isn't necessary for an actor to know these things, but I think it helps. It makes him able to appreciate what's going on, and be able, possibly, to relate a little better to the director. Of course, Jack has now directed and has written; Jack wrote several scripts for me, and will eventually have a career as an actor and a writer-director.

Question: On the other hand, do you think you picked up anything from working with Jack?

Corman: Yes, I probably did. Because I think Jack is both an intelligent and an intuitive actor. He has the ability to plan and to develop his character, yet at the same time be able to come onto the set and make changes under pressure, to be free, and to improvise, and I think I gained a little more insight into the actor's problems from working with him. I also think I gained some flexibility, because I started as a writer and did not have much experience working with actors.

Question: How much time did you give an actor to prepare for a role?

Corman: Not a great deal for this reason: the Screen Actor's Guild says if you put an actor on salary for rehearsals, you must pay him for that time. So there wasn't much formal rehearsal time, but I would try to get the script to him at least a couple of weeks before the picture, so that he could read it and so that I could discuss it with him. Then we had one or two actual paid rehearsal days. A good actor like Jack would spend time on his own working with the script, and working on his character, and meeting with his leading lady and doing some rehearsals or improvisations together.

Question: Why do you think he remained virtually unknown until *Easy Rider*?

Corman: It's hard to say. I think it might be because he isn't the standard type of leading man that was popular when he started. When he started it was the tail end of the Rock Hudson-Tab Hunter school, with the straight, clean-cut, all-American actor playing the lead. Jack was an offbeat lead. I think in the long run he's a more intelligent and more versatile and more interesting actor, but when he was very young, say in his twenties, and a lot of other people were going under contract with major studios primarily because of their look, he didn't have that look. Now in the long run that may have helped him, because he then worked around town in independent pictures, in low-budget films, sometimes in television, sometimes in major films, and he got much more experience and developed as an actor. He developed his craft playing many different roles, not always the lead. He very seldom would play the straight juvenile that a more traditional classic face on a man might have lead him to play.

Question: Do you think he'd be where he is today if it hadn't have been for these films?

Corman: I wouldn't say all of these films are responsible for his success, but I think they helped him. I think they gave him more depth as an actor, more assurance, more confidence, so that when the time came he was able to grasp it. For instance, in *Easy Rider* it seems quite clear to me that much of what he brought to that role, he brought himself, that he added to what was there in the script. The script provided something; Dennis Hopper, who's a talented director, provided something; but Jack, himself, provided more and put it all together. The role was, to a large extent, a tribute to his work. Although I wouldn't discount, in any way, what was in the script, because I was originally connected with the script, but through a variety of reasons faded away, primarily due to an argument betwen Peter Fonda and AIP.

Question: What was the last movie you and Jack worked on together, and why was it the last one?

Corman: The last one was *The Trip*, which he wrote, and the film immediately after that was *Easy Rider*, and the reason that *The Trip* was our last film was because *Easy Rider* was an instant success and his salary went sky-high.

Question: What happened between the written page of *The Trip* and the screen version?

Corman: First of all, the written page had some more difficult things in it to shoot than could be done on a low-budget picture. I shot the picture in three weeks, and we couldn't shoot everything there, but I'd say we shot ninety per cent, maybe ninety-five per cent, of what was there. Peter Fonda was essentially right when he said that AIP ruined the film. AIP became frightened in the middle of the picture. They let us shoot essentially what was in the script with one or two minor changes, which we went along with because we felt they didn't hurt, but then after the film was over they demanded greater changes in the cutting. And then after I had finished the film and had gone to Europe on another project; they made some drastic changes in it. They cut several sections out that we felt were important. They changed the ending in a slightly innocuous way. They put some sort of an optical break across the film to imply that it had been a bad trip, and the break or crack would mean that the character's personality and his life were now cracked and destroyed, which was total nonsense. The original ending was to leave it open, and let the audience decide whether it had been a good or a bad trip.

AIP was very worried at the time about the anti-drug propaganda, and they turned the ending, which hurt the film cinematically and also changed the meaning. I think they also put some preface on it saying, "We are against drugs." Though the changes did hurt, they didn't destroy the picture completely.

Question: Where do you think Jack Nicholson ranks among American actors today?

Corman: I think he's one of the most important American actors for this reason: he's one of the few leading men who will take a chance on extremely unusual and offbeat material, and I think that's one of the reasons he will probably stay a major actor for most of his life, or as long as he wants to work. He will not run the danger of being typecast and tossed aside when that particular type of film fades from favor. His willingness, if not eagerness, to go to offbeat material will stand him in good stead. I think somewhere along the line he will make a mistake, and one or two of those films will be unfortunate choices, but I think this is the nature of the game.

Question: Do you have a favorite performance of his?

Corman: Either *Easy Rider* or *Five Easy Pieces,* but then again, *Carnal Knowledge* was very good. And I wouldn't discount his work in *Little Shop of Horrors.* He was very good in that. See, that's the funny thing. Jack was very good in a lot of little pictures that were forgotten. There was one little picture that was directed by a high-school drama teacher in northern California called *The Wild Ride* that had an essentially amateur cast, in which he played an "alienated youth" and was really very good. And he proved, as he's proved other times, that without an experienced director, but with a role he could understand, he could do good work by himself. So I would not discount some of those early pictures, which might be said to be in the learning process, but in that learning process he turned in some extremely good performances.

Question: Do you think Jack Nicholson's screen personality has changed over the years?

Corman: I think the personality has remained, but I think it has changed and modified, become a little bit more sophisticated, a little more polished, as he became more sure of his craft and himself. But the basic man is still the same man.

Question: What was the funniest experience you had working with Jack?

Corman: I remember in *Little Shop of Horrors* he was in a scene in the dentist's office, where he and another actor were dueling—one of them had a dentist's drill and the other one had a scalpel, and in the master shot they knocked over the dentist's chair, and I was shooting this picture in a

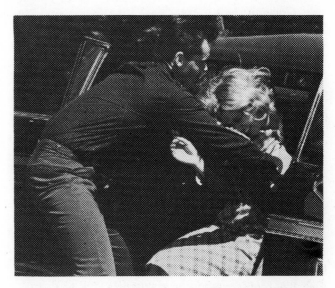

Nicholson as hot rodder Johnny Varron in The Wild Ride

two-day schedule, and I turned to the prop man and asked him how long it would take to reassemble the dentist's chair, and he said it was about two hours' work, and Jack and I said simultaneously, showing how much his thinking was like mine at the time, "That scene ends with the collapse of the dentist's chair."

Question: What kind of relationship do you have with him now?

Corman: We're still friends. I don't see as much of him as I did at one time, simply because his career has gone in one direction, and mine in another.

Question: Do you foresee any future collaborations?

Corman: There might be. If I had the right project for Jack, I certainly would be delighted to work with him, but at the moment I really don't have anything that I think would be suitable for him, and then I would not want to offer him a script that I thought was not right.

Question: Can you characterize Jack Nicholson in one sentence?

Corman: You know, I don't think I can.

Karen Black

Karen Black has worked with Jack Nicholson on several occasions. She was seen briefly in *Easy Rider* as one of the prostitutes in the New Orleans cathouse who tripped out with Hopper and Fonda on LSD. She didn't really have any scenes with Jack, so they saw each other very little. A year later Ms. Black played Nicholson's leading lady in *Five Easy Pieces*. Her performance as the naive, but loving Rayette Dipesto opposite Jack's scolding Bobby Dupea was quite touching. She later appeared in Nicholson's own film, *Drive, He Said,* where she played Olive, a lady mixed up in two ultimately unsatisfying love affairs. Offscreen, Karen Black and Jack Nicholson are close friends. They live less than two miles from each other.

Ms. Black was first seen on the big screen in the film *You're a Big Boy Now,* which was directed by Francis Ford Coppola (*The Godfather, The Great Gatsby*). She also co-starred with George Segal in *Born to Win,* a film by the Czechoslovakian director Ivan Passer. It's a shame that the film version of Philip Roth's *Portnoy's Complaint* was so bad, because Ms. Black's performance as The Monkey was first-rate, and she did not really receive credit for it, though many critics singled her out as the film's sole saving grace. Karen Black recently completed *Rhinoceros* with Zero Mostel and Gene Wilder. The film was directed by Tom O'Horgan (*Hair, Jesus Christ Superstar*) for the American Film Theatre. After that came *The Great Gatsby* with Ms. Black playing the role of Myrtle Wilson in the F. Scott Fitzgerald classic. In spite of, or perhaps because of, the advance hoopla surrounding *Gatsby,* the film didn't score at all at the box office, but Ms. Black received fine notices for her supporting role. Karen Black is now one of the busiest actresses in Hollywood, following *Gatsby* with a co-starring role in John Schlesinger's *The Day of the Locust* and also *Airport 1975*.

We scheduled an interview with Ms. Black through David Wardlow, her agent at William Morris.

The meeting was to take place on Saturday, July 15, at her home. On our first arrival at Ms. Black's home off Mulholland Drive, we were greeted by her manager, Peter Rachtman, and the message that Ms. Black was ill and that we should call her in a few days. Talking with Karen Black is a pleasure. She always knows who you are immediately when you call, and sounds as though she's glad to hear from you. We rescheduled the interview for the following Monday. This time when we arrived at Ms. Black's house we made it inside and met Karen Black. The living room has a beautiful view of Los Angeles, and there was a funky old upright piano and a large Coca-Cola sign on one wall. Unfortunately, after a few minutes taping, it was evident that Ms. Black was still not feeling well, and we decided to return at a later date.

Ms. Black was then tied up doing *The Dean Martin Show* and a *Ghost Story* episode for television, and then she left to do *The Pyx*. We found out where she was staying in Montreal and called her there to find out when she was going to return to Los Angeles. Her schedule being as hectic as it is we decided to do the interview over the phone. We set a time on Friday, September 29, and held our first three-thousand-mile interview.

Question: How long have you known Jack Nicholson and how did you meet him?

Karen Black: I met Jack at the Old World [a Sunset Strip restaurant] sitting in front with a whole group of people, and I thought he had a very good confront, so to speak. He just looked right at you, and he had a lot of space, and he was very sort of yellow. He was very beautiful. We went to his house and teeter-tottered. He had a teeter-totter. He said, "I've got this game where you look into each other's eyes, and you're gonna love it." So we did that for a while. I liked him a lot. Then he took me home, and he really sort of wanted to date me for awhile, but I didn't even think of him that way, because I was going with Peter Kastner at the time. We were going to do a thing at the Actor's Studio, but we never did, and I didn't see him at all. Then I went to do *Easy Rider,* but I didn't see him, because we didn't have any scenes together, and then we went to see the showing of it, and I saw him out in the lobby afterward, and I started crying. And he said,

"Blackie, you're crazy." He didn't understand that, but what it was was that I really loved him a lot, and I didn't know it until I saw him again, because it all welled up. So I really cared a lot about him. I think most people do.

Question: Did you have any problems working with him on *Five Easy Pieces?*

Black: No, it was very exhilarating. We were having a very, very beautiful and good time of it. Sometimes, though, when you're working with Jack, you can see that he's wrestling around with the realities of the character to make it jive with his own reality, so that he can believe it and know that it's his.

Question: Do you think Jack identified closely with his character of Bobby in *Five Easy Pieces?*

Black: I think that he really has very little in common with Bobby. I think Bobby has given up. I think Bobby doesn't look for love, actively. He runs into it, but he doesn't have enough hope to look for it, and I think Jack does. He's very interested in love, in finding out things. Jack is a very

curious, alive human being. Always ready for a new idea. I think Jack and Bobby are, very, very, very, very, very, very different. The only thing I do know is that the scene in the restaurant was practically something that Jack did, but you'll notice that it's slightly out of character for Bobby anyway, because he cared, and Bobby is a person that doesn't really care. He kind of lets things drift him around.

Question: What was the reason behind Bobby's not wanting to marry Rayette?

Black: There was a lot of truth in his not wanting to marry Rayette, because from Bobby's viewpoint Rayette was creating a person in Bobby's image that wasn't even Bobby, and loving that. Her whole reality was entirely different from his, and included in hers was that his was like hers, and it wasn't. That made it a really impossible situation. Classic, but impossible. I think he was quite right.

Question: What happens to Rayette at the end of *Five Easy Pieces?*

Black: I don't know. I think she survives

Nicholson and Karen Black in Five Easy Pieces

somehow. I think she'll be all right. I think in a way she'll be a lot more all right than he ever will be, because she really can love, and she is alive. Like, can you imagine Rayette with a kid? She'd be great. Can you imagine Bobby with a kid? He'd be shitty.

Question: Do you think that the ending that's in the film is the best possible ending?

Black: I never had to make up my mind about that, because there it was in the film. It's funny that you ask, because Rafelson did come to me and we had a whole long discussion about that one evening, and the ending that I preferred over the one that they chose was an ending where you'd suddenly see Bobby in a tie store. Did Jack tell you about that?

Question: No, he mentioned one about the car going off a bridge and Bobby being killed.

Black: Shit, I'd forgotten that. That was in the script, too. That would have been very interesting for Rayette, because she came out of that river very angry with Bobby for having died, for leaving her like that; and screaming at him looking like a wet rat. That would have been wonderful to do.

The other one discussed was with Bobby going away from me, and then you'd flash to him in a department selling ties, dead as ever. Another dead end. What Jack wanted to do was to just walk away. Start walking, and use a long lens so that no matter how far he walked or how fast he walked he still looked the same. I liked that one a lot; just the walking, and walking, and walking. I guess that's the one I sort of chose, but they didn't use it. The one they used was awfully good, I thought.

Question: Was there a lot of improvisation in the film?

Black: No. It sounds like there was improvisation because Carol Eastman writes so legitimately, so congruent with life's voices.

Question: You've worked with both Jack and Bob Rafelson as directors. What are the differences between them?

Black: It's hard to differentiate between director and script. If Jack had directed me in the same script as Rafelson, I could really tell you the difference, but every director changes with the script just

Nicholson going over Drive, He Said *script with (l. to r.) William Tepper, Karen Black, and Robert Towne*

like I would change for the character. *Drive, He Said* is kind of a multi-imagistic picture, so you have to do a lot of switch-offs and change-offs and things. I guess Jack talks more to you, because Rafelson pretty much left me alone. He talked to me when I needed it, but I needed more talking to in Jack's film, so you really can't compare, because if I had needed less talking to, I might have been talked to less. Jack's very sensitive to the actor; he knows what you're going through.

Jack didn't have a strong producer in that movie for some reason, and he had a lot of running around to do, picking up costumes for the day of shooting and stuff. So he was being run fairly ragged, and I don't think Rafelson was being run that ragged. His was a more well-planned project. It just sort of happened that way. There weren't really enough people in my consideration for the jobs that needed people, so they kept sliding over into other peoples' jobs, which left Jack with more of a burden than a first-time director really should have to have. I think he's very talented as a director, and I'm sorry that his first project wasn't easier and more highly greased, so he would feel more like doing it again. The Director's Guild wanted him to join in the middle of his picture, but he didn't want to, because he didn't know if he wanted to direct again. It's like somebody who paints their first picture, and you say that they're going to be a painter for the rest of their life. Well, Jack didn't sign for that reason, and they shut down production. We were shooting in the gymnasium, and they turned the lights out, and he just sat there and stuck to his viewpoint, and he won. That's really kind of terrific; I respected him for it.

Question: We understand that Rafelson is one, if not the favorite director of Jack's. What do you think is the reason for that?

Black: Jack once told me that Bob and I have the creative genius that children have, but children grow out of it, and we never did. I remember he said that once. It's just something about being close to source with Jack and Bob. There's probably an aesthetic viewpoint agreement; that happens between people sometimes, and he's lucky that he's found it with Rafelson, because sometimes you can find it with a director and never work together, because of circumstances. Like, I've found it with Ivan Passer, a Czechoslovakian director, where he knew what worked and what didn't as far as our aesthetic viewpoint was concerned. And I think Jack's found that with Rafelson, you know, where

if he says, "I don't think that will work," then Rafelson will say, "That's right," and he'd see it that way, too. The thing about what works and what doesn't work is a floating subject; there are no absolutes, rights or wrongs, black or whites. It's just whatever seems to you to work, is what seems to you to work. And that's all you'll ever know about it. I think that kind of agreement is very beautiful, and something that I think could make very fast friends among men. Like I would think that John Lennon and Paul McCartney are still very fast and very true in some ways, because once you find that thing where the viewpoints match up, where aesthetically it looks the same to each, that's quite a union of mind.

Question: How was the switchover from working with Jack as an actor to working with him as a director?

Black: I fell in love with Jack while we were doing *Five Easy Pieces,* but I was going with somebody, and Jack was going with somebody, and we were both in love anyway, so we never got together. I think that working with someone as an actor kind of turns that thing on. You find a lot of leading ladies marrying their leading men. Well, when someone works with you as a director that kind of thing doesn't get turned on usually.

Question: What is that?

Black: I think one thing is that actors get convinced of their own mockups. They mock up the guy as their husbands; every day they go in and mock him up as their husband, and the next thing you know they marry them. It's very easy to create somebody as something for yourself.

So I think that that's part of it; there's a kind of magnetism between men and women that are playing opposite each other, but that doesn't happen with the director. And also by then I'd gotten used to the fact that he was a friend, rather than ever going to be a boy friend.

He's very light in his acting and his directing, you know. If it seems good at this moment, let's do it. If it seemed to have been good right at that moment, let's keep it. It's not, "Well, I wanted you to frown on the word 'pea' here, and you didn't so we've got to do it again," and "You dropped a word here, and you can't do that." Jack doesn't do that, and that speaks to me of a lot of talent. Also, he would say the right thing at the right time, and he cared a lot. Like the scene with Tepper in the car, Jack just said, "I want a nice, organic imagination. Just imagine that this is really happening, and go ahead and do it." That's all I needed to hear.

Question: How do you think that scene came out?

Black: I never saw it. I only saw the film when he ran it for everybody, and I overslept and was twenty minutes late, and I never saw that scene.

Question: What was the problem between Olive and Richard in *Drive*?

Black: What the problem is, is that he dumps. He's a dumper. What that is, is somebody that when you say, "Let's go on the Ferris wheel," says, "Well, Olive, I don't know about the Ferris wheel. The last time that you went on it you did not enjoy yourself, and therefore I think you oughtn't to try it again." Olive is swift. She's swift; she thinks fast and does fast, and she's a little edgy. It's like someone who always has to wait a little too long to get an answer to a question.

Question: How about Olive and Hector?

Black: Hector had a little of the same problem. He's freer, and happier, and livelier, but he's a little bit of a "schlump." He's a guy that would absolutely forget that he was going to see you Sunday at four o'clock. But that's her game. She's got two guys that irritate her, so she's got to do a thing where she gets irritated. It's hard to get all the characteristics that Olive carries with her. I think they were there, but there just wasn't enough time to really get them.

Question: Why do you think *Drive, He Said* failed?

Black: I think partly because of timing, prejudices, and the movie itself. I think that the movie had certain things about it that I liked a lot. I mean, I believed that house. I believed that place. I kind of liked those people. There was an interior feeling. It wasn't like people being puppeteered through a plot line.

I think it was released at a ghastly time. I remember protesting loudly. And there wasn't much of a build-up. It should have been released in the fall, because it's nothing but a college picture. I shouldn't say "nothing but," but it is a college picture. It should have been in Westwood (the UCLA area) in the fall, and it was released right after everyone left for home, like in July.

People that I know liked it a great deal, because it was satisfying in that the people were real and the places were real. Where the prejudice comes in is that we expect to see one actor who we know as a leading character, and he does this, and

he does that, and then he does the other. I'm not saying that that is a right or a wrong assumption to make when one goes to see a movie, but if it is an assumption, if it is an expectation, then they are going to be disappointed when they go to see this movie. There isn't any exposition in the movie. You don't really know if Olive's married to Richard, but I liked that. I always liked the fact that you dropped in on these people, much like you would drop in invisibly with a camera into peoples' lives, because they would never say, "I'm married," because everyone she would talk to would know that she's married, so how could you ever find that out, unless you wrote up a scene where she went to a hospital, or went to get a job as a secretary, you see?

A lot of things like that were going on, where there wasn't much exposition and it kept shifting from character to character. I think it is a good idea to stay with one character, not because it's a good idea for the sake of being a good idea, but because there is no work of art without viewpoint. And again, the viewpoint is neither right or wrong, good or bad, or anything, but it is just a given viewpoint. And that's why you need to have one guy, so you can have one viewpoint on any work. If you read any book that's well-written, it has something that's contiguous, and continuing about it, and that's the viewpoint. I think the movie needed that, but it had some good things in it.

Question: If you were to work with Jack again, what kind of a project would you like to do?

Black: I would like to be, in relation to Jack on screen, a woman similar to those women that he tends to like. For instance, Catherine in *Five Easy Pieces*. It would be interesting to play that with him. Some natural-blonde lady, with a cool brow, and an offhand natural manner.

Question: What kind of characteristics does Jack have that make him attractive and/or repulsive to women?

Black: I don't know that he's repulsive at all. I think what makes Jack attractive makes Jack attractive to anybody. I don't know about the differentiation between the sexes. What makes Jack attractive is that he's a very big person. He's, sort of, very shiny, and he has a very white aura that kind of glows and shines. He requires of himself to try and truly understand others' viewpoints, rather than dismissing them before he hears all about it. He always grants people beingness, so to speak. He grants them their-ness. He grants them you-ness

Nicholson and Karen Black in another scene from Five Easy Pieces

and me-ness, and a lot of people don't do that.

He really expects nice things from people, because he has a basic kind of respect for others. People feel that they are liked by Jack, and they're right. Each person is kind of special in his own way to Jack, and they know that. One time we were on a plane, and I looked up and saw him talking casually to someone. Well, I assumed Jack knew that person very well for a number of years, but I found out that he had just met him. He gives that off; he gives off familiar, friendly, old, always, friendship, trusting, loyal, and on, and on, and on, and people pick that up. The best description of a Taurus I ever heard was that if there's a garbage can nearby, they don't ignore it, and they don't contribute their garbage to it, and they don't bury it, and they don't call somebody to take it away. A Taurus will go up to that can of garbage and look in it until they find something that they can consider beautiful, and that's Jack. I mean, Jack sticks his nose in; he doesn't disconnect, he doesn't move away. He makes things acceptable for himself somehow. I don't know if he knows that he does that, but it's kind of a big person that can do that, you know. Jack taught me a lot. He taught me mainly that I was just fine, just the way I was. He taught me that I could have a conversation with the king of Spain, and probably outdo the son of a bitch. He really made me realize that I'm one of them. I'm one of those people and I'm needed. That's nice. I'm sure he's a great giver of confidence to people that know him. I think Jack buys too much crap. That's where we disagree in philosophy. I would reject some things. I would just say, "That's crazy. Good-by. I don't want you in my life. I don't want this and such in my life." And Jack doesn't. He takes it all. Tries to wear it all. Tries to grow big enough to put it somewhere in his universe where it can fit, and not kill and destroy. I don't do that. It's a very powerful game he's playing. Powerful in a sweet way.

Question: Is there one thing that attracts you most to him?

Black: I like what attracts anyone to anyone; it's him. That being. That soul. With whatever qualities, and textures, and characteristics, and meaning and significance it has to me or to you or to anyone. That particular being; there's only one like it, just like there's only one like any of us in the universe. And his is just him. It's too simple to talk about in a way.

Question: Do you have a favorite performance of his?

Black: I guess I liked *Easy Rider*.

Question: Why?

Black: I've never thought about it before. Well, I'll tell you why, because the guy was warm. The guy was expansive. The guy smiled a lot. Jack is a smiler. He's a warmer. He's a turning you happier. He's a finder-outer, you know? He's a get in

there and liver. The guy in *Carnal Knowledge* was kind of sick. He's fairly worn down with unsalvageable concepts, and Jack's nothing like Bobby (his character in *Five Easy Pieces*). I was worried about him when we were doing that picture. I thought, "How is he ever going to be like Bobby?"

In *Easy Rider* the guy is bright, and warm, alive, and he's sticking his neck out going along with these guys. That's more like Jack. If Jack would just be shot like Jack, it would be the greatest thing you ever saw in your life. The way he talks, the way he listens, the way he moves. Even just the physical manifestations of his funny smile with his nostrils flaring, and the sort of prideful way he stands on both feet with that cigar in his mouth, and stuff like that, and yet he's very sweet at the same time. There's nothing like it; he's just special.

I used to want him to go on talk shows very badly, so the world could get to see the real Jack.

Question: What were the differences between the making of *Easy Rider* and *Five Easy Pieces*?

Black: Oh, well, *Easy Rider* was nuts. *Easy Rider* was crazy. You didn't know who was going to be fighting with whom, or if there was going to be a street fight, or if they were going to throw a television across the room. You had to give Dennis a vitamin E because he's been up so long he's completely paranoided-out about it. Gee whiz, it was crazy, but some of the creative work was good, well-intentioned, and Dennis is really a gorgeous, beautiful man. He's really darling. I might just pop in and do a little part in his next movie just for fun. I haven't told him about it yet.

I'd like to be an actress who just pops into films, and does little stuff, and then does leads, if you can get it together in this country and work it out that way. But they're so silly. They figure if you're a leading lady, then you have to be a leading lady.

Question: Can you characterize Jack Nicholson in one sentence?

Black: The boy from New Jersey in the corner, who everyone at this party is gathered around, who comes on like Will Rogers, and may just be our Will Rogers, except with more talent, who fills up the whole room with his presence.

Richard Rush

Director Richard Rush

Richard Rush is an integral part of Jack Nicholson's development as an actor. Very early in Jack's career, Rush directed him in a controversial film about abortion, *Too Soon To Love*. Though this film went virtually unnoticed (as many of Jack's early films have), it was the first in a trilogy of free-spirited, socially conscious appraisals of then-current phenomena. Producers tend to label this genre "now movies."

In 1967 Rush directed Nicholson again in *Hell's Angels on Wheels,* a much better film than the title suggests. It was at this point that Nicholson first suggested glimpses of a future role, Jonathan Fuerst in *Carnal Knowledge*. Rush's fine-line direction offered Nicholson freedom to search inside his character, but he was still being guided toward a definitive end result.

Psych-Out concluded the trilogy with an intense performance from Nicholson and calculated craziness from Bruce Dern.

Richard Rush has the same levels of energy and complexity that pervade the seemingly simple characters in his films with Nicholson. He is totally in control of his thoughts and words and their directions, but he still permits himself to be in awe of something well done.

The feelings we received from him carried over from our first phone conversation to our interview at his office at the Burbank Studios, where he was preparing to direct *Freebie and the Bean,* his first film since the enormously successful *Getting Straight*.

The appearance of his office suggested that he would be stationed there only temporarily (he had only recently moved from the old Columbia Studios on Gower Street in Hollywood). The wood-paneled walls were sparsely decorated, and our attention focused on one section featuring newspaper ads of all sizes for *Getting Straight*.

Rush was completely at ease as he ushered us into his office, and we quickly began the interview.

Question: How many films have you done with Jack Nicholson?

Richard Rush: Well, we did *Psych-Out* (1967), and *Hell's Angels on Wheels* (1965), and in 1959, my first film, one of those little low-budget wonders called *Too Soon to Love*. It was an exploitation film made for about fifty thousand dollars, which we were pretty successful with. We sold it to Universal for a couple of hundred thousand, and it hit at just that magic time when the critics had invented the "New Wave," invented it in the sense that they had decided to call that whole wave of creative work in Europe that. It was sort of elevated out of the genre critically. It was talked about at the time as the first American New Wave. It was a good, little combination serious-exploitation picture, with some excellent performances in it, and Jack played a secondary role in it. Aside from the two leads it was perhaps the most important role.

I ran the film after several years, and it was stunning to see Jack as a kid, twelve years younger, with almost a butch haircut, and a very strong hint of the style, and techniques, and character that emerged later.

Question: How did you decide to cast Jack later in *Hell's Angels* and *Psych-Out*?

Rush: I had liked Jack's work as an actor when I worked with him then. It wasn't a twelve-year span between that and *Hell's Angels;* it was only six. I had kept in touch with him vaguely during that time, but it was strictly from my knowedge and memory of him as an actor, and his heavy Actor's Studio work, and his style and technique that very much appealed to me about Jack.

Question: How closely do you think Jack identified with his role of the gas-station attendant looking for something else in *Hell's Angels on Wheels*?

Rush: In personally developing the things he could use for the role, Jack always was the same kind of iconoclastic rebel that that kid was. He was the same kind of askew, hip, romantic hero. However, Jack is a much, much brighter man than that kid was. It's always been one of Jack's most unique abilities to almost lower his IQ by grade points according to a meter. He has a way of dropping it without becoming less interesting and it's a very difficult trick. There are a lot of fine actors who simply aren't tuned in to that ability.

Question: Then do you think that went along, too, with the rock musician in *Psych-Out*?

Rush: Yes, except that the rock musician in *Psych-Out* was, at least in my mind, a much brighter guy than the kid in *Hell's Angels*. He also was a little bit older, and a bit more worldly. He was a little more ambitious, and in conflict about his ambitions. He was walking that crossroad that we all do between our intellectual rationalization and our emotional upbringing.

Question: In *Psych-Out* and *Hell's Angels* there is a feeling of almost non-direction, of eavesdropping on the proceedings led by Nicholson. How did you create this feeling?

Rush: It was a deliberate style that I was playing with, which I actually used those three pictures to develop. At that time I had the somewhat dubious reputation of being the best of the two-dollar hookers; I could always get a picture for a hundred and fifty thousand dollars, as long as it didn't cost more, and I was very interested in some visual experiments and storytelling experiments, and made the deal that way on *Hell's Angels*. I said I'd give them all the razzle-dazzle fights and action that they'd need, and in return it would be hands off, let me play a little bit with what I want to do. That sort of proceeded through the next three pictures, and through them we developed a long-lens visual style, and what was happening then, which was pertinent to Jack and his particular talents, was a whole, excitingly different level of acting that relied less, although there was a definite relationship, on the Actor's Studio stuff that Brando represented, and more on the Second City group which was doing a kind of behavioral improvisation. There was something very appealing about the Second City's style, but it called for a very spontaneous, improvisational work, which until then nobody was really handling on film, because of the necessity of doing repeat takes, and different angles, and so on.

I had a great cameraman, Laszlo Kovacs, who I had worked with once before, and with whom I've worked many times since, and a whole unit that was very in with what we were trying to do. Kovacs was like magic with a hand-held camera, so we started working out ways of staging, within the context of the written material, improvisational extensions, and covering them with a combination of hand-held and production work, where you went back to recapture and extend the best moments of what had emerged, and to work that in with the straight storytelling.

Jack works very well in both styles. He is extremely adept and bright and creative in that improvisational field, because he's not only a good actor but a good writer.

Question: How much did you go by the script, and how much was improvisation?

Rush: In *Hell's Angels* a good deal of it was improvisation, because the screenplay was a very episodic piece. The subject matter itself was fraught with concern, because unlike the couple of bike films before us, we had the real Hell's Angels working with us rather than the imitation ones. The material and the subject matter were a bit edgy, but almost because of that you didn't feel quite the sense of responsibility to it. I'd say about half the material was improvised. At one point we left the script, and I think it was about two and a half days before we could work our way back to it. I remember the whole cast and crew cheering when we announced, "Hey, we made it."

Question: With relatively short shooting schedules, how much of a rapport were you able to build up with Jack?

Rush: A very solid one in those pictures, because it was tremendously essential. If everyone was going for something special, or some private fantasy of quality, it really all relied on performance, and a unique kind of storytelling through performance. That meant a sort of total understanding with Jack, his creative efforts, and an instant responsiveness to circumstances that we were winging.

Question: Where do you think *Hell's Angels* and *Psych-Out* fit into Jack's spectrum as far as learning experiences are concerned?

Rush: I'm likely to be prejudiced, naturally, but Jack sure as hell didn't learn how to act on those pictures. He came to me as one of the really accomplished, although unknown, actors, and he's a guy that had always worked real hard, very seriously. But he acquired a certain kind of release mechanism that allowed him to take chances that he might not have had the chance to take before on film, or to do more serious, demanding material. By working with a good director who's trying to get the most out of the material, the actor has a good chance to teach himself through the working experience. I think Jack had a chance to try more dangerous things, more demanding things, on those films than he had before. There were a few characteristics of his that particularly appealed to me. He had certain physical habits, tendencies, mannerisms, that intrigued the hell out of me, and seemed very right for the character. There are things that I don't think he had used in his work before on film, but that remain in his work as part of the Jack Nicholson personality on film since then, which pleases me, because I like to see them when I watch him work.

Question: We found a lot of similarities between the characters that Jack played in *Carnal Knowledge* and *Psych-Out.*

Rush: Very much so.

Question: He kind of injects the same mores that he has in *Carnal Knowledge* into the acid-type society he was living in in *Psych-Out.*

Rush: Right. And I know that he showed Mike Nichols *Psych-Out* before they did the picture. They watched it together. I don't know whether he showed it to him before or after he was cast, but it was a strong part of his calling card because of the obvious relationship between the two roles.

Question: Why do you think Jack remained virtually unknown until *Easy Rider?*

Rush: I've got a theory about that. It's almost a standard phenomena that most of those bright new discoveries have really been around for about ten years, and working very hard, and I really think it was something to do with the fact that men get to their most appealing peak when they get to be about thirty, and sort of swing from there. Whereas the girls hit in their early twenties, and it's downhill from there. The men can play younger. We're almost always looking at Redfords or Nicholsons and figuring them to play early twenties; and they're not. Their faces have become stronger, they've gotten rid of a lot of their hang-ups, and have waded through enough shit to have interesting character lines show up on their faces.

Question: Having written a few scripts himself, did Jack convey his feelings to you about the content of *Hell's Angels* and *Psych-Out?*

Rush: There was particularly a relationship in that area on the second one, *Psych-Out*, because Jack was in that project before I was. He had written a screenplay on it. Unfortunately, AIP, who was financing the film, turned it down. I'm not surprised. It was a very imaginative, somewhat esoteric, fairly brilliant piece of writing. It hardly qualified as an exploitation film in the genre as it was known then. So the project had gone dead at that moment. I was hung up on the phenomenon of the whole scene at that time. I thought it was the most exciting social phenomenon that had occurred in the last forty years, and I still do. I was hung up on doing a glorifying examination of the scene, an examination on the emergence of a new non-aggressive male, and took the picture as a chance to do that. I later sort of did a screenplay on it, but as a director I don't like to get into screenplay credits. I did use two or three scenes from Jack's original screenplay.

I'm sure Jack felt that his original screenplay would have been a better treatment, and I liked his original work very much. I would have been delighted to do it had someone been willing to finance it at that moment. My screenplay on *Psych-Out* was heavily lacerated with the injection of AIP exploitive sequences. I was extremely fond of that piece as it exists privately the way we shot it, where it doesn't become that heavy chase piece but really a focused study of the values that were in conflict at the time.

Question: Do you think it was a pro- or anti-drug film?

Rush: The way the picture was structured, it was really attempting to look at the entire scene through two windows alternately. To look at it through the stained-glass window of the idealized version, which was handled in the first thirty or forty minutes of the film, and later on similar circumstances were seen through a different window: the disillusionment of the girl, disillusionment because of her relationship with the guy. But without the early balance it tended to be more of an anti-drug picture than it was designed to be. It was designed with a lack of bias, saying, "It's beautiful if you look at it through here," and "It's destructive if you look at it through here." Nevertheless, the phenomenon has a great deal of richness to it.

I think Jack was pretty much in accord with what the picture was saying, but he felt the same uneasiness that I did about some of the overlaid exploitive fights and chases and bullshit things like that. I was sort of amused by the knight-in-shining-armor-acid addition to the fight scene in the wrecking yard, but the guys chasing the Bruce Dern character to get rid of him became a drag.

Question: Do you think Nicholson's script for *Psych-Out* was a forerunner to his script for *The Trip*?

Rush: I wasn't aware of a feeling of connection between the two, although they did deal with the same scene. Stylistically, I almost feel that there was a closer connection between the screenplay he had done for *Psych-Out*, or *The Love Children* as it was originally called, and the picture he directed, *Drive, He Said*.

Question: As far as the production of the film, *Easy Rider* has a very communal feeling about it. How would you describe the production of *Psych-Out* and *Hell's Angels on Wheels*?

Rush: There's an inevitable relationship between my two films and *Easy Rider*. That crew, which included Laszlo Kovacs, which at that point was a nonunion crew, and almost a stock company of actors, which involved Jack Nicholson, Adam Roarke, and several other good people, sort of had a continuity in that trilogy of films, *Too Soon to Love, Hell's Angels on Wheels,* and *Psych-Out*.

Bert Schneider actually took those three films to New York and showed them to Abe Schneider at Columbia, and said, "Look, these are the budgets Dick has been working on. These are the people he's been using. I'm going to use the same people, and I've got Dennis Hopper and Peter Fonda, and turn out a film that was right for the market, because the grosses on those were so phenomenal." He actually used those three films to package *Easy Rider*. As a matter of fact, the day before they left on the road for *Easy Rider* they screened all three films for the cast and crew. The comment was, "Well, we're gonna go make a Dick Rush picture." It was based on that combination of elements—motorcycles, communal living, the same crew and cast, and a shooting style that had emerged from those three pictures, which was that method of episodic storytelling using rock music as background scoring, and so on.

They had that in common, a lot of the storytelling style of proceeding episodically through the piece, where the impact of whatever you're saying emerges through the results of the episodes—that business of playing against material, like using motorcycles and cutting out the sound effects, and handling them lyrically with the right kind of rock-music accompaniment, rather than scored music; a certain amount of improvisational work; and of course a lot of the techniques that Laszlo and the crew had developed with me through our past pictures.

I think that Dennis [Hopper], as a director, works fairly differently than I do. They're both equally valid systems. Dennis tends more to use the camera as a stationary eye and work his action in front of it. He's very heavy improvisationally, because of his own acting training, so he'll shoot a great quantity of improvisational work and footage, whereas my style is a much more compulsive one as far as controlling what's in the frame. Everything in the frame is somewhat predesigned, even in the improvisational work and the hand-held work. It all fits very tightly into a designed pattern. I'm much more likely to use the camera subjectively, because I tend to tell the story from the view of the central character. In both *Hell's Angels* and

Psych-Out you were seeing it through Jack's eyes. Not literally point of view, but he's in every scene. You only know what he knows. You don't get additional information. That type of thing. I think that's where Dennis and I would differ, and I think that's where the production differences would come.

Question: How much did Jack relate his own drug experiences to that of the character in *Psych-Out*?

Rush: I'm sure as heavily as in any other area, like relating his own sexual experiences to a love scene. You work with everything you've got. Jack certainly knew the drug scene, and knew the whole sociological scene. Jack, in a sense, was a vanguard. He always had a sense for what was happening on the street in people's minds, and was usually with it before it happened.

Question: Do you think you utilized Jack to your satisfaction in those films?

Rush: Yeah, definitely. Within the limits we had to work with I was extremely pleased with where we got. There are scenes in both *Hell's Angels* and *Psych-Out*, which, isolated from the rest of the picture, are little performance jewels. In *Hell's Angels* there's one moment with Sabrina Scharf where she lures him into the apartment, and there's kind of a cunty game going on. In that scene Jack is absolutely stunning. I can read fifteen levels of confusion and tension in every second of what's happening in that two-minute scene.

Question: Despite his seemingly naturalistic approach to acting, do you think Jack has any gimmick, any crutches as an actor?

Rush: Yes, however, probably not in the same sense that a critic might say it if the critic felt hostile to Jack for some reason. I think he has crutches and mannerisms that he relies on in the same way that each one of us does as human beings. Our natural front to the world is absolutely loaded with personal, recognizable characteristics. One of the things that makes him an appealing leading man, as well as a brilliant actor, is that the particular front that he uses for the world is one that excites people and intrigues them. I think without the crutches and the characteristics he'd be somebody else.

There is a laugh of Jack's that I confess I wanted very much to be a part of his character in *Hell's Angels*, and which he was kind enough to oblige me with, which is one of his recognizable characteristics. It's kind of a mindless giggle, which is terribly real. It says, "I'm covering up my self-consciousness about what I'm saying. I'm trying to be cool. I am vulnerable," which works well with that low-mentality character that he knows how to play.

I haven't met a good actor that won't create a certain amount of friction, personal anger, tension, that he can use in a scene. Jack does that like the few dozen other good actors there are in the world, but he keeps himself pretty much under control, so he doesn't become a burden outside of the immediacy of the scene he's doing. Occasionally, lines don't work for him. One of the nice things about Jack is that if a line doesn't work for him he will usually throw in something better, and nine times out of ten it will be something that I'll like better also, rather than something I'll have to con him out of.

We had some funny numbers that happened on *Hell's Angels*. In the initiation scene, which was something that was brewing in my mind as we were doing it, Jack didn't know what was going to happen when they grabbed him, pinned him, and started pouring crap all over him. Normally one wouldn't do that kind of a number with Jack, but it happened in the flow of the scene and it was appropriate for that moment. Jack doesn't have to be tricked into something; he's a good enough technician to trick himself into it.

At one point in the climax of the film, where the guy rides the motorcycle through the window and tries to run him down, there was a freak phenomenon. It was a one-time shot, because there was only one window. We had decided about a half an hour before how to end the picture. It had been a matter of two alternatives until that moment. The mortocycle had a dummy on it as it went through the window, but Jack was walking outside. All we could do was to calculate and predict what would happen, and clue Jack and Sabrina in and let them improvise the results. The final hope being that they had final marks to end up facing each other through the broken pieces of glass. What happened was, the motorcycle went through the window, veered off, and hit Jack, knocked him down, toppled over, and burst into flames. Jack climbed to his feet, rushed to the motorcycle, and attempted to rescue the dummy, dashed back to the window, tears streaming down his face, and Sabrina, who was also in a horrified panic, hit her marks with the fire raging between them, and it was the most brilliant moment I've ever seen. And it's the only time in my life and ten pictures where we yelled cut, and had someone hand-rush it to the lab in L.A., it was that precious. But for some insane reason, which we've never really figured out, the camera had stopped after the scene began, and it wasn't on film.

Question: Films like *Hell's Angels* and *Psych-Out* started out as "do your own thing in your own time" visual fantasies for affluent, half-educated American youths, but have become, by way of the film cultists, pieces of art.

Rush: That's very nice.

Question: Why do you think that change has come about?

Rush: I think it's a combination of a couple of things. One, that film has been emerging as an art form. It has tended to replace the novel for a whole generation, maybe two. In that sense it almost becomes the artistic medium for this generation. Forty years ago everybody had a novel they were writing up in the attic or under their bed. Today, everybody's shooting a film. They really think in those terms. And even though it is a commercial medium, the two aren't necessarily contradictory. It is emerging as an art form.

On those pictures, even though they had the surface characteristics, we were trying for much more. Apparently we got some of it in. They served their purpose at the time, because they were released that way, and it's great that they were remembered.

Question: Did you have the audience in mind when you were making these films?

Rush: Yeah, at least in terms of the agreement to fulfill a commitment to what were called exploitation pictures. All that really meant was that we were going to attract a youth audience. Of course, the absurd thing was that they were finding out about that time that the entire movie audience is a youth audience. There are the exceptions like *Airport,* where once or twice a year families will go out to a movie, and will go out in droves, but it's only once or twice a year, and that won't support an industry or an art form.

Jack is very much a part of the young people's feeling and thinking. At the same time, playing his real age and present conflicts in a picture like either *Five Easy Pieces* or *Carnal Knowledge,* he knocks off the next-ten-year age group very well with that split feeling about learned inescapable values and intellectually accepted ones that are in conflict. That is one of the most valid, important themes going today, and both of those pictures happen to deal with it.

Audiences tend to identify with actors according to the roles they play, and I think they identify heavily with Jack for those roles, and also for that combination of the cool man that we all grew up knowing was the one we had to be, and who is still going to be vulnerable and suffering. Jack somehow combines those truths into his work.

Question: Can you characterize Jack Nicholson in one sentence?

Rush: I tend to think of him as the man who plays the way I feel about things.

Jeremy Larner

It is hard to describe Jeremy Larner's appearance because we've never seen him. Nor have many other people.

Larner is always behind some project but never our in front. He was a speech writer for Eugene McCarthy during his campaign in 1968. Many of Larner's experiences on the political trail were transformed into a screenplay, *The Candidate,* which starred Robert Redford. Larner won the Oscar for best original screenplay.

In 1970 Jack Nicholson chose a fairly obscure, yet controversial novel to make his directorial debut in film. The novel, *Drive, He Said,* was a character study of an eclectic group of people at a university. Although it was the best of the campus movies, which included *Getting Straight, R.P.M.,* and *Strawberry Statement,* it received mixed reviews and was a box-office failure. Nicholson, besides producing and directing the film, also co-wrote it with Larner.

Larner, who makes many campus appearances around the country as a lecturer, was in Boston at the time we first spoke to his agent. After having written to Larner once, we mutually agreed that it would be easier for all parties concerned if we were to conduct the interview through the mail.

Question: Can you tell us how Jack became interested in your book and approached you about it?

Jeremy Larner: There were a number of people around my own age who from time to time wanted to produce a movie based on *Drive, He Said.* Jack Nicholson was the first who got the power to raise the money to do it. In 1967 Fred Roos tried to get backing for a production. He got Jack and me together because at that time he wanted Jack to do the script. When it was obvious that *Easy Rider* would make Jack a star, Bert Schneider offered him a chance to direct. Jack then came to me in New York where I was living —in the fall of 1968—and asked me to write the script. [Fred Roos became the associate producer and worked on the film from beginning to end.]

Question: How close is the movie to the book as far as plot and characters go?

Larner: You can answer this question for yourself by reading the book. The Bantam edition is best.

Jack and I agreed from the outset that the movie would have to be different. I envisioned two major areas of change: (a) the violence, which was prophetic when the book was written in 1960 to 1962, had already come to pass and even been exploited in a series of Hollywood movies. The action would have to be more subtle, suggestive, and comic; (b) I wanted the love story between Olive and Hector to be richer and more realistic.

Jack agreed, and kept warning me throughout the entire process to get away from the book. Yet in the clutch it was he who went back to it, in spirit if not in perfect exactness.

Question: How did the writing of the film proceed? Did you write with Jack on a day-to-day basis?

Larner: I wrote a first draft of the script which was deliberately long and overdone, in order to get out every possible idea. Jack, working along, produced a second draft which drastically cut and simplified the material and added some new bits of his own. Jack by this time was working under time pressure and other pressures connected with his suddenly expanded career, and the second draft remained incomplete. However, this draft became the shooting script. I had produced a third draft which was an expansion and polishing of Jack's second draft, and as the film was shot, pieces of this third draft were interpolated.

Jack and I worked together for the first time on the set, where we frequently rewrote scenes, sometimes while the actors were waiting. The screenwriter Robert Towne was on the set playing Richard Calvin, and he and I rewrote half a dozen scenes together, which were then edited by Jack before being shot. Towne also wrote one short

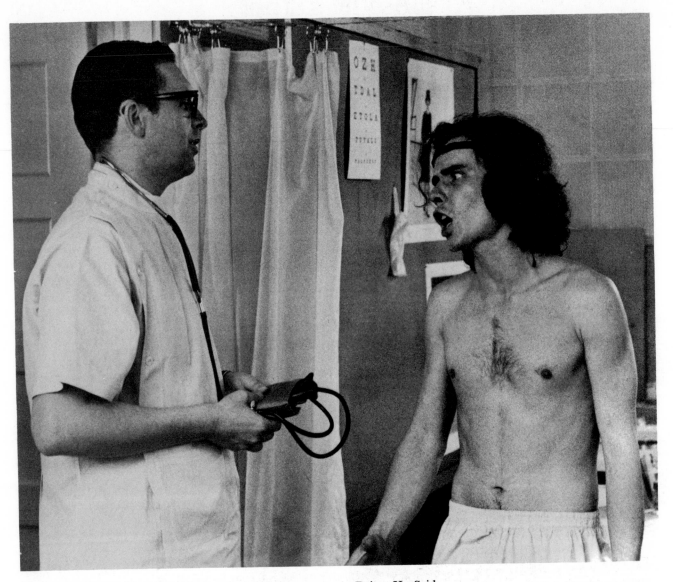

Michael Margotta (r.) in the hilarious draft induction scene in Drive, He Said

scene for himself and Hector.

A few scenes, and many lines, were improvised by the actors. Sometimes the actors didn't
know their lines, like, when Gabriel attempted to
recite Creeley's poem.

I have the feeling when I see the film that
most of the material originated from my own
imagination, but that its final form and shape is
the work of Jack Nicholson.

Question: Did you have any say in the casting
of the film?

Larner: No.

Question: What were your feelings about Jack
directing this as a first-time director?

Larner: Jack's experience, intelligence, and
theatrical instincts obviously qualified him for a
chance to direct.

Question: What do you think of the final
product? Is there anything that you'd like to
change?

Larner: To me the film is full of marvelous
action and surprise. Occasionally, when it tries to
get serious, I wince. I think, given the footage at
hand, the film should have been cut entirely as a
comedy.

Question: Why do you think the film failed at
the box office?

Larner: The movie could have been more
integrated. But no one knows.

Question: Getting specific for a while, what

did the shot of Michael Margotta (Gabriel) lying on his back in the sand signify?

Larner: I was strongly in favor of removing that shot. Regardless of how it was intended, it cannot help but remind the viewer of Jesus Christ —a comparison which should be made by Gabriel himself, not by the film.

Question: What significance, if any, is there in the repetition of the last line in the film, "Your mother called"?

Larner: Like all the best lines, it has no "significance."

Question: What were you trying to say through your two stealing scenes in the film (i.e., the pickpocket at the basketball game and the dance instructor at the market)?

Larner: Those two items were created by Jack.

Question: How were the basketball games shot?

Larner: This would be a long story to no good end.

Question: What do you think *Drive, He Said* was basically trying to say?

Larner: To ask that question is to hate art. But you might have a look at Creeley's poem.

Question: Did you ever encounter any problems working with Jack on the script?

Larner: Sometimes I was like the cross-eyed batter who sees two balls and hits the wrong one out of the park. (Have you noticed how many people in the flick are cross-eyed?)

Question: Was Gabriel's growing insanity supposed to be seen as comic?

*Larner*s Partly—at times, in its effects.

Question: Do you think the film's comic moments help or hinder the statement of the film? For instance, the draft sequence is very funny and yet deadly serious. Do you think they cancel each other out?

Larner: The film is not making a "statement," I hope. I can only refer you to the nature of comedy.

Question: Can you give us a few of Nicholson's personal additions to the film that you think helped or hindered it?

Larner: Jack has an eye for the bizarre and original visual touch which keeps the film interesting to look at even in its dubious moments.

Michael Margotta avoiding induction

William Tepper as Hector, the basketball star, in **Drive, He Said**

Question: After the film did Hector go on to play more basketball, or did he become a radical?

Larner: Hector lives with his dog on a small farm in Maine.

Question: What was Richard's [Robert Towne] problem with regard to Olive [Karen Black]?

Larner: The problem with Olive in the movie is that she is a hysterical bitch who screams all the time.

Question: Were the basketball sequences scripted?

Larner: Yes, more or less.

Question: What did you think of the movie's promotion? Would you have handled it differently?

Larner: BBS and Columbia deserve credit for sticking with the film and continuing promotion for longer than one might expect.

Question: Do you foresee any future collaborations between you and Jack?

Larner: Sure, I'd love to, if the gods are willing; in different roles next time.

Question: Can you characterize Jack Nicholson in one sentence?

Larner: "The truth was that Jay Gatsby of West Egg, Long Island, sprang from his Platonic conception of himself. He was a son of God—a phrase which, if it means anything, means just that —and he must be about his Father's business, the service of a vast, vulgar, and meretricious beauty. So he invented just the sort of Jay Gatsby that a seventeen-year-old boy would be likely to invent, and to this conception he was faithful to the end."

Bruce Dern

Bruce Dern gained widespread popularity for killing John Wayne. He did it in the Mark Rydell film *The Cowboys,* where he played a lunatic cattle rustler.

Dern, like his good friend Jack Nicholson, became an overnight success after about ten years in the business. He has risen to stardom through a lot of low-budget horror and exploitation films, and by playing numerous small roles in major films. In the first category there were films like *Wild River, Hush, Hush Sweet Charlotte,* and *The Wild Angels* with Peter Fonda. And in the second there were *Waterhole #3, Will Penny,* with Charlton Heston, and *The Cowboys.* Dern has worked with Nicholson on quite a few films, from Roger Corman's *St. Valentine's Day Massacre* and Richard Rush's *Psych-Out* to his fine supporting role in Nicholson's *Drive, He Said.* Jack and Bruce also did a small film together called *The Rebel Rousers,* which has yet to be released here, despite the fact that it was made in 1966.

Although Bruce Dern is a quiet, peaceful man offscreen, he has the ability to play the most disconcerting madman you'd ever like to see on the screen. He did it in *Psych-Out* and, as mentioned, in *The Cowboys.* He also was a spaced-out astronaut in *Silent Running,* his first starring role in a major film. After that film, to display his remarkable versatility as an actor, Dern did a complete role reversal. He co-starred with Jack Nicholson in Bob Rafelson's extraordinary low-key film, *The King of Marvin Gardens,* and there was a lot of speculation that he might have an Oscar nomination for it, along with Nicholson, but the film was sorely overlooked in the balloting.

Having broken the psycho stereotype once and for all, Dern went on to co-star with Walter Matthau in *The Laughing Policemen,* a real-life look at two homicide detectives. Then, in *The Great Gatsby,*

Bruce Dern

Bruce Dern played Tom Buchanan opposite Mia Farrow and Robert Redford. Dern's portrayal of Fitzgerald's upper-crust Buchanan brought rave reviews and talk of an Oscar, but the film was hardly a success at the box office. From the Fitzgerald twenties Dern went on to star with Kirk Douglas in a Western called *Posse,* which Douglas directed, and then he did Michael Ritchie's look at the beauty pageant world, *Smile.*

We spoke with Bruce Dern at BBS Productions and arranged to meet him there for the interview. Bruce speaks in an engaging manner, but every so often you catch a glimpse of that calculated craziness that has marked so many of his roles. We held the interview on the third floor at BBS, Dern providing riotous moments with a fantastically manic impersonation of Jack Nicholson.

Question: How long have you known Jack Nicholson and how did you meet him?

Bruce Dern: I met him in 1961 in the summer, when I first came out here. He was studying in an acting class that Marty Landau was teaching, and Marty Landau went to Europe to do *Cleopatra* so his acting class fell apart. I was living at Normandie Village, which is a pathetic little place up on the Strip—it's torn down now—and I had just come out from New York and I was a member of the Actor's Studio, and I was like the only other bona fide member of the Actor's Studio who was

Nicholson (l.), Cameron Mitchell (c.), and Bruce Dern in a scene from the bike film, Rebel Rousers

Nicholson relaxing between takes

into knowing some of these people, though I didn't know Jack Nicholson. So I met this guy who studied with Jack, named Eric Morrison, and they were going to do this play, a Calder Willingham play, *End as a Man*, which was later made into a movie called *The Strange One*, which starred Ben Gazzara. It was about a boys' military school. So I went to his house because of the Actor's Studio, and when I went to the house they were casting the play out of Marty Landau's class, and all these guys were there, and Jack was there. And his wife, Sandra, was there, and that was the first time I ever met him. Jack, evidently, was revered as a good actor at the time, as were two or three other people, as was I, although I was like an outsider coming in, and they were all very happy that Jack could not play the part of Jocko. Jack's Air Force unit was just activated and he had to go away for a year, which was a crusher to him and to everybody else. He made the most of it. I think he went to some basic kind of thing, and then went to Van Nuys, so he was close by all the time. I'm not really sure, because I lost track of him after that.

Then I didn't see him again until 1966, five years; never saw him, not a day. In 1966, when I was doing the *Wild Angels,* I think I saw him a couple of times, he was around somehow, because it was a Corman film. He had, by that time, done all his Corman films except a couple, and soon after that he started writing *The Trip* and I started seeing him regularly. He wrote *The Trip* and he wanted the part that I played, the part of the guide, he wanted to play, because he wrote it for himself. The original script that he wrote for *The Trip* was just sensational. He had really way-out ideas and stuff. I think the thing that brought me closer to him than anything was in January of 1967, before we did *The Trip*. I had just done *Wild Angels* and he had just done *Hell's Angels on Wheels*. My ex-wife and I had a manager named Marty Cohen, and he was going to produce and direct this little low-budget motorcycle picture, and I told him I wanted Jack Nicholson in the picture to play the leader of the bad guys. It was a good part, so I got him. I put three or four other guys like that in to make up my motorcycle gang, and we did a little picture called *The Rebel Rousers*. It's just recently been released in little tiny places; I don't think it's ever played here. It was in Frisco and Little Rock and a couple other places like that. He was starting to go through his separation and divorce then, and that was a very rough time for him, and he needed the job, and that kind of gave us a common bond. I guess kind of way back in his mind he's one of those guys that registers, you know, well I owe him one now, someday. That was kind of the way it was left. About three months later we did *The Trip*, and in one scene in *The Trip* he has the guy's bedroom, Peter Fonda's bedroom; he has memorabilia, pictures on the wall, and his list in the script of who is on that wall just made me love the guy. It's every little hero I ever pulled for, from guys like Eddie Stanky and all these fuckin' baseball players and football players to Robert Oppenheimer and General Groves, Huey Long, and all these people out of the past of Americana. Just memorabilia of people who did things, like John Dillinger. I mean everything was there. And that made me realize that he was much more in tune with what I was in tune with, and me with him, than ever before.

My problem was that I was not a doper; I don't take dope, I never have, and they were into a very heavy LSD experimental thing. I don't really know how much Jack was. I mean, I'm sure he's taken LSD and stuff. I kind of withdrew from that, so I wasn't around much.

We finished *The Trip*, and then that fall we both played tiny parts in *St. Valentine's Day Massacre*, and we both did it simply because of the money, not that we made a lot of money, but Roger Corman worked it out so that we could both go to work on the first week of the movie and work on the last week of the movie, so therefore, because of the Guild rule, we got carried for the whole movie, which ran for seven or eight weeks.

At that time I never went to his house and he never came to my house. We never visited each other. We were just friends, and got along great when we were together, but we kind of intimidated each other a little, I think. The next thing I know, I'm doing *They Shoot Horses, Don't They?* in January of 1969, and Jane Fonda everyday is telling me how great Jack Nicholson is in this movie, *Easy Rider*. I'm saying, "Yeah, sure, another fuckin' motorcycle movie. Tell me all about it, I've only done two billion of them." She says he's got this marijuana-smoking scene, and I say, "Sure, it figures they're going to film one of those someday, for Chrissakes." I didn't think much of it, and then *Easy Rider* comes out and goes "blam!" Then he made *Five Easy Pieces*. Well, he's a major fuckin' star now, and I'm in the toilet. And I'm thinking, "Great. Now if this fuckin' guy can make it, anybody can make it."

He did a scene at the Actor's Studio from a Lewis John Carlino play. He did it with Luana Anders. It was just a scene, but it was the best work I ever saw an actor do in the Actor's Studio. I mean it was a heavyweight scene; he was just right on that night. It's about a guy whose wife henpecks him all the time, and he finally turns into a chicken. He does good chicken imitations, and finally he does his chicken thing, and he really gets into it; and then at the end of the play he lays a fuckin' egg. He actually squats down and lays an egg. He was really great in it. I really admired him for that. And I always thought of myself as the best actor, ability-wise, of all the guys in my generation, and that was the first time that I felt that here's a guy on my level that I've got to hang right in there with to stay with. And he went through all the work, and all the preparation, through all the years; he studied, he learned about acting, he always had interesting points of view about acting.

Then I got a call one day in 1970—from him. I was doing a *Land of the Giants* TV show. I was zapping people with a zip gun, making them time travelers that could go back in time, or some goddamn thing like that, and I got a phone call from him, saying [Here, Dern does a great impersonation of Nicholson], "Hey, we're doin' this goddamn movie. C'mon Derns, we got it here. We're doin' basketball players. Gimme a fuckin' break. Hey, we're up there, what a bunch of fuckin' lames; gonna get me a mil. We're goin' up makin' movies." So I said, "Oh, Jesus Christ." Now at this time, *Easy Rider* is the only thing that's broken big. He did that pitiful thing with Barbra Streisand, which I saw, and it was a total toilet job for him. I mean the movie was awful, but you could see he was uncomfortable and awkward and Minnelli intimidated the shit out of him, and he just couldn't do any work. It was too bad, because it scared him a little bit. In no sense did he and I ever have a rivalry. It was me that had the rivalry, in that I wasn't making it and all these other people were making it; I mean, Redford, Beatty, Jimmy Caan. Every fuckin' guy in the world but me. Anyway, he says we're doing this movie, and so forth and so on, and I find out it's legitimate, and they make me an offer, and I go up to Oregon to do *Drive, He Said*.

He was the first director that I had worked with, even though I had worked with Kazan and Hitchcock, who really made me feel that, even though

I was not the star of the movie, I was as important as anybody else in the film. He was very good with actors. He was particularly good with me; he was encouraging, and he was the first person that actually directed me, in that he said, "Don't do this, try this." He gave me things to do, quite little mannerisms, little bits to do. But then again, he let me go, he let me improvise certain things. Consequently, we got on very well on the picture. He was fairly disorganized in making the film. He was definitely ready to direct his first picture, but he was not ready to direct it without more help than he had going in. He was not a guy who was readily acceptable to outside help at that time, whether it was from producers, asisstant directors, script girls, or whoever it was. He would listen, but I don't know whether it was that he wasn't big enough yet in his own head as a person to say, "Boys, I need help. I don't know." He just didn't do that, and it hurt him a lot. And it hurt the movie a lot. Not really in the performances so much, because he always hung in there with the actors, but in the point of view of the film and everything. I think its' a good film.

This might be cold to say, but I'm not really that proud of the movie. I'm proud of the fact that the director did not compromise, at least in the making of the film. He said in the making of it what he wanted to say. Now between the making of it and the time it came out and the editing, I don't know what happened. That's not my department. But I do know that he insisted on his point of view, and what he wanted to say, and what he wanted each character to say in the scenes, and he's the first man that really fought for that, of that vernacular of directors. I mean, with a Kazan or a Hitchcock, they'd done so many films it was already something that you do. Bob Aldrich or somebody like that, they just do those things. But Jack really fought for it on his first film, and he didn't give in in those areas, and that was heavyweight.

Question: Why do you think *Drive, He Said* failed both critically and at the box office?

Dern: Well, I think for three reasons. I think first of all it got a bad reception at Cannes. I don't know why, I don't know what happens at festivals, I wasn't there. It got a bad reception. When it came to New York then, to open, the word was out that they had a toilet. And there wasn't an outlandishly big ad campaign out then to override that.

Number two was that it was the last of the campus revolution pictures, to use a really corny phrase. *R.P.M.* was out, *Getting Straight* was out, *The Strawberry Statement* was out. It had been said.

And number three, I think Jack suffered from his excellence as an actor as a first-time director. I think somehow they expected more than what they saw. Had he not had *Five Easy Pieces* out yet, or *Carnal Knowledge* out, which opened the same time *Drive, He Said* did, I think he'd have probably gotten off much better. But somehow you live by the sword, and you die by the sword, and if you have excellence in one area of the profession, and if you're an outspoken guy—and he is—well, that all travels around. So when you make a movie, and you say that movie says certain things, when they go to that movie they better see it. They better see the greatest fuckin' movie that's ever been made, or else you're in trouble.

The perfect example of it is, I went on then and did *Silent Running*. Now there is no question about the ability of the directors. Jack is a far superior director to Douglas Trumbull, far superior, and look at the difference in the two movies. And look at the credit Doug Trumbull gets and the credit Jack gets. Some really hip critics gave Jack good reviews, and other really hip critics ripped him; but he survived in it, whereas Doug Trumbull has big deals at Warner's and Metro. He is a great film-maker, Douglas Trumbull, I really believe that. He's got an enormously gifted imagination in that area of making drones, and putting little people in there, and making the rings of Saturn, and doing it all out in a workshop in Canoga Park for seventy-five thousand dollars, which was his effects budget on the movie—it looks like six million dollars, I mean it's incredible, and so they gave a lot to him for that. But as far as dealing with me as an actor, or the other actors in the movie—what I consider the directorial aspect of films to be as important as the overall aspect and the look of the picture, is the behavior of the people, and the involvement of the people—Jack is superior at that. Jack is as gifted as almost anyone I've ever worked with, up until Rafelson, in that area. He's just brilliant that way. But they didn't give that to him; they shot him down.

Question: Do you resent the fact that "directed by Jack Nicholson" was billed above all the actors in *Drive, He Said?*

Dern: No. In certain situations I would have resented it, but you find any way you can to sell a picture, and they feel nobody will see "directed by" and they'll just see Jack Nicholson, *Drive, He Said,* and they'll figure if he's got pull from *Easy Rider* and *Five Easy Pieces,* they'll get them into the theater. I mean, that's what they're looking for, so you can't resent them for that; it's a business. Now had it been someone else, some lame or something like that that I'd worked for, then I would've resented it. But, then, that's part of the deal you make as an actor when you begin. Now I had no power then to make any kind of a deal. When I did *Drive* I'd done twenty-one films, but I was always number seven or eight man. That's another difference between Jack's career and my career. Now, *The King of Marvin Gardens* does for me what *Five Easy Pieces* did for Jack; *Silent Running* did for me kind of what *Easy Rider* did for Jack. *Marvin Gardens* makes me a major star like Jack is. The difference in getting to that point that we're both at now is that he did a zillion B movies and no A movies, but when he did a lot of the B movies, he was the star of them, like *Psych-Out* and *Hell's Angels on Wheels.* I did a few B movies; I call them B movies even though they made a lot of money—any movie Roger Corman makes to me is a B movie. I mean, when they're scammin' around for three hundred thousand dollars that's B. Give us a break. When you're sharing box lunches that's a B movie; when you get a box lunch it's an A movie; when you get a real lunch it's millennium.

Jack was kind of like the king of the underground movies, although they weren't underground movies, the king of that vernacular of film, and he hardly did any television at all. Whereas I've done twenty-five films, over a hundred television shows, I did a series for a year and all that, and I logged all that time climbing the ladder bit by bit by bit. I did what I call fourteen or fifteen A movies; multimillion-dollar-budget movies—two, three, four million-dollar pictures, but in those pictures I was always the ninth or tenth man, and I always had one or two scenes that I was very good in, but so, who gives a shit? By the time they get around to explaining about my character, the movie's over. So, it's an interesting parallel in that we both started at exactly the same place actually, and we both climbed the ladder on totally different sides of the business, me through television and then converting that television work into little parts in movies and building up the ladder that way, and he to kind of hanging in there and always doing

Bruce Dern promoting a scheme to Nicholson in **Marvin Gardens**

good work until his people finally gave him a shot in *Easy Rider,* and *Easy Rider* hit. If *Easy Rider* doesn't hit, then he's got to wait for Curly [Bob Rafelson] to make *Five Easy Pieces,* and Curly maybe don't make *Five Easy Pieces* if *Easy Rider* don't hit. So it's all a matter of logistics and timing; it always has been and it always will be. If you're there at the right time in the right spot—there are many, many gifted people in this business.

I don't know what a genius is. I think at times I've done genius work as an actor; I feel Jack has done genius work as an actor; I feel Brando has constantly done genius work. I mean, there's a bunch of people. I don't mean to just name us three. But somehow Jack has always been a guy, along with myself and maybe a couple others, who has maintained an excellent standard of acting, no matter how trashy the vehicle that we've been in. And the fact that we both climbed the ladder independently, and in different segments of the business, is a very unique thing, because you can never say now that you have to be George Hamilton or Rock Hudson or Bob Redford or Warren Beatty and come from a certain kind of luck-out at the beginning of your career. I mean, everybody lucks out. I lucked out to be in *Marvin Gardens,* Jack lucked out to be in *Easy Rider,* I mean he's actually a replacement for the Rip [Rip Torn].

Question: How did that come about?

Dern: When Schneider and Rafelson got involved with *Easy Rider,* they pushed very heavily. for Jack. I don't think Peter and Dennis wanted

Jack in the film originally. Curly insisted that Jack be in the film because he always thought Jack was a brilliant actor. He's a guy that always goes with the people he thinks are that way, and he went with Jack in *Five Easy Pieces* and proved it, and in *Marvin Gardens* he went with both of us; and Ellen Burstyn also. He put her against Bogdanovich's will, he made them use both her and Cloris Leachman in *The Last Picture Show.* Bogdanovich didn't want to use either one of them. Rafelson used Ellen again in our picture.

Jack has done well. He's excellent in *Marvin Gardens,* just excellent. In *Carnal Knowledge* he was very good, but a little lazy, I felt, a little lazy. But I think he got caught up in the Nichols syndrome, that's what the work looks like to me. I've seen the pictures just once, so I can't tell—I enjoyed the picture, it was nice, but he did not have anybody to hang in there with him, you know what

Shocking climax scene from Marvin Gardens *with (l. to r.) Ellen Burstyn, Bruce Dern and Nicholson*

Nicholson and Dern mount hourses symbolic of their roles in The King of Marvin Gardens

I mean? Ann-Margret was in way over her head, and consequently he pulled her up and she did the best work of her life. Candice Bergen was about what she always is, I mean my feeling about her is that she's never been used properly in film. She's got interesting gifts and interesting talents, but they never really deal with her vulnerability, which to me would be really exciting. And Garfunkel was kind of wandering.

As far as I'm concerned, Jack's a guy I would jump at to work with again as an actor. From now on, hopefully, I will always be the star of the movies that I'm in, and I would never want to give that up; I've worked too fuckin' long to get where I am. I would love for Jack to direct me. I would say, up to date, he and Rafelson are the best two directors I've ever worked for. Rafelson definitely first and ahead of him, but Jack's right in there. Now, it's not fair to compare them to Hitchcock and Kazan, because when I worked with Hitchcock and Kazan I was just playing little parts, and they didn't have any time to work with me, so in actuality I can't say I really worked with them. You know, unless you have a big part, and go through the everyday give and take of an actor-director relationship, it's not the same thing.

The difference between Rafelson and Jack right now is—ability-wise they're both equal—Raf-

elson is a film-maker. Jack is not yet, and that's the difference. Bob understands the overall film; what it says. Jack understands it, but his brightness of understanding it somehow gets in the way of translating that into what he wants it to say on the screen.

Question: What's the difference, if any, in working with Jack as a director and working with him as an actor?

Dern: Well, he fucks around a little more now than he used to. He's more fun also, he's not as grim now when he's working as an actor. When we worked in the *Rebel Rousers*, which is the only time we really worked together, because it was the only movie where we had scenes together even though we'd been in five movies together, he fucked around, but then it was kind of neurotic fuckin' around, each guy into his own little bag, showing how tough he can be, making everyone think he's getting more pussy than anyone else. But somehow I was always married through all that, so I never horsed around as much as the guys that weren't married. But now, his horsing around is more relaxed and more enjoyable, and I can understand it, but it's tough sometimes on other actors. I know when I do it myself it's tough on other actors, and it's rude, and it's cruel, but I can't stop myself from doing it sometimes, and neither can he. He doesn't

Nicholson and Dern in the Atlantic City convention center for a mock Miss America pageant in Marvin Gardens

quite have the patience that he should; when you go to take four or five he gives you one of those, "Oooohhh, fuck." I get the feeling that the biggest difference is that he would ultimately rather direct than act. I mean, that's the feeling that I get. Now that he's proved that he can be a major motion picture star, and that he can be a major actor, I think he'd rather move on, whereas that's not my desire at all. I'm in what I want to move on in. I think he's a guy that wants to say it all and do it all, and the next step, obviously, is to make films, and if he wants to appear in them, fine. But I don't think anybody should put that burden on themselves, particularly him. He is an actor desperately in need of direction. I don't think he should ever attempt to direct himself.

Question: So do you feel, then, that Nicholson has reached a plateau as an actor?

Dern: No, I figure he has a lot more things he can do and say as an actor, but my feeling is that he feels that he's reached a certain level with the kind of roles that he's getting now, and he should go on and go into new areas. That's what I keep talking to him about; go director, go director. He always thinks I'm saying, "Sure, what am I? Get another fuckin' guy out of the way, so you get another part by default." Well, that ain't a bad idea, but I love to act with him. Together we're really great. In *Marvin Gardens* you'll see it. You probably won't see two American actors as right on as we are in that film. And both cast totally different than either one of us has ever been cast in our lives, and that's the exciting and fun thing about acting. *Marvin Gardens* is the first time that Jack has really been cast differently, and been asked to do different things than what he normally does, which is [again the Nicholson impersonation], "Hey, come on . . ."

Question: Can you sum up, then, what kind of offscreen relationship you have with Jack?

Dern: Since *Marvin Gardens* we have become very good friends. He comes to my house a lot, I go to his house a lot. He lives with kind of a strange girl; Michelle Phillips is a lot younger than we are, even though she's probably only eight or nine years younger than we are. She also comes from a whole

52

music scene that we never knew anything about. She wants to be an actress now; that's tough on him, it's much tougher on her, but it's tough on him. He loves her and everything, and I'm sure she loves him, but it's very tough times for him in that respect, because she's a tough lady. I think he would like to get married again. I think he would like that thing of settling down and having dinner to come home to every now and then and not having to go out and buy everybody's meal. But right now, he's just about as good a friend as I have. We check in at least two or three times a week. We never talk more than about three or four minutes at a time, whenever we feel the conversation slipping, that's it. We just say, "Well, I'll see you." And the next day he'll call me and say, "Sure, who am I? Don't call me. I'm just a piece of shit." And we'll talk for about five minutes and we'll jack each other off and then hang up, and then two days later I'll call him and say, "Yeah, why call me? I'm nothing. I'm only billed second in the fuckin' movie." We have very good thermometers of when we've had enough of each other, and it's never having enough, it's just that he's a guy that takes vibes from whoever it is that's around, and I'm a guy who's always been kind of a private liver and a private person, and I have a tough time hangin' in there when he dopes with them, a tough time. I got him into running in Atlantic City—long-distance running is my hobby—so much so that he ran six miles once.

He gets very depressed very easily, and very down on himself, and down on the world, and the business, and everybody around. *Drive, He Said* was a big blow to him. *Drive* hurt him. He thought, "Hey, we're in; eleven mil," and it hurt him. He has to understand that he's reached a lot of people with his films, and his films have made a lot of

Nicholson, Dern, and Julia Anne Robinson on the beach in a scene from Marvin Gardens

money. He was surrounded by a lot of people that wouldn't tell him the truth, and that was sad. And at times I've felt that I haven't told him the truth, because he's one of those guys that gets so depressed if you lay one on him that it's just not worth it. You figure that you'd rather slide a little bit with him than do it. I'm gonna stop it. I have stopped it. I've been much more honest with him in the last couple of weeks. But when he's here and you're here, a little below him, or anybody's like that, it's very tough in this business to hang in there and be brutally honest with people, because you feel the guy won't like me and he'll never use me. You know, it's that whole psychology, and it's very sad. I'm guilty of it; everybody's guilty of it.

Jack is a great middle-of-the-road person. I mean, he rides the white line better than anybody I ever saw. Inside he commits himself, but outside he says, "Well, those are nice jeans you've got on, and not bad Levis you've got on." He never says, "Hey, what are you wearing? Take a wash." He never does that, and when he does it you think, "Jack Nicholson put me on today." So he always protects himself. He says, "Aw, I was givin' you a jack job in a paper sack." That's the way he covers himself, but he's really a terrific guy. I mean, I really came to love him at times on *Marvin Gardens,* and I've never had a relationship where I've felt like that. Now, the role had a lot to do with that; we play brothers and I'm always after him in the movie to get him to love, and I had just never come across a guy like that. He had some rough times there when it was lonely, and of course none of his people are left, his mom and dad are gone and my mom died during the making of the movie, and we both always refer to Mom. "Sure, let's get this one for Mom." And he could never really do that with me, and then after my mom died, I came on the set the first day and he said, "O.K., we're getting this one for Dern's mom." It just cracked me up, because both of our moms couldn't have cared less. They thought we were in a totally plumber business, a total septic tank.

Question: Can you remember one particularly funny or weird experience that happened while you were working with Jack?

Dern: In *Marvin Gardens* when we were on the boardwalk in Atlantic City, both in one day, a guy came up to him and one guy says to him, "You Jack Nicklaus?" and the other one says, "You Mike Nicklaus?" and they didn't know whether he played golf or what. One guy came up to him and said,

"What are youse doin' here? Filmin' a golf commercial?" And then they'd call him. They'd say, "Hey, come over here. You Mike Nicklaus?" And they weren't putting him on. They thought that was his name. And he never gets into it with them and says, "No, I'm Jack Nicholson."

That was one. Another day we were staying in this hotel with one of the teams from the small college football play-off, C. W. Post. We were working all day Saturday on the day of the game, and C. W. Post got crushed by Delaware seventy to thirteen, and they were staying in our motel. So we're walking down the street, and we'd just done a great scene, Jack and I, and we were very up and Curly was very up. But I'm a lay-back; I don't want to go around punching people. Curly's a very big man, physically. He walks into the hotel, and just before he walks in he turns to me and says, "Hey. How's about we just beat the shit out of one of these football players." And just as he says that we go through the front door, and Jack walks in with this fuckin' briefcase he was carrying and goes, "Hey, how'd you do against Delaware?" And all these guys are standing around, and he had this old coat on that he wore in the movie, and this woman yelled out across the thing, "About as good as you did when you bought that coat." That totally shut him up.

And sometimes people will come up and know me and not him. Since *Silent Running* he's gotten a little more of that. People say, "Oh, that's the guy . . ." and he'll turn around and say, "Sure, give it all to him. What am I? I'm just a major fuckin' movie star, and you're looking at a man that talks to refrigerators."

Question: What kind of ambitions did Jack have when you first met him?

Dern: I don't know. I didn't know him that well. I wasn't aware of any ambition other than he wanted to be an actor, and work all the time. He wanted to be a respected actor, I know that. And it hurt him that he could never get a job in television. He did *Sea Hunt* and those shows like everybody else, but he never did the big TV shows, and it hurt him. He was a tough sale for a long time.

Question: Is he pretty well liked around Hollywood.

Dern: I don't think he has an enemy in Hollywood, except a guy that's jealous of him. I don't think he's ever made an enemy. I think he went through, when they were doing *Head* and all, a kind of crazy period where'd he come on the set

The Monkees from the ill-fated Head

and say [again the Nicholson voice], "Hey, come on. Give me a fuckin' scene. Yeah, give me Monkees. Come on, anything. Out the window. Zit can. What's the difference?" I don't think he's ever alienated anybody. He's not a cruel man. And he's not an impersonal guy. He did a very, very heavyweight thing for me.

When we were doing *Marvin Gardens* we have a little scene where I have to drive one of these furniture carts out of the convention hall with big carpets on it, and the two girls—he and I are sitting in the car, and the two girls get on the back of the car, and as soon as they're on I have to drive off. The girls get on, and as soon as they sat down I drove it off. Well, one of the girls was stoned, and the other one was trying to hang on for dear life, and the car jerked, and the girl that was stoned, she was out of it, just went over on her head. I went about twenty feet and stopped, and everybody ran to the girl, and Jack didn't move. He just put his arm around me and said, "Are you all right, Dern? Are you sure?" He was more concerned about me, because he knew what I was

going through, than he was about the girl on her ass. And that was the most heavyweight thing in a crisis that anyone had ever done for me in my life. That was *the* most heavyweight thing.

It wasn't a big thing, the girl was fine. But I didn't know that at the time, and he didn't know it. It's like in the automobile accident; you always go to the person that's injured. You never go to the person that hit the person that's injured, and that's who he went to, and that was heavyweight. That's an inexplicable thing that will make me love him for the rest of my life no matter what he does. He can drown my puppy, and I'll still understand him a little bit.

Question: Do you think he has any offensive characteristics?

Dern: I think he offends certain women sometimes. I think he pissed off a lot of them with his *Playboy* article. He refers to them as "pussy," and it's a little beyond that now for them. And yet he has a great deal of respect for women, and I would think was one of the pro women's lib type people ten years ago. He's always for liberated women, but

55

he's very dependent on them. They're chicks and bimbos and this and that. They're pieces of ass, and he's in a big contest about that. At thirty-five years old he's still big into, like Friday night, "let's get the car." He doesn't say that, but that's what it is. I think that's one of the reasons why he'd like to get married. I think he'd like to cut all that out. I think he'd like for Michelle and him to have it all. I think he'd like to just give everything to her. But it remains to be seen whether it'll ever happen; I don't think it will. I think somehow that they won't make it throughout the years. I hope they do.

Question: Why don't you think they'll make it?

Dern: I don't know. I just think there's too big a gap. I don't know whether it's age, or what. She's been there in the music business and it's all over for her. Her music career is gone. That era of music is almost gone. She wants to be an actress, and she studies, and studies very hard, and I don't know how good she is. But I do know that it's a big burden to put on him that he should have to put her in a movie with him. And it's a big burden for her to not ask him to put her in a movie with him. It's that terrible husband-and-wife relationship with both people being in the business. I was married to an actress and you can't do it.

Question: How much of the film-making process did you and Jack learn from acting in B movies such as *Psych-Out* and *Rebel Rousers?*

Dern: Seventy-five per cent of everything I learned about the business, I learned from those movies, because you weren't directed in those movies. The guys that were directing them didn't know. They were just making a scam film to make bucks. They were involved in the deal somehow. In *Psych-Out* Dick Rush was a serious film-maker, but he had no conception of how to deal with an actor. He just didn't know. He didn't know what to say to you; he'd just say, "Do it again," or "Try it again," and any kind of enthusiasm or energy he would mistake for talent, and he would just love that. He was the most sensitive of the early directors that I worked for, although he wasn't the best. Corman was far superior to him. So what you did was to learn to do it yourself. You learn how to survive, and be real, and be good, and be interesting, and exciting, and to promote your career, and continue on. That's what you learn, and that was seventy-five per cent of the ball game.

Now, consequently, later, that becomes a problem, because then you get with a guy who's a director and you don't trust him. That's because you couldn't trust these other guys because they'd ruin you. So you have a tendency to nod, "yes, yes," to a director, but inside you're fighting him, and you can't give it all to him and listen to him. And that's hard. And that was hard for Jack, and that was hard for me. And you can see it in a lot of Jack's work. You can see it in *Five Easy Pieces.* He did not trust Bob in the early part of the film. In *Marvin Gardens* he totally trusted him. He trusted Nichols, I think, because Nichols has a bullshit reputation of being a genius, and a boy-wonder, and all that kind of stuff, and that's one of the reasons that I think his work is as lazy as it is. Not that he shouldn't have trusted him; he should have, but he trusted him for the wrong reasons. Nichols is the top jet-set director, you know what I mean? I mean, he's in with the Lizard [Elizabeth Taylor] and Richard Burton, and he's in with Jackie probably, and all them kinds of people. It was a trip, and Jack was on the train. It's the same thing he was on with the McGovern thing. He loved that. He loves that style and grace. He's got to be in there with the big ones. He don't want to have the four guys from the Mobil station up to his house for dinner. Make no mistake about it. He definitely wants the guy that shot Reuben Salazar, and Daniel Ellsberg, and he wants all them kinds of people there. He loves that, and he knows how to handle that. It's not crafty, it just excites him.

I mean, he went down to Miami Beach for the event, and also because he was tied to McGovern. That's his way; he's a public person. He may tell you that he loves to live privately and is very reserved, but he's a totally public person. He's show-time; he's a showman—a great showman, and that's the thing he never gives himself credit for. He's a P. T. Barnum in his own element, and that's why he should make films. Everything is out front, it's all open. The real Jack Nicholson ain't out front, because he'd never let you see that, unless you get to know him really well and you're watching a football game with him or something like that. All I have to say to him is "John Brodie," and he goes totally fuckin' nuts and can't even deal with it. He says, "I've got a man throwing a pass to the opposing fuckin' tackle in a ten-billion-dollar football game."

I think the best thing that ever happened to him is, he has probably come further from what he was raised in than any of these other guys that have made it. Jack comes from very rough times, although not as rough as say McQueen or somebody like that from Hell's Kitchen. But he lived on the bad side of the tracks until he was about thirteen, and then somehow shook it out, and he's always tried to impress people with how sharp he is, or how intelligent he is, and how quick he is, and how he knows this person—and actually knows him—and actually is as sharp a guy as I've ever known in my life, and is very quick-witted. That's why it's sad about the dope. I don't mean to make it sound like he's a heavy doper or an addict, because he isn't. But it's just a substitute he doesn't need. He's too big a person for that. He's just too big a person for it, and it's sad, because he loves athletics and he loves sports. And he'll win almost any god-damn thing he can do. He's a tremendous competitor.

Question: Does his competitiveness put strains on your relationship at all?

Dern: Not mine, but it does with everybody else he comes in contact with. When somebody reads some bad news about Jack and Michelle being here or there, and Jack Nicholson showed up looking like dog shit, there's about a hundred guys going, "Yaaaaaayyy!"

He's got one friend, Harry Gittes, who is the most productive and sensitive guy that knows both of us, and is just a super guy. Jack loves him, and I love him. He's the only guy in Jack's circle who is an honest, true friend of Jack's, as far as giving it to him straight. And for a while Jack had a tendency to make a bunch of these guys feel like he was gonna do it all for them. Harry was a big advertising executive in New York and came out here to help produce *Drive,* but then all of a sudden it was all over. He's left a job, all his money's gone that he earned on *Drive,* and he has nothing to do. And so now he's trying to break in as a producer on his own. Jack gave him the biggest break he could, and he should have understood that. But he can't take him on every picture; other people are making the pictures. I don't think either one of them ever sat down and had a dead serious conversation about the bottom line, which is when it's over, it's over. It's like I worked in a play with Paul Newman for a year once, and he told me how great I was and that I could call him when I got out here. Well, I've never worked with him. You mean, there wasn't a part I can play in *Cool Hand Luke* as a prisoner or a guard, when I'm bleeding on my ass broke?

But Jack's weeded out the freeloaders. He

used to have some. But, I mean, he travels in a very fast group. They live a fast life; they're out to dinner every night. You got to be in good shape to hang in there with them; they go. I live out at the beach, and they're out at the beach from two to five. While they're out at the beach from two to five, they're at two or three different houses, and then they say, "Hey, what do you say we go into town, have a little supper, then go Lakers. Then we go over and have a little joint, and then go Troubadour it up. Tomorrow we're over Maxfield Blue, buy a suit—" I mean it—it's just go, go, go, go, go. To me that's a little sad, because there's no home. He's got a nice house, Michelle lives right next door. That's kind of bizarre, but that's the way she wants it.

Question: Tell us something you can't tell us about Jack Nicholson.

Dern: I don't know any sordid things about him. I've never seen him at an orgy, I've never been to an orgy, so I don't know whether he's been to one or not. I don't think he ever has. He sure talks about them a lot. I think the only thing I can tell you is that he brags about a lot more pussy than he's ever gotten. His opinion is that, "Hey, come on. I'm out of here, in five minutes I'm hip-deep in pussy over on Highland Avenue." But I question that. I know that girls tend to throw themselves at him at parties, but you have to remember what girls they are, and what parties they are. He goes to a Hollywood producer's party someplace, there are girls there that throw themselves at Jack Nicholson. If he went to the Fairfax High School senior prom, he gets nothin'. That's about the only thing I'd say. I'd say if you cut half of his pussy in half, you'd have it about right, and still he probably gets more than anybody around. He and Beatty have contests about it. They talk in those terms. Jack'll say, "Hey, I left Hefner's—" Well, anybody gets laid at Hefner's, come on, you know what I mean? Michael Dunn probably scores big there. I don't mean to put Michael Dunn down, but, I mean, if you're at Hefner's and you don't get laid, get out of town.

Question: Do you think Jack is basically an honest guy?

Dern: Yeah. I think he's honest to other people, and I don't think he basically honest with himself. It's just conjecture on my part. But I don't think he's honest with himself, and I think that's why he has a lot of tortured days. I don't think he tells himself the truth about what he thinks about

Nicholson, Ellen Burstyn, and Bruce Dern in The King of Marvin Gardens

other people, and what he feels about other people, and I think he always tells himself only the negative truth about what he feels about himself. In other words, he constantly needs encouragement and pats on the back, constantly. We all do, but he needs it a little more probably than a lot of people. Actors as a whole need it more than anyone.

I don't think he's honest about other people's work to them, except in certain situations, but I'm not sure anybody is. You have to sometimes find ways to say things without telling the guy it's awful, and that's hard, because we've been in everything that's awful and we can measure it. I mean, I did *The Two-Headed Transplant* so I know what that was like. I know what the bottom flooor is; I've been on it, and so has he.

I would just like to see him have a home life. I'd just like to see him feel that he can get off the train now and then, because he is on a train. I think the happiest time of his life is when he's on

location doing a movie. Because then he's on salary, he's relaxed, he's got money coming in, he's working, he's productive. He's a movie star, he's got girls coming down to see him, he's got everything he wants.

Question: Do you think at this point you could pick out one performance and call it his best?

Dern: Easy Rider.

Question: Why?

Dern: It was the first time that we'd seen him. He was definitely the character. He was more a deep part of Jack than what we've seen before. Now his overall performance in *Five Easy Pieces* was outstanding, but it was closer to Jack. He didn't have to reach as far. I think probably the years will tell us that the work in *Five Easy Pieces* was greater than *Easy Rider*. But for me, *Easy Rider* was the World Series for him, and he won the car. I mean, that's what it's all about. For me, *Marvin Gardens* is the World Series, and I won the

58

car. They may not know I won the car, but I won the car, because I know I was great in the film. I've never done as good work in my life. And we're talking about two guys that always do great work, but somehow the thing that's the most gratifying is when a guy does it under the pressure of knowing that this is his shot. A guy like Redford will always have a shot, that's why his work ain't never worth a shit. He's good; he's always good, but he ain't never great. Beatty's the same way, only I think Redford is a good deal better actor than Beatty is. He's always Warren Beatty. He'll give you a couple of variations, but Jack was not just Jack in *Easy Rider,* nor was he in *Five Easy Pieces,* and there's no way he's Jack in this, and there's no way I'm Bruce in this. But there'll be a whole new flock of fans that will see this movie and say "That's Jack Nicholson, and that's Bruce Dern." That's why I think *Easy Rider* was the best thing.

Also, because any time you're in a movie with Peter Fonda it's very hard to do quality work as an actor, because he's just not an actor. He just doesn't have a clue. I don't know why they stand for it; I don't think they will much longer. I think his career has definitely waned as an actor. He might be a pretty good film-maker some day.

Question: Can you characterize Jack Nicholson in one sentence?

Dern: [Again the Nicholson impersonation] "Heyeyeyeyeyey, we got it."

Jack H. Harris

Producer Jack H. Harris in his plush Sunset Blvd. office

A great deal of the time spent on this book was done so in a search for pictures and materials from Jack Nicholson's films. Jack Harris is the producer who currently is distributing the two Jack Nicholson-Monte Hellman Westerns, *Ride in the Whirlwind* and *The Shooting,* and he not only granted us permission to use the stills and posters from those films, but graciously agreed to be interviewed by us. Some of the other Jack H. Harris productions include *Dinosaurusi, The Blob,* which starred Steve McQueen, the 1968 Claude Chabrol film *Les Biches,* and a series of films entitled *The Oldest Profession.*

Though he did not become actively involved in the two Westerns until almost five years after their completion, he had had a growing interest in them well before he had the opportunity to acquire them in 1971. Jack Harris had great faith in the two films, especially since they did so well in Europe, but was greatly surprised when they fell flat here.

As evidenced by the offices on Sunset Boulevard, Jack Harris Productions is not accustomed to failure. Mr. Harris' office is elegantly furnished in rich woods and French provincial furniture. It was in this office that we held the following interview.

Question: How did all the elements involved in the two Westerns come together?

Jack Harris: I want to present the facts in their proper light, so everything I tell you is part hearsay and part personal experience. Hellman and Nicholson were ready to do something, and they came to Roger Corman, and Roger said, "Why don't you make a sex-oriented film. That seems to be doing something now." That takes us back five or six years. They went out and wrote a script, and Corman read it and said, "I think it's a good script, but I think it's too hot. Instead of that, why don't you make a Western?" They were in the middle of writing the script, and Corman calls one day and says, "How much do you think you can do that Western for? Really do it for, with no fooling around?" And Nicholson said seventy-five thousand dollars. After Corman recovered from that he

said, "How would you like to do two of them?"

So they went and wrote the scripts, and as I understand it, Corman was too busy to even read the scripts, so he just told them to go and do the pictures. So they got all their friends, and they went to Kanab, Utah, and they started production on the first picture, and they wrapped that, and then went right into production on the second picture. And that's how the two pictures came to be made.

When they finished the films they showed them to Corman, and he thought they were very good pictures, but he felt they were wrong for the market; so he sat on the pictures.

Nicholson took the pictures to Cannes, and he found a Frenchman who said he would distribute the pictures in France, and they opened first one and then the other, and they did very, very well in France. The problem was the guy they did business with had an office in his hat, and when they came to collect the money they couldn't find him. They're still trying to find him, as I understand it. Corman was still unimpressed, so he decides to get out, and he makes a deal with a guy who's no longer in the picture business, Walter Reade. Walter takes Roger off the hook, and takes over the pictures. Reade's general manager, Jerry Pickman, made a judgment that the pictures were not fit for the market, and then Reade got scared, and then they tried to sell them to television. At this point Hellman and Nicholson are pretty upset with what's happening to the pictures, because they both feel that they're two damn-good motion pictures. I happen to agree with them.

I'd been looking for the pictures. I knew Roger Corman and Walter Reade, but who knew they had them? Then one day I heard they were available. I was talking to Millie Perkins, and she asked me if I'd heard of the pictures, and I said I had, and she said she would find out about them and get back to me. Coincidentally, a few days later I got a call from Hellman's attorney asking me if I wanted to distribute the pictures. I said that I'd like to, but I thought it was proper that I see them first. I saw the pictures, and I was duly impressed, and that's how I came to be involved in the pictures. I had nothing to do with the production of them, and I had nothing to do with the stupid television arrangements, or the Cannes festival. I came in very late in the day, and I felt that the main salability of the films was the box-office appeal of Jack Nicholson, even though I thought they were good films.

Question: What year was that?

Harris: Nineteen seventy-one.

Question: Why did it take so long for them to be released in this country?

Harris: It was judgment, and very frankly, the pictures have not done well. That's a blow to me, because I don't have that kind of experience. All my pictures do real well, but those two just didn't make it.

Question: Do you have plans for redistributing them?

Harris: Yes. We constantly play the pictures, but cracking in a big way is not available to us. We broke both pictures here in L.A. in February, 1972, and did nothing. The film buffs turned out, but that's all.

Question: Why do you think they were such hits in Europe?

Harris: The respect for horseflesh is peculiar to Europe and the Far East. People in this country are fed so much of it on TV every week that Western films per se have been at a steady decline at the theater box office, so I think that's the principal problem. Also, we tried very hard with the pictures. I was going to break them singularly to correspond to his winning the Oscar nomination. The day after the nomination we were in Dallas, and we had every possible press break. We took over the VIP lounge at the airport and worked there for nine solid hours. It surpassed anything I've ever been able to accomplish promotion-wise. The nomination came on a Monday; we did all the promotion stuff on Tuesday; and on Friday we opened, and it was very disappointing. I figured, horses, Nicholson, and Texas. It should be a good parlay. At the same time, *Five Easy Pieces* was in its fourteenth week in Dallas. We had one week and out with our picture. They didn't want to see Jack Nicholson on a horse.

Question: Did it do well critically?

Harris: Fair. The critics didn't break their backs over it.

Question: Do you prefer one over the other?

Harris: No, I think they're both good films. Where *Ride in the Whirlwind* is a more formula-type Western, *The Shooting* is a thinking man's Western. It's more of an action-suspense film than it is a Western film in the formula sense.

I think they're two separate things. To give you an idea, I would like to open *The Shooting* in an exclusive run, and open *Ride in the Whirlwind* city-wide at theaters and drive-ins.

Question: Do you think Hellman and Nicholson were looking for artistic pieces at the time, or money-makers?

Harris: They were looking for both. You see, when you get in the position that Nicholson is in today, you can't say that profit motive is his foremost thought. It just doesn't work. He feels that they're good pieces of work, and that they should be exposed to the public as examples of good work. But how do you reap the benefit? You reap the benefit by virtue of your ticket sales. In other words, you can have favorable reviews up to the ceiling, but if people don't buy tickets, that's the definitive vote that counts.

Question: Can you explain the ending of *The Shooting*?

Harris: First of all, there was a whole prologue that Roger Corman cut out that would have

(above) Cameron Mitchell (l.) and Jack Nicholson (r.) in Ride in the Whirlwind

(below) Nicholson and Cameron Mitchell (r.) at their hide-out in Whirlwind

Jack Nicholson and Will Hutchins in The Shooting

explained a lot of things. I can tell you what I thought when I first saw the pictures. I think that would be valid, because nobody had discussed it with me. I didn't meet with Monte until after I had seen the pictures. When I first saw it I thought it was symbolic of Warren Oates chasing himself. In other words, it was a man's duel with his own ego. He demonstrated to himself that he was in an impossible life that had no ending but a violent one. That's what it said to me.

Question: Did Jack's main motivations for doing these two projects lie in the producing-writing end of it, or in the acting end of it?

Harris: I think the writing-producing. This is by inference, you know. I think the writing-producing aspects were foremost. He still hasn't gotten away from wanting to be a film-maker, and that does not necssarily include performing. This was an opportunity to do that, because he was the producer on both pictures.

Question: What do you think these two films were basically trying to say?

Harris: Looking at the films today is a bit unfair. It's a damn shame that the films weren't released five or six years ago, when they were actually completed and ready for the market, because

(above) Warren Oates and Nicholson in The Shooting

(below) Nicholson and Millie Perkins in Ride in the Whirlwind

then they had a lot of brand new things in them. The films were trying to say that a Western doesn't have to have good guys and bad guys, and a man in love with his horse instead of a girl, and that sort of thing. It can be about people who have unique personalities, and images. Also, they were to demonstrate the way with a buck. These pictures were done with very little money, which proves that spending a lot of money does not neces- sarily make a slick product up on the screen. And also the inventiveness of Nicholson and Hellman as producer and director.

Question: Can you characterize Jack Nicholson in one sentence?

Harris: A truly dedicated motion-picture-industry person, who fully believes in the industry, and being connected with it, the industry has taken a very big part of his life.

Sally Struthers

Though she was on the screen for less than five minutes in *Five Easy Pieces,* we felt that Sally Struthers would be able to give us an interesting point of view about Jack Nicholson. She did not know him prior to the film, and only worked with him for what amounted to about a week. In that short period, however, she was able to make some definite observations about the man.

Ms. Struthers is probably best known for her portrayal of Gloria Stivik, Archie Bunker's daughter, on television's miracle show *All In The Family.* Before that she was seen as the Tim Conway dancer on *The New Tim Conway Show.* She also appeared on the *Smothers Brothers Show.*

As far as motion pictures are concerned, Sally has done only one film since *Five Easy Pieces,* and that was a fine and really different performance as Fran in Sam Peckinpah's *The Getaway,* which starred Steve McQueen and Ali MacGraw.

Arrangements to interview Ms. Struthers were made through her publicist, Rose Pichinson, and we agreed to meet Sally at CBS Television City where she was rehearsing for the week's taping of *All In The Family.* Sally greeted us like old friends, and after chatting for a few minutes in the commissary, we found our way into an unoccupied dressing room. Unlike her garrulous and excitable character Gloria, Ms. Struthers is thoughtful and composed. She likes to talk, but enjoys listening as well, and after a few minutes we were all very relaxed, so we turned on the tape recorder.

Question: How did you get the part in *Five Easy Pieces*?

Sally Struthers: I don't know. There's a man by the name of Fred Roos, a casting man. I'm sure he's done a lot of things, and apparently from a session, or a scene, or a time in my life that I don't remember, because I, like a lot of other actors, block out an interview that you want that you don't get, and apparently I read for something, or did a scene once at a studio, and Fred Roos saw me. Well, nothing ever came of it, so I never remembered meeting Fred Roos. But one day, three years ago, a phone call came when I was living with this lady and her daughter, and working as a secretary, and this man said, "I'm Fred Roos, and I saw you audition a year ago, and we're doing a movie over here at Columbia call *Five Easy Pieces,* and can you come read for it?" And I said, "I'll be there in five minutes." So I went over there, and I read it, and he liked it, and he said he'd let me know, and he called me a few days later. Then they brought another girl in, and I hate to say it, but I have blocked out her name, and I have blocked out her name for two reasons. Number one, because I didn't get to know her that well. And number two, because since then she has killed herself. But we both read for the two parts of the bowling-alley girls, and we got them. But I never did understand the part, because the part in the script was called "Pigmy," but when I introduced myself in the movie to Jack I said, "My name's Shirley, but my friends call me Betty." But the script said "Pigmy," and I never understood it, but I played it.

A few weeks later we all left on a bus for up north, and I did my part, which was just my bowling-alley scene with Jack, where I had to pat him on the head and flirt with him and pretend like I thought he was wearing a wig. And the other scene where we were sitting around in our underwear telling funny stories, and then I left location. It was like four or five days' work. I got back into town, and I got a phone call to get right back up to location. And I said, "For what?" "Well, for the love scene between you and Jack." And I said, "No, no, no, no, no. That's the scene between Twinkie and Bobby, and I'm Pigmy." And they go, "We know. You're doing it." And I didn't have an agent, so I had nobody to call and say, "Should I or shouldn't I," and I got up there, and they rushed

Sally Struthers (l.), Nicholson, and Marlena MacGuire at the bowling alley in Five Easy Pieces

me off into body make-up, and I wouldn't let them make me up, and I wouldn't open the bathroom door, and I wouldn't take off my clothes, and it was just awful. And the part that infuriated me the most was when they finally got me stripped down to my underpants and I refused to take those off, I came out and Jack was fully dressed. At that moment I was full of such anger for him. I thought, how can this actor, knowing how uncomfortable I am being stripped down to my underwear—I'm holding my breasts facing the wall, and sidling along the wall out to where I'm supposed to stand, he's standing there in a T-shirt, jeans, and boots. I was angry at him, but he turned out to be a dream, because he didn't stare at me, and he was very professional about it. He just set me up on a kitchen counter, and I wrapped my legs around his waist, and we went. The director said, "Go, and spin, and flail, and moan, and cry, and get her somehow into

the bedroom on the bed, and we'll just follow you with the camera." On the first take, Jack got a little crazy with me and whipped me into a Venetian blind, which is very sharp if you hit it that fast, and it cut my leg. So then they let me put on my jeans, so at least I had something on to protect my legs. The second time, Jack lost his balance, and went through a plate-glass window and cut his hand open horribly. That was just awful, and they took him outside and did butterfly taping on his hand to keep it from bleeding. The third take we got it.

If it had been someone else, I think it would have been hard for me to do, but Jack Nicholson is so sort of boyish and shy, and gregarious at the same time, if that's possible, that I guess I got through it all right. It was good for me.

Question: Was it anybody's particular idea to have Jack wearing a Triumph T-shirt?

67

Struthers: Yes, I'm sure it was the director's idea. It might have even been Jack's. I don't know how much Jack threw in and how much Bob Rafelson threw in, but they both added a lot. We all added a lot. The story that I told about the dimple in my chin was my story. It wasn't in the script. I had told it to Jack and Bob the night before we were going to do that scene, and there was nothing in the script for that scene other than four people sitting around, drinking and having a good time. There weren't any words. Oh, Jack was crazy that day. He was so funny. First we decided that we would do it in our underwear, so we two girls had to strip down to our bras and underpants, and Jack decided that he wanted to do the scene with just a cigar and his boots on, but he refused to take off his undershorts until the crew took off their clothes. He said, "Hey, now, listen. If actors have to work nude, and they're embarrassed about it, it should be union rules that the crew be nude, too, and then nobody will be staring at anybody." Well, all the guys on the crew love Jack, so they all started ripping off their clothes, and then Bob Rafelson said, "Hey, wait a minute. We can't do this here." So nobody took their clothes off. So Jack was embarrassed; he's very shy. So he left his shorts on through the scene, but if everybody had undressed I'm sure he would have taken them off.

So they turned the camera on us, one at a time, and said tell a story while you're singing a beer-drinking song. There was no script, and I already knew ahead of time that they wanted me to tell the dimple in the chin story, so I was prepared. Jack wasn't prepared. He just started out, "Well, I remember when I was fourteen years old and I went to a party in New York, and ran into this twenty-year-old xylophone prodigy, and she grabbed me by the front of my pants, and she took me out of that party, and wanted me to have my first sexual encounter. She took me into a hotel room in New York, and we did it, and all the time we were doing it, all I could think about was how bad I had to go to the bathroom. So when she was all finished with her orgasmic compulsions, or whatever you call those things, I got up, and I had to go so bad, and I couldn't find the bathroom, so I threw open the window and from this day on you could read my name rusted in that screen." Well, it was hysterical. We were all on the floor, it was so cute. And when I started thinking about it when I left, I thought if that scene is cut at all,

and I'm sure a lot of it has to be, they'll cut out my story and everybody elses', and leave Jack's. But I guess Bob Rafelson felt they had enough of Jack in the movie, and they didn't need that, so they left my story in, which amazed me. But he's a very, very clever young man.

Question: What is Jack Nicholson like off camera, during the course of a film?

Struthers: Well, Jack is not your basic flirtatious type. He's a man's man. Jack likes to joke around with Bob Rafelson and the crew. I think why he's so attractive to me, and to a lot of other women, is because he doesn't have to sidle up to you and say, "Hey, Baby," and pull a smooth move. He's so boyish and has such a beautiful grin —to me, he reminds me of a young Henry Fonda, I don't know why. But he didn't have to ever flirt, and by never flirting with me, or doing any of that thing, then it makes a woman like a magnet zap onto him, and that's what happened to me. I was so attracted to Jack I couldn't stand it. I'd find myself one night at about midnight, knocking on his door going, "Jack, what are you doing?" I mean I was crazy for him. But all I got to work with him was for a week, and then I was gone. And the only other time I've ever seen him was about a year ago when he was driving on Wilshire, and so was I, and he was in front of me, and I started honking, and he turned around and honked, and then he put it in park in the middle of traffic, jumped out of the car, ran back and kissed me, ran back to his car, and drove off.

I haven't seen him since the movie. I wish I could. I'd love to sit and talk to him. I'd just really like to get together with him sometime, because then I was really, much more than now, very immature, and very little-girlish, and didn't know how to hold a decent conversation with anyone, and probably turned him off in that respect. I was much heavier. I was about ten pounds heavier, and I had that Shirley Temple in heat hairdo, and I was just an object to people. I wasn't human. I was a funny little thing that ran around and did nutty things. Now I'd like to sit down and talk to him as a person.

Question: What other qualities do you think he has that make him a star?

Struthers: I'm not sure. To not know someone well, to never have spent any social time, or been at a party, or gone on a date, or not even knowing anyone that knows Jack well enough to tell you anything about him, you just have to live with first

A piano on the back of a truck entices Bobby Dupea (Nicholson) in Five Easy Pieces

impressions. And my impression was that Jack, a lot like the character he played in *Five Easy Pieces*, is a bit of a loner. And people that are loners, or people that keep to themselves, and aren't always in the news or doing publicity stunts or going on telethons and lots of talk shows, become mysterious. And if you can create a mystique about yourself, then there's twice as much intrigue from the public, and Jack has never overexposed himself, literally or figuratively. But behind that smile you don't know what's going on. There's that smile and the twinkle in his eye, but you don't know if there's a bit of a maniac there, or a genius, or a madman. You don't know, but he's got this wild look to his face all the time. It's a great look.

Question: What were your thoughts about Jack Nicholson before you met him?

Struthers: I think *Easy Rider* had already come out by the time we started filming *Five Easy Pieces*, and I had seen him in that movie, and because of the character that he played in that movie I thought he was a lot older. I was prepared to meet a forty-something-year-old, balding, real Southern-lunatic type, because he played that character so well. And then there was Jack in his Levis and a T-shirt, and very boyish walking around, and all of a sudden I felt attracted to him. And at that point in my life, I didn't like anybody that was any older than two years older than me. I hadn't matured enough to find an interest in older

men. And then all of a sudden there was Jack Nicholson, and there I was knocking on his door in the middle of the night. "Hi, Jack. What're you doin'?" He sent me right away, by the way. He didn't even invite me in. I wish I knew him better.

Question: What kind of atmosphere surrounds the set?

Struthers: Well, I just noticed that the crew loved him, because he didn't pull any star shit. He didn't walk on cocky and say, "Hey, let's do my scene and get out of here." He was very helpful to other people who seemed to be having a hard time. He was patient, and he's good at joking around, and it kept everybody at ease, which is a real trick. If you get the crew to like you, and they're on your side, they'll just jump over backwards to help you or light you right or do a scene over again. And that's where Jack has them, in the palm of his hand, by being nothing more than himself and not having any airs about him. That makes some people immediately unattractive; I don't like people with airs.

Question: Acting-wise, did you learn anything from working with Jack?

Struthers: Yeah. Don't push. Don't push a scene. He underplays so beautifully, he's so natural. He's a combination of a lot of marvelous actors; a lot of the way he moves around with his head, or his hands, or doesn't always look at the person he's talking to is kind of a Marlon Brando thing, and

I hate to even put him in that category. I don't know how many acting lessons he's had, but he's a very natural actor. I don't know if he looked over his script at night in his room, but I just had a feeling everyday when we were doing a scene that he would just glance at it once and kind of know where the scene was supposed to go and just do it. He didn't overtax his brain with being meticulous about lines. He let them come out naturally. That's when you get your best moments in film, not when the actor and director marry themselves to the page, but when you take the written page as a guideline and then explore it while you're doing it. He did a lot of that in the film, and he taught me to have the confidence to do that.

I did a film with Sam Peckinpah called *The Getaway*, and remembering Jack, and remembering a lot of *Five Easy Pieces*, which was the last film I did, I did that on camera. I didn't follow the script at all. I made up lines. I made up attitudes. I made up extra props that weren't there. And I learned a lot of that from Jack just from watching him. He's got to be aware that he's being that natural, a kind of studied unstudiedness. It's hard to be natural when forty guys and a hundred lights and a camera and a clapboard and script girls and stopwatches are all around you, and yet it comes off so easy that it's real.

Question: You mentioned *The Getaway*. Could you compare working with Jack and working with Steve McQueen?

Struthers: Uh-huh. Like I said, working with Jack was a joy, and working with Steve McQueen was different.

Question: Why?

Struthers: Steve is outwardly what you might suspect Jack is inwardly. Like I said, behind that boyish grin of Jack's and his twinkling eyes might be a madman, but you don't know, and that's what's intriguing about him. Steve is outwardly a crazy guy. In between takes he jumps on his motorcycle and rides straight up dirt mountains and through crowds of people, and does things not to only endanger himself but to endanger a film. You don't hop on your motorcycle and do crazy stunts when you're halfway through a film and there are a lot of actors and crew members counting on their livelihood for the next three months by you being in good health and being able to shoot everyday. And he did that a lot.

Question: Changing the subject for a moment, do you have a favorite performance in *Five Easy Pieces*?

Struthers: I can't say. I won't say. I won't say just from my viewpoint of awards and saying who's best actor. If you took each male actor in that film and had each one do a five-minute scene of the same character, then you could judge which one of them played that character the best. I don't understand awards. How can you compare Jack Nicholson playing Bobby to George C. Scott playing Patton? They're five different people playing five different characters. How can you say who gave the best performance? And so, it's not fair of me to say who's the best actor in the film. Obviously, Karen Black and Jack Nicholson and Susan Anspach had the biggest parts, but sometimes having the biggest part doesn't make you the most memorable. All I can say is that I think everybody in the film gave it their best and was a great actor, or the film wouldn't have run for a year in the theaters. I was on the screen for less than four minutes in that film, and I had been on television for a year already and nobody ever recognized me. Four minutes in *Five Easy Pieces*, and I couldn't go anyplace anymore without somebody saying, "Hey, aren't you the girl in *Five Easy Pieces*?" And I feel that all the characters in the film were memorable right on down to the father who never said a word and burped once in a while in a wheelchair. Jack had the largest part, and gave it his all, and he was beautiful, but I feel that it was the ensemble that made the movie. And it was Jack's graciousness of letting everyone make it an ensemble, and not making himself stand out, which an actor can do. The way to stand out is to let everybody else around look so good that you can't help but look good, too. That's what Jack did.

Question: Would you like to play opposite him now?

Struthers: Mmmmm, yes. Yeah, I'd like to play opposite him. But not necessarily from the man-woman standpoint, because I hope I've gotten over that. I hope I never get into that thing where you see so many leading actors and actresses falling for one another while they do a film, and then the film's over and they break up. I'd like to work with him from the standpoint of a natural, easygoing actor who would help me relax and not be up tight.

Question: Do you have any fantasies about what kind of a role you would like to play with him?

Struthers: There's so many ways to go with Jack. It might be interesting to do a husband-wife number with him. It might be interesting for the two of us to be maniacs in a mental ward trying to escape. It might be fun to—oh, I don't know. I just think that playing anything opposite him would be great. It would also be great if he called me up for a date. That would be nice.

Question: Does Jack have any qualities that make him difficult to work with?

Struthers: No, not unless you're an up-tight person. I mean, if I were fifty or sixty years old and from the old school of acting, and if the script said, A, B, and C and I learned A, B, and C the night before and came in prepared to do it just this way, and the director's going to tell me to move this far, and I'm going to hit it exactly, and there's Jack Nicholson lolling all over the place and joking around with the crew and doesn't want to rehearse, and let's just go do it, and making up lines, he'd drive me up the wall. But he's of the young, new school of acting, where you just make it happen for the first time on film. If that could be termed as a fault, then it would only be a fault with somebody that couldn't handle it.

Question: Can you characterize Jack Nicholson in one sentence?

Struthers: Jack is a little boy trapped in a man's body.

Dennis Hopper

In the last decade, perhaps no American film has had such a significant effect on film-making and filmgoers as *Easy Rider*. Certainly the instrumental force behind this monstrous success was writer-director-star Dennis Hopper. Besides receiving two Academy Award nominations, the picture has grossed in the neighborhood of $25,000,000.

Hopper, who was born in Dodge City, Kansas, made his acting debut at the age of eighteen in *Rebel Without a Cause* with James Dean. Hopper worked with Dean again in 1956 in George Stevens' *Giant*. It was during the shooting of *From Hell to Texas* in 1958 that he was branded a troublemaker in Hollywood, and he was soon blacklisted. In 1965 he worked in *The Sons of Katie Elder,* his first acting job in almost eight years. In rapid succession he followed this film with *Cool Hand Luke, Hang 'Em High, True Grit,* and *The Trip,* where he first worked with Peter Fonda and Jack Nicholson.

While Fonda was on a promotion tour for *The Trip,* he telephoned Hopper suggesting they make a film about two guys who score some cocaine and split to Florida to live in retirement. The final result was a film called *Easy Rider,* which was certainly a career milestone for Hopper and Fonda, and catapulted an unknown actor named Jack Nicholson into an Academy Award nomination and instant recognition.

In 1971, after much publicity, *The Last Movie,* directed by and starring Hopper, was released in two cities and almost instantly shelved. Much of the acclaim for Hopper as a director had disappeared, and it could well have been his last movie.

But one producer in particular didn't feel that Hopper was a risk as an actor. In the spring of 1972, Hopper completed a starring role in *Kid Blue* for director James Frawley.

After speaking to Ed Gaultney, Hopper's representative in Taos, New Mexico, an interview was arranged at Hopper's home a few minutes from the center of town. (Hopper discovered Taos in 1968 while filming *Easy Rider*.)

Hopper and his wife of less than a year, actress Daria Halprin (*Zabriskie Point*), live in a small, two-story adobe house situated on land owned by the Taos Pueblo Indians. Hopper pays the Indians $125 a month to live here, despite the fact that he also owns a larger house less than a mile away. The larger house had been owned, at one time, by Mabel Dodge Luhan, and was frequently visited by D. H. Lawrence among other notables.

Hopper also owns a movie theater in town, the El Cortez, where he can screen his own films and other classics for the film buffs of Taos. In addition, he is a devoted lover of art, and owns a gallery, The Dennis Hopper Art Gallery.

Instead of meeting the violent, unstable man suggested by his public image, we met a modest serene man who graciously welcomed us into his home.

After looking at some of the art lining the walls (Indian, Andy Warhol, Jasper Johns, Dennis Hopper) and some of his movie memorabilia (a huge poster for *The Last Movie,* an *Esquire* magazine cover featuring *Easy Rider,* various photographs from film festivals he had attended), we retired to his primitive but comfortable living room.

Question: How long have you known Jack Nicholson, and how did you meet him?

Dennis Hopper: I'm sort of bad on time, but I think I met him around nineteen fifty-six. We were sort of coffee-house actors or bullshit artists, or something. I remember him long before either one of us had ever done anything, obviously, when we just sat around talking about what we'd like to do, or act in, or whatever, criticizing the movies being made. So I knew him from sitting at other tables and so on, in the beginning, and so I really got to know him on a social level. I knew Bert Schneider and Bob Rafelson, and I was married at that time and my wife was friendly with their wives, so we were thrown into social situations. But then I really got to know him better when we did *Easy Rider*.

Question: To clear up some controversy, who edited *Easy Rider*?

Hopper: Well, I edited it for a year, and then

Bert Schneider decided he didn't like it the way it was at that time. He came in himself and did some things on it. Jack did some things on it. Henry Jaglom did some things on it. Bob Rafelson did some things on it. There were quite a few different people who worked on it.

Question: How close is the version that's out to the one that you put together?

Hopper: The scenes that are in it are the same as when I had it. All the rides, which I feel are all kind of personal editing trips, are all the way that I edited them to the music. The scenes themselves, like the restaurant sequence, are different. Various scenes, dramatic scenes, were changed. They came out a little bit more like what I call television editing. Or right out of the book kind of editing, which I really wasn't into. I can't really say that it isn't more dramatic, perhaps, or easily understood or easily followed, but the structure's the same.

The dramatic scenes have been changed to protect the innocent from whatever.

Question: We understand that Rip Torn was originally set for Jack Nicholson's role, and when Jack was named to replace him you and Peter Fonda were against it.

Hopper: I didn't want him; Peter really didn't have that much to say about it.

Question: Why didn't you want to use him?

Hopper: I wanted to use a real Texan. Rip and I had a fight, and he wanted some rewrites, and I said, "Screw you," and that's basically what came down there. And Bert Schneider, who was giving us the money, said, "I haven't asked for anything," which he hadn't, and he said, "I want Nicholson to play the part," and I fought it and said that I didn't want him because I wanted a Texan. But I'm really glad that Jack did it, man, because he was great in it. It was my first picture,

Dennis Hopper and Karen Black in a New Orleans whorehouse in Easy Rider

Nicholson as George Hanson tries marijuana for the first time in Easy Rider *with Peter Fonda*

and I was really hung up in the idea of getting someone who had the accent—I'd never seen Jack do anything like that before. I saw him as a Hollywood flasher, not as a country bumpkin.

Question: Do you think it would have been the same with Rip Torn?

Hopper: No. I think that Rip Torn and I would have had a lot of fights, and Jack and I never hassled at all. Jack was right there. No problems.

Question: What kind of off-screen relationship do you have with Jack?

Hopper: I haven't seen Jack in a long time. I think the last time I saw him was when he came up here and stayed overnight in the big house and left early in the morning. I consider him a good friend.

Question: What's the strangest thing that's ever happened to you and Jack?

Hopper: I think when we were shooting *Easy Rider.* We were up here, and we had the day off, and we dropped acid at D. H. Lawrence's tomb. We laid down in front of his tomb and got into a conversation. I noticed that the insects were circling right over us in relationship to the sun, and Jack said that's really what we are, just insects. Then we later went to a hot spring, where he proceeded to marry me to an Indian girl. And a Chicano guy, who was drunk, came up and said, "I want to watch you hippies." I pulled a knife, and got into a whole trip with the guy. Then we got everybody back in the car, and Jack and I were running down the road in front of a truck at night, and Jack said, "We're geniuses. We're both geniuses, Hoppy." Without any sleep we arrived in Las Vegas, New Mexico, and shot the scene where we got out of jail in *Easy Rider.* And Nicholson came up with the line, "Well, here's the first one of the day for old D. H. Lawrence."

Question: How much of Nicholson's character was laid down by you, either in the script or through your direction, and how much of it was created by Nicholson?

Hopper: Well, the whole "Nic, nic, nic, fire. Nic, nic, nic," thing was his. We had a biker working with us, who every time he couldn't start a bike he went, "Nic, nic, nic," you know, and did one of those for the crowd, and Jack picked that up. The scene that most people think was improvised, the thing around the campfire with all of us getting high, I wrote that. And that was word for word out of the script except for the "Nic, nic, nic, fire."

Jack, like a good professional, stuck mostly to the script, and whatever he would add most people would like. But most of it was a script. I like to improvise, I like to do those things, and I like to have people feel free to improvise, and then I set them and say, "O.K., do that." I mean, Jack's seenes were very keyed to me in the picture. When I wrote the picture I wanted people, if they couldn't identify with the longhairs, to be able to identify with this character that Jack played, because it would be like they were killing their own son. That might be more tragic for them than Peter and I getting killed.

Question: So you feel that was the main reason for the character of George Hanson, as a third alternative?

Hopper: Yeah, right. So that the audience can say, "My God, you can kill this other guy, but don't kill him." I mean, if the rednecks saw the film they could dig, and laugh and joke with him, because they can understand the alcoholic level and the small-town lawyer whose father's rich, and he can't make it, and he's out of place and doesn't know what to do about it. Then when he gets killed they feel the loss.

Question: Did you have any complications with Jack as far as your director-actor relationship?

Hopper: No, Jack and I had no problems at all. It was really easy. I've heard that he and Rafelson were getting into trips, but I don't know that Nicholson.

Question: Peter Fonda has said that he thought you gave the best performance in *Easy Rider*, and that everybody gave the credit to Nicholson because his role was the most obvious. Who do you think gave the best performance in *Easy Rider*?

Hopper: Jack. Besides, what does Peter know

Nicholson strikes a Gable-like pose during A Safe Place *(Photo courtesy of Henry Jaglom)*

about acting? No, really, if I thought that I had, I wouldn't say it anyway, and I don't really feel it. I mean, what comes off on the screen is who gave the best performance. I don't know about best performance. I think it was a part that was calculated really have the response, and as far as getting the response from the audience, I don't think anybody could have done it better than Nicholson. Nicholson's got a tremendous personality. I think that sometimes his personality can get in his way, or get in my way, maybe not in his. I could disagree with a life-style that I may find rather frivolous, but it certainly is a great plus as an actor and a personality, and that's what people want. I mean, Jack is a throwback to the old-time movie stars. When I say old-time, I mean twenty years ago. He's a personality like Cary Grant, Clark Gable. He enjoys Hollywood; he enjoys the partying; he enjoys the life; he enjoys the whole thing. And he admits it, and has a good time at it. I hate it. I really hate it. I resent it. I find it terribly frivolous. But Nicholson digs it, likes it, loves it, and should be there, and he is.

Question: Do you resent the fact that Nicholson got most of the praise from *Easy Rider*?

Hopper: Well, I won the Best New Director Award at the Cannes Film Festival, and I was very disappointed when Jack didn't win best actor. I have tremendous feelings for Jack. I was very hurt when I was in Cannes and I saw *Drive, He Said,* which he directed, and saw the response of the audience, booing him. I identify with him. I'm very sympathetic to Jack. Jack's a really talented guy. He's a talented director, to.

But anyway, I directed the movie, and I wrote the movie, and I acted in the movie, and that's all. What more can you ask for? And Jack gave a performance in that movie.

Question: Just from your viewing of *Drive, He Said*, can you tell anything about the differences between your directing habits and Jack's?

Hopper: I don't know. It's a very professional movie, isn't it? Very slick. Very right on. I have a tendency to be much more esoteric and aesthetic and artistic, and sometimes I trip over it. Jack's a really slick professional person all the way down, from his personality to his socks. It's amazing that

Nicholson's sparkling portrayal of drunken lawyer George Hanson in Easy Rider *brought him his first Academy Award nomination*

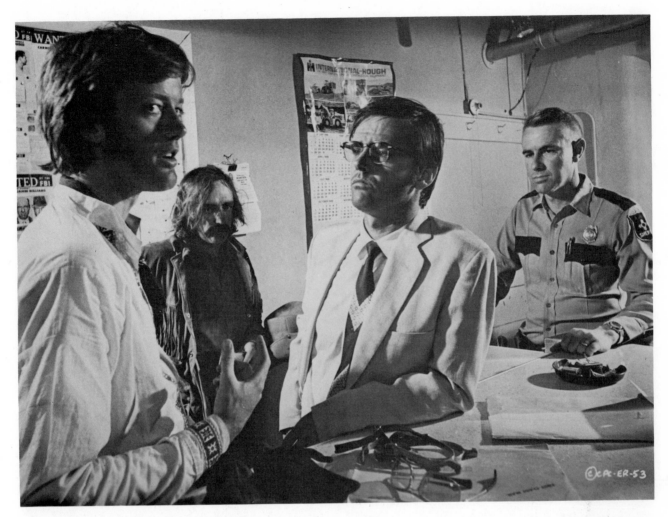

Fonda, Hopper, and Nicholson being released from jail in Easy Rider

his picture didn't make it. I don't quite understand it. I mean, there wasn't anything really wrong with the movie, and there were a lot of things that were great about it. It wasn't difficult to understand, and it seems like the right subject matter to me, too. I liked it. I like his work.

Question: Do you have a favorite performance of his?

Hopper: Well, I didn't see *Carnal Knowledge*, but I liked him better in *Easy Rider* than in *Five Easy Pieces,* and not because I directed the movie. I just think the part was better for him. It was difficult for me to make the transition between the guy in the oil field and the concert pianist. I thought he was really good. I thought Karen Black was really good, too. Karen played the prostitute with me in *Easy Rider.* Besides, I think Bob Rafelson is a pretty talented guy. I was very happy for Bob. I mean, Bert Schneider and Bob Rafelson

gave me the money to do *Easy Rider.* I think more or less for a tax write-off, but that's O.K., too. Bob was directing *Head,* which Jack was writing with Bob, and it was a disaster, and *Easy Rider* made it. And his next film, *Five Easy Pieces,* was a success, and I was happy for everybody concerned, because I want to see Rafelson have his up, too. It's sort of a bummer to be on the other side.

Question: What do you think are the basic differences between Jack's film-making principles and your film-making principles?

Hopper: I think the differences are inherent in our life styles. I'm not a charmer. I don't go out of my way to charm people. I'm sort of like poison to most social events, and Jack has a tremendous personality; he enjoys the game. He enjoys the diplomat role, and I don't. I think I'm a little bit more like Lenin, and he's sort of like the czar, to put it on a weird level. I would be very happy to live in a very small place and make films, and not have to worry about whether the films are going to make money or not make money, but feel that I am involved in the evolution of film, which is a very young art form, which is a big business, but should be an art form.

I feel that Jack would hate that. He loves the glamour. He loves the fame, the wealth, the limousines, driving him to and from. Whereas I get terribly embarrassed riding in a limousine.

You know, my kind of seriousness is grabbing someone and shoving them in a corner and screaming and yelling at them, and his is, like, to tell a joke and blah, blah, blah, blah, and then walk over to a corner and they follow him over. It's just a difference of approach, I guess. If I feel something, then I really feel it, and I can't hide it. Jack, I'm sure, really feels it, but has a way of playing out the game and getting what he wants.

Question: Do you think the fact that Jack goes around with Michelle, your ex-wife, hurts your relationship with him?

Hopper: I think it probably hurts it from his point of view. It doesn't from mine.

Question: How honest do you think Jack is?

Hopper: I really don't know him that well. But I think Jack is very honest to Jack. I don't think a guy can be that talented and not be honest with himself. For example, he was concerned about Michelle, and he called me up, and asked if his seeing her was going to screw things up, and I said no. That's pretty up front. Beyond that, I haven't seen him since. Film is one of those things that when you're working together, you're together, and when you're not, you're not.

Question: Can you tell us about your early days in Hollywood with Jack?

Hopper: I think of that whole period of time as a period of anxiety, and thinking that I'm never going to direct a film, and never going to get it together. Jack was really already getting it together, even though people didn't realize it. I mean, he had already produced a couple of films, which were successes in Europe. He had been around the Cannes Film Festival. Those things were just dreams to me. That was a very desperate period of time for me. Just before *Easy Rider* I was going off to teach school in San Jose. I'd given up hope of ever directing. I'd written three films, but nothing had ever happened.

Jack was very responsible, in a way, for getting the money for *Easy Rider*. He and Rafelson were writing *Head* and getting that together and getting ready to shoot it, and Peter Fonda and I brought Michael McClure in to ask Rafelson to put up fifty thousand dollars to make a movie called *The Queen* that Michael wanted to do. And Peter started talking about a deal we might have to make for a movie with AIP, and Bert asked what it was about, and we started talking about it, and Jack and Bert and Rafelson went into another room, and then Rafelson called me in and said, "Call me later. Bert might be interested in putting it through."

Question: What did you think of the script for *The Trip*?

Hopper: I thought the script was much better than the movie. As a matter of fact, that was the first time I got to direct when I went out with Peter on weekends and shot second-unit stuff. Corman gave us the camera and film, and we did it for free. We went down to Palm Springs and shot all the desert stuff with Peter running around on the dunes. But that was because we identified with the script much more than the film, because Corman wasn't really willing to shoot the film the way it was written. It was just too complicated. But the script was, I think, a thousand times better,

Question: Do you foresee any future collaborations with Jack?

Hopper: I saw him at a party in New York at the film festival, and I said that I'd like to do something with him, and we sort of joked about it, but I don't really know. I'm not sure that Jack would like to do anything with me. I don't know why, I just felt it from his attitude when we talked. He's obviously very career-conscious, and he'd probably prefer doing something with someone else. Rafelson and him seem to have a good working relationship. I think there's probably a great question in people's minds about my editing, and I think that would be a consideration.

Question: Can you characterize Jack Nicholson in one sentence?

Hopper: Well, when I think of Jack Nicholson I think of a big smile and flashy clothes.

Ann-Margret

It took a long time, but Ann-Margret has finally put down her sex-kitten image and has tried to emerge as a serious actress. The public and the industry's recognition of this metamorphosis came after her fine performance as Bobbie opposite Jack Nicholson's Jonathan in *Carnal Knowledge*. For this she won an Academy Award nomination in the best-supporting-actress category.

Until that time Ann-Margret had starred in a great many films, but none that were ever really taken seriously. Her early films included *Pocketful of Miracles, State Fair,* and 1963's *Bye, Bye Birdie,* the latter bringing Ann-Margret well into the lime-light. From there she went into a series of motorcycle-sex films, and a stereotype she found it difficult to overcome. Some of those films were *Viva Las Vegas, Kitten With a Whip, The Pleasure Seekers, The Swingers,* and *Murderer's Row.* Ann-Margret was also featured in the 1965 film *The Cincinnati Kid,* which starred Steve McQueen.

By the late 1960's, Ann-Margret had virtually disappeared from the big screen, though she was still doing occasional films like *C. C. and Company,* in which she co-starred with Joe Namath, and like Joe's knees, the film was pretty weak.

Her marriage to actor Roger Smith (*77 Sunset Strip, Mister Roberts*) was the primary factor in the redirection of Ann-Margret's career. Smith, along with partner Allan Carr, put together a top-notch nightclub act for Ann-Margret, which we had the pleasure to see at the Sahara Tahoe.

Another facet of Ann-Margret's talent that the public was not aware of until *Carnal Knowledge* was that she could be a fine dramatic actress. Mike Nichols called on her to test for the part of Bobbie in *Carnal,* and she did not disappoint Nichols, for she turned in the finest performance of her career. Since that film she has gone on to star with John Wayne in *The Train Robbers* and Jean-Louis Trintignant in *The Outside Man.*

After quite a few phone calls to Allan Carr, and to Paul Block (Ann-Margret's publicist)', we decided that the most convenient place to conduct the interview would be at the Sahara Tahoe where she was to open her new Ann-Margret Show. We arrived in Tahoe and spoke to Allan Carr, and

Stunning Ann-Margret backstage at the Sahara Tahoe
(Photo by R. D. Crane)

arranged to do our interview between shows on that Friday night. When we arrived at the Sahara, we were escorted downstairs and shown into the comfortably elegant dressing room to meet Ann-Margret. After the interview we stayed for the late edition of the show, and discovered yet another side to this talented lady. Though she speaks in tones just above a whisper, she really can belt out a song, not to mention the spectacular choreography in the revue. And, even though we saw only the sixth performance of this particular show, it was smooth and very together. Incidentally, it was only two days later that Ann-Margret fell from the scaffolding and was hospitalized for eight weeks. As of this writing, she has totally recovered.

In the dressing room Ann-Margret greeted us in a sleek red robe with pearl buttons, and we instantly discovered how striking this lady is in person. She settled into a corner of the couch and the interview was underway.

Question: First of all, how did you land the part in *Carnal Knowledge*?

Ann-Margret: Mike Nichols called my agent and said that he wanted to see me. He had seen a lot of ladies for this role, and I went to New York to see him. I had met him perhaps once or twice before, just saying hello and that was it. I was frightened, so frightened. I was scared witless to go in there and meet him and talk with him. I had read the script, and I was so nervous. We talked for about two hours, and then he had me read one of the scenes. Of course, I never thought

I'd see him again, and then I got a call the next week from my agent saying that he wanted me to test for the part, and then I got all nervous again. I did it, and I found out later that I had the part before I took the screen test, which was thrilling. That whole thing is like a dream sequence.

Question: Had you ever met Jack Nicholson before you worked on that film?

Ann-Margret: I had met Jack one time in a doctor's office. I was introduced and I just said, "Hi," and that was it. Then I met him up in Vancouver, where we did the movie, and we went right

Nicholson and Ann-Margret on their first date in Carnal Knowledge

into rehearsing, and all those love scenes, and everything.

Question: Aside from your brief meeting in the doctor's office, did you have a mental picture of what Jack Nicholson would be like, and how did he compare to that image?

Ann-Margret: I had seen him in *Easy Rider*, and he just flipped me out in that role. And the way he spoke, with that slow drawl of his. I was so pleased to find out that he spoke exactly the same way in person as he did on screen. He was extremely easygoing. The thing that I admire so much in him is that he's so unselfish. When I would have a close-up of a very rough scene, like the scene when we were shouting and screaming at each other, and we had to do it a certain number of times, he actually went home with laryngitis that day. He did everything to evoke the right kind of emotions from me. So unselfish.

And what I like, too, is that he looks directly into your eyes and talks to you.

Question: Going into the film, were you intimidated knowing you'd be working with Mike Nichols and Jack Nicholson?

Ann-Margret: The thing that gave me strength was just knowing that Mike had faith in me. That's what got me through the entire picture.

Question: Can you pinpoint some things that you learned about acting from working with Mike Nichols and Jack Nicholson?

Ann-Margret: What's wonderful about Mike is that he makes you feel like you're the one that's come up with the idea, when it is actually he that has come up with it. He has a marvelous way about him. He watches every single thing you do. He has a marvelous eye for complete honesty, and a marvelous ear for it. If he sees that there's something that looks a little false, that the character wouldn't do, he tells you very softly—not in front of the entire crew—very softly what it is. You feel like you're doing nothing, but you're really being extremely honest.

What amazed me about Jack was, I tried so hard to be as relaxed as Jack, but there's just no way. I don't know how this man can do it. Before one of the most difficult scenes in the movie he'd be discussing some other subject, and go immediately into a scene where he had to, let's say, burst out crying. Total concentration, and the whole body and mind was relaxed, and I was sitting there shaking. I really studied him to see if I could do the same thing. I guess I will always be a race-horse.

Nicholson brooding in Carnal Knowledge

Question: As a spectator, were you able to tell what kind of things Jack learned from Mike Nichols?

Ann-Margret: That's so hard to know. I know that they're extremely good friends, and I feel that Mike knows Jack very well. We didn't have to do any of the scenes more than, I'd say, twice. It wasn't the kind of thing where, "There they are folks, on the seventy-fourth take." He knew what he wanted from Jack, and from me, and as soon as he saw it, it was a print. I know that they would have long, long discussions before we started shooting.

What's good is that Mike is a Broadway director, and we had complete rehearsals before we started shooting. We had about two weeks of rehearsals, so everyone knew what they were doing.

Question: Carnal Knowledge had mixed reviews. What was your feeling about the final product?

Ann-Margret: I thought it was a very honest portrayal of two kinds of men from age nineteen to age forty. They weren't trying to say that that was every man, but you certainly can see those two types of men around you. If you're honest with yourself, I'm sure there are parts of both of those men that you can identify with.

It was a very emotional, very shattering, very personal kind of subject. Maybe a lot of men were afraid to face it.

Question: What do you think the film was trying to say?

Ann-Margret: Let's talk about Jonathan, since we're talking about Jack. Jonathan's character is so pathetic that it's brutally honest of a certain kind of man. You know what's so strange about it, is that it's so entirely different from what Jack is, because Jonathan is completely selfish. Everything is for him. He just uses people all of his life, and Jack is so unselfish. Fantastic job of acting.

Very sad ending for Jonathan. I just don't see how it can be any other way though, because he wasn't willing to give anything of himself, nothing. He didn't know what it was to give.

Question: He didn't love Bobbie, then?

Ann-Margret: He loved her in his own way, but he loved himself more.

Question: Did he love Susan?

Ann-Margret: Not as much as he loved himself. It was always him first.

Question: So do you think that Jonathan was viewed as a negative character?

Ann-Margret: I can only say, for myself, that I felt very sorry for Jonathan, because what he did he have in the end? What really did he have? He was a maniac. He was a complete psycho by then. He was so bitter and cynical, and so many people had loved him, really, truly loved him. And he had taken that love, and misused it, and not appreciated it.

Question: As Jack played Jonathan, do you think that Jonathan had a positive view of Jonathan?

Ann-Margret: He had a positive view only because he blocked everything else out. He refused to look at any negative side. But his world got smaller and smaller the older he got, and there were more and more things that he had to block out. Finally, he was so brittle, and cynical, and callous, that he couldn't even live with himself. Everything irritated him. I have a feeling that he could barely look himself in the mirror.

Question: Do you think that Bobbie was a ball-buster?

Ann-Margret: No.

Question: What do you think she wanted out of life?

Ann-Margret: She wanted to get married and have children.

Question: What caused the divorce between Bobbie and Jonathan?

Ann-Margret: I think it came to the point of no return, where she realized that this man kept getting older, but did not change. I think any woman will agree, that if after a few years a man like this hasn't changed, and she's done everything she possibly can, then there's no changing him. The fact is that he doesn't want to change, or he's unable to change. So, it's a question of Bobbie living in a world where she was giving everything she had, and he was giving nothing. She wasn't a dummy. She wanted love in return.

When they got married she thought he loved her. She didn't know to what extent he was mentally disturbed. That didn't come out until much later. It was very frightening to Bobbie to watch this person that she'd had so much fun with in the beginning just change into a maniac.

Question: Was your section of the film shot sequentially, building up until the end?

Ann-Margret: Yes, thank goodness. It made it so much easier.

Question: How did you prepare for the explosive argument scene with Jack?

Ann-Margret: Very carefully. I was dreading that scene from the very beginning when I actually had my first reading with Mike, and I thought, "What if I get this role?" It's that one scene where you just have to depend on every kind of emotional experience you've ever had, or read about, or heard about, because your emotions, your nerves, everything is raw. You're just spreading those emotions out in front of everyone, and you've got to be hurt. They're just there, raw.

Mike and Jack both knew that I was terribly nervous about it. I would stay in my dressing room the whole time, when I wasn't in front of the camera, and think morose thoughts and just stay in the character. It was very nice, because the weather at the time in Canada was a kind of somber, cool climate, and it helped. I just sat there, going over my lines in my head, not talking to anybody, just so I could stay in that kind of mood. I was impossible to live with.

I remember one scene where I was sitting on the bed, and I said I wanted to get married. Well,

I don't know how Mike knew this, but I'm an only child and I'm very close to my father, and my father is a very quiet, gentle man, and he has a way of just putting his hand on my head that makes me just fall apart. It just makes me feel all loved and protected, and just everything. It just rips me apart. I don't know how Mike knew this, but before the scene he didn't say anything. He just came over to where I was sitting, and he put his hand on my head, five seconds before the camera started. And he stood there, and then said, "O.K., roll 'em." And the tears just started. He didn't know me. He didn't know that part of me. It shook me up. And Jack. On my close-up he bounced on the bed. He actually stood on the end of the bed, and bounced, and threw pillows, and screamed and yelled. I actually got frightened. I thought he was going out of his mind. Both he and Mike are extremely unselfish.

Question: How close are you to Bobbie?

Ann-Margret: I'm her age. She's extremely emotional, which I am. Very sensitive, which I am. You look into her eyes, and you know how she's feeling, and I think I'm the same way. It's very hard for me to mask it.

Question: What about differences between you and Bobbie?

Ann-Margret: I would never become a doormat. I have more fight in me. It might just be once a year, but I can be belligerent.

Question: In the film, we see the skater in white twice. What do you think she represents?

Ann-Margret: Just another girl. He was just forever looking at "another girl." He looked at every girl that walked by, or skated by, or crawled by, or jumped by. He was just obsessed.

Every woman that he got into a relationship with, he just destroyed it; he couldn't handle it. So, therefore, he was always looking to see if there was a relationship that he would not destroy.

Question: Would you say that Jack is a sexually oriented person?

Ann-Margret: He's earthy.

Question: In what ways?

Ann-Margret: Oh, I don't think I need to explain.

Question: Except for your nomination, *Carnal Knowledge* was nixed at the Oscars.

Ann-Margret: That's so incredible to me.

Question: Why do you think that was?

Ann-Margret: Perhaps jealousy. I really don't know. But to me it was incredible. I was shocked.

Ann-Margret and Nicholson in a lighter moment from Carnal Knowledge

Who knows what the reasons are? I think it's horrendous to overlook the work that was done. I really do wish that people could—I know this sounds like Pollyanna—I wish people could get rid of all their prejudices and jealousies, and try when they sit down to vote and to choose, to just think of the performances, and what happened behind the camera, and just see it as a piece of work, judging it with no bias, no prejudice, and judge everything that way. Not how much money the studio spent on it, or whatever the reasons are that people don't vote for something.

Question: Was there very much improvisation done on the set?

Ann-Margret: During rehearsal Mike told us to do whatever we wanted to do, and he only stopped us if he thought it was wrong. He said he chose the actors, because he thought we were very much like the characters.

I remember one vivid thing that Mike had me do during the screen test. He had me do the very first scene, where Jack and I are having wine and dinner, and he had me do that scene four different ways, four different characters. That was so much of a challenge for me. He'd say, "O.K., do it as an airline hostess would do it."

Question: Which one did you finally choose?

Ann-Margret: The one that I initially did that was just kind of a tease.

Question: How did you approach the sex scenes?

Ann-Margret: With trepidation. Obviously, it was an integral part of the movie to show their relationship. That was the main part of their relationship, and to not show it would be dishonest. I feel that's a very sacred part of a relationship between two people, and I was very nervous. Mike realized that, and so did Jack, so it was just Mike, and the cameraman, and the soundman.

Mike was always very warm to me, as was Jack, and spoke very softly. I think if someone had spoken harshly to me I probably would have run out the door and run out of Vancouver, because I was on the edge anyway.

Question: What part of Jack's personality impresses you?

Ann-Margret: He has a marvelous quality of not taking himself too seriously. Of the movies that he wishes to forget, he just makes fun of those, and that certainly was a big part of his life.

Question: Can you describe his acting techniques?

Ann-Margret: Deceptively simple. He's doing many, many things. I think the fact that he's so relaxed throws a lot of people off. He's concentrating like mad. He knows exactly the beginning, middle, and end of the scene he's doing. I think he definitely does his homework, and also he's brave, in that he tries new things.

Question: Would you like to be directed by him?

Ann-Margret: I think it would be very interesting. The fact that he's worked with me as an actor would be beneficial, because, being an actor, he knows what actors are feeling, and evokes all these kinds of emotions. He knows exactly what to say and what to do in each situation, whereas someone who has not been an actor might have to try take after take after take to get the right kind of feeling.

Question: Can you characterize Jack Nicholson in one sentence?

Ann-Margret: He's a secure man, who's gone through a lot of insecurities to get that way.

Monte Hellman

Unknown in his own country to all but a small handful of film buffs, wildly praised in France, Monte Hellman is the latest of a number of American directors to have his reputation made in Europe.

His association with Jack Nicholson has resulted in four of his last five films. In 1964 he traveled to the Philippines with Nicholson to direct him in *Back Door to Hell* and *Flight to Fury,* which Nicholson also wrote.

In 1964 he produced, directed, and edited back-to-back films starring Nicholson: two European-flavored Westerns written by Adrien Joyce and Nicholson. The two films went on to receive acclaim at the Cannes, Montreal, and San Francisco film festivals, but went virtually unnoticed by the general filmgoing public.

It wasn't until 1970 that another Hellman film appeared, *Two-Lane Blacktop,* starring Warren Oates, which marked James Taylor's acting debut and little more. Hellman reteamed with Oates in 1974 to film *Cockfighter,* a Roger Corman production set in Georgia, co-starring Millie Perkins and Richard Betts of the Allman Brothers Band.

After talking via telephone to Hellman at his Malibu home, we set up an interview at the office of his agent, in the IFA building on the Sunset Strip in Hollywood.

Hellman, unaccustomed to interviews, nevertheless appeared relaxed as he greeted us into the office. He settled down on a long sofa, moving a folder full of material for an upcoming project aside, stared at the microphone, and leaned back.

Question: How long have you known Jack Nicholson?

Monte Hellman: I think I met him back around 1958. We just met socially. We were all trying to break into show business or something. Our first working relationship was on a picture called *The Wild Ride,* which he starred in, and I had just directed my first movie, and I was associate producer-film editor on *The Wild Ride.* We got to be quite good friends, and I told him he was going to be a director, and twelve years later he was. Then we began working together on various projects. We wrote a script together that we wanted to make starring him, and we kind of had a deal on it with Roger Corman, and in the meantime I was hired to direct two pictures in the Philippines, *Back Door to Hell* and *Flight to Fury,* and they hired Jack to write one script and act in both of those pictures. When we came back from the Philippines we talked to Roger about doing the script that we had written, and Roger said he was no longer confident in the commercial possibilities of it, and he wanted us to do something else instead, so he gave us some money to do two Westerns. So we've done really four pictures together as director-actor-writer-producer. Apart from that, I'd

also directed him in some scenes from *The Terror.*

Question: Can you tell us briefly about the script that was turned down by Corman?

Hellman: Yeah, it was kind of autobiographical. It was about a young actor who was working a little bit in television and movies, and we were going to use a lot of footage from Jack's movies. Jack has really made a lot of movies that people aren't aware of. We were going to use footage from *Studs Lonigan,* and from the Westerns that we had done, and tie it in with the character that he was playing. The picture was really ahead of its time, and now it's old hat.

Question: How did it come about that you did two back-to-back Westerns?

Hellman: Corman said he didn't want to do our Hollywood story, but he said that if we wanted to do a Western, he'd back it. And before we had finished with lunch he said, "Well, as long as you're going to do one Western, you might as well do two." Jack and I immediately went out and rented a little closet office in the writer's building in Beverly Hills, and we started working on one script and Carol Eastman started on the other one.

Question: How long did it take to get the projects going?

Cameron Mitchell telling Nicholson "They went thataway" in Ride in the Whirlwind

Hellman: Well, we made the deal with Roger between Christmas and New Year's, and we rented our office on January 2, and we had both scripts ready by the end of February, and we began shooting the first week in May, and we finished shooting both pictures by the first week in July. Then we spent about six months editing both, and they came out of the labs in January of the following year. That was 1966. It took a full year to do the two pictures. And it took another year to sell them. Jack spent a long time taking them around to festivals in Europe.

Question: Why do you think it took so long for them to be released in this country? [They were released in the United States in 1972.]

Hellman: One reason was that we didn't make the American deal until a couple of years after we had finished them, and Walter Reade, who bought them originally, was only interested in promoting them to television, which we didn't know at the time we sold them. Finally, Jack Harris bought them from Walter Reade, but he hasn't been very successful with them. He's only played them in two cities.

Question: What were the two Westerns trying to say?

Hellman: We weren't really trying to say anything. What we were trying to do was make a couple of Westerns that were pleasing to us, and attempted to do a lot of the things that we would have liked to have seen in other Westerns. We always felt there was a lot of Hollywood, phony bullshit in Westerns. I mean, they always had the women wearing those kind of blouses that conform to the breasts, which was not historically accurate. Men's clothes would always be tailored in the style

86

of the particular period that the picture was made in, not the period that they were depicting. We tried to have a greater reality in the look of the picture, and also we tried to do away with some of the obligatory Hollywood scenes that aren't realistic. We just decided to do away with a lot of phony traditions. Like the scene in *Ride in the Whirlwind,* when Jack takes the farmer's daughter out to the barn; well, that has always been a sex scene, and we decided not to do it that way.

Question: How much of Jack's script made it to the screen?

Hellman: Some dialogue was snipped out of certain scenes, but we shot the whole script.

Question: Which of the two Westerns do you prefer?

Hellman: I think, because they're so different, I don't have any preference.

Question: What did you think of Jack's acting ability at the time?

Hellman: Well, I've always thought that he's the best actor that I knew. He really developed a lot as an actor from the first time that I met him, say through the two Philippine pictures, so by the time we got back from the Philippines, he was as good an actor as anyone in America.

Question: How was it decided that he would be in both Westerns?

Hellman: That was the idea in front, that he'd be in both pictures. It was the same for the Philippine pictures; he'd be in both of them, and write one.

Nicholson and Millie Perkins in The Shooting

87

Question: Do you think that the Jack Nicholson screen personality has changed over the years?

Hellman: I think that in recent years he's been playing characters that will allow him to use different aspects of his personality. I don't think that his particular screen image has changed, but he's got a broad range. He can be a really villainous heavy, or a really sweet, nice guy. He likes to seesaw back and forth. I think he's a terrific heavy.

Question: Why do you think it took so long for Jack to be recognized by the mass of the theatergoing public?

Hellman: I think it's really a combination of the picture and the role. I think that *Easy Rider* obviously was a picture that appealed to what I call the politics of the audience, a picture that the audience could root for. It has nothing to do with anything but where their heads are, so they can say that this is a picture that really represents their feelings. And Jack played a really appealing character, in a picture that had those elements. The picture probably would have been a success no matter who played the part, but I think that Jack certainly contributed to the success of it. He was just as good in a half a dozen other pictures that he's played in.

Question: Do you have a favorite performance of his?

Hellman: Yeah, I guess *Flight to Fury*. It's a role that he wrote for himself, and there's a lot of Jack in it. It's really one of his most subtle performances. He's had more emotion in some of his other films, but overall I think it was his best.

Question: Can you tell us a little bit about the role?

Hellman: He plays a kind of psychological criminal. He's just a middle-America nice guy, but he has this quirk, and it's just interesting to see Jack's personality with this craziness in it.

Question: What did you think of Jack's directorial debut with *Drive, He Said*?

Hellman: I thought it was terrific. I don't know of two or three directors in America that I admire more than Jack.

Question: Why do you think it failed at the box office?

Hellman: I think it was promoted wrong. I think it was a terrible advertising campaign; it looked nice, but it didn't mean anything. It wasn't something that would bring you in to see the picture. It didn't have any stars to do it, so when you have a picture like that you need the right image; you need the right catchphrase. I went to see *Willard* even though I'd heard it was a terrible picture, because I couldn't resist "where your nightmares end, Willard begins." How can you resist that?

Question: Do you foresee any future collaborations for the two of you?

Hellman: I'm sure that we'll work together. We just haven't found the right thing, or else he's busy or I'm doing something. At one point it looked like Warren Oates wouldn't be able to do *Two-Lane Blacktop,* and I wanted Jack to do it.

Question: What do you think Jack's chances are of becoming a full-time film-maker?

Hellman: I don't think he'll ever stop acting, and I don't imagine that he would like to direct himself. I think that he'll probably go back and forth between the two.

Question: Can you characterize Jack Nicholson in one sentence?

Hellman: There's something diabolical about him; Jack's evil.

Henry Jaglom

Henry Jaglom and Jack Nicholson have been friends for a long time, and when we approached him about doing an interview, he was happy to oblige us with his insights into Jack's character.

Jaglom, a member of the Actor's Studio, is currently garnering many fine reviews for his cinematic exposé of the female mind, *A Safe Place,* in which Nicholson co-stars. Jaglom wrote and directed this motion picture, which in addition to Nicholson stars Orson Welles, Tuesday Weld, and Philip Proctor. Jaglom is currently in Europe working on a project called *Return to Oz.*

Though *A Safe Place* is the first film that Jaglom has made himself, it wasn't the first time that he and Nicholson had worked together. Their first asso-

ciation on film came in Richard Rush's *Psych-Out,* where Jaglom played Nicholson's sidekick in Haight-Ashbury. Credited as consultant, Jaglom played an important role in the editing of *Easy Rider.* Then as Conrad, an instructor of guerrilla theater, Jaglom appeared in Nicholson's directorial debut, *Drive, He Said,* before they switched roles to do *Safe Place.* Henry Jaglom also appeared in Dennis Hopper's *The Last Movie.*

We contacted Henry at his home in Hollywood and arranged to do an interview at the offices of BBS Productions. We met there, and found our way into an empty office where we engaged in a very enlightening two and a half hour conversation.

Henry Jaglom directing Orson Welles in A Safe Place
(Photograph by Josh Weiner)

Jaglom (l.), Tuesday Weld, and Orson Welles at Central Park Zoo shooting A Safe Place
(Photograph by Josh Weiner)

Question: How long have you known Jack, and how did you meet?

Henry Jaglom: Where I met him originally, I don't know. It was out here in California. I came out here in about 1965, and I met him that year. We used to hang out at Barney's Beanery [a Hollywood night spot] together. We were both at the Actor's Studio, but that was a little later on, I guess. I've known him for my whole time out here. At that time I remember him vividly as writing *The Trip,* because I remember reading the first draft of it, which was really much better than what they finally did with it. We've just been really good friends for a long time, so I don't really remember how I met him. We used to hang out at the same places; Barney's Beanery was an important spot in our lives for a few years there, before Barney died.

And the beach, too. Bobby and Ellie Walker had a place down at the beach, and they used to have people down every weekend. Jane Fonda had her house there, during that period when she was still with Vadim. Tuesday Weld had her house nearby. And somewhere in that whole axis of people came Jack.

Question: At what point in Jack's career was *A Safe Place* made?

Jaglom: It was made after he directed *Drive, He Said,* and somewhere simultaneous with his *Carnal Knowledge.* It was around the time of *Carnal Knowledge,* because he did me this huge favor of being in my movie, where he charged Nichols whatever he gets, which is a lot of money now, and for me he did it for a color television set.

He had known about it for a long time before, that I had wanted him to do this. We had not specified what it was he was going to do, because I didn't want to. I just told him that he was going to be coming in, and that I wanted to use him prototypically for what he had become in the American film, where he would be the "hero." He would fuck the girl, fuck the audience, fuck the movie, save the girl, save the audience, save the movie; that role that he's come to do, except that I wanted to betray that role and use that role to show the lie of that myth of the white knight. He really comes and fucks the girl, fucks the audience, and then leaves in reality, and doesn't fulfill the fantasy at all, but he seems to. And I wanted to use Jack that way, because he's become Clark Gable. He's become the hero. He's become the star that is based upon not just his talent, which is enormous, but beyond his talent, his charisma, his style. He's that old-fashioned kind of star that Gable and Bogart were, which there are very few of now. People like Dustin Hoffman and Elliott Gould have careers that go up and down, based on how their movies are doing. Jack could be doing movies that are great; that do do well, or that don't do well. It's his image that they're responding to. It's a strange thing how America needs certain images. That's why I used Orson Welles in the picture to be this great, ultimate parental figure, which he is to all of us as directors. I wanted to use Jack as the hero. Everything's going to be all right when he comes into the girl's life. Everything's going to be all right when he comes into the movie's life. Everything's going to be all right with the audience, like he did in *Easy Rider*—saves the movie, saves the audience—except for me that's a lie. It's another myth that's unfortunate, because Jack's being scaled down by it in my opinion, and that's why he's making very brave attempts to break out of it, like he's just done in *Marvin Gardens,* and he's getting violently attacked for it. Some of the critics have said, in essence, "How dare he play a role that is so far removed from himself." They've forgotten he's an actor, and it's really significant, because they don't do it with others. They don't do it with Brando and *The Godfather.* They don't say, "What a weird part for Brando." But they do it with Jack. They want him to be that hero. They want him to fulfill the role, they don't want him to betray it. It's a shame, because it's limiting to him. But he'll get out of it. He is getting out of it, because he's enormously versatile as an actor, and he's got a lot of years to show it. I think in twenty years they're going to be talking about him the way they're talking about Brando now. I really believe that.

Question: We felt that Jack's performance in *A Safe Place* represented the truest picture of the real Jack Nicholson.

Jaglom: That's why I told him what I wanted to do was to use him really for what he does in life, and how his style works in life, and how the glimmer of that has made him such a big actor in such a short time. It's that quality that he has in life, I think, that they've touched upon in the movies that makes him such a big star, and I wanted to use that whole quality. I like using actors, rather than imposing characters on them, for what they have. What Jack is, is exactly what I wanted to deal with emotionally there. I tried to get him to be just what he is, and he did, including the language. Ninety per cent of that is his own lan-

Mock Miss America Pageant presided over by Nicholson and Julia Robinson in The King of Marvin Gardens

guage. We worked very closely. I just gave him an outline of what I wanted. I wanted a certain thing with him and Tuesday, and I wanted a certain thing with him and Philip Proctor, a certain attitude about where he was coming from, what had transpired, and where he was going, and I wanted it in his own language.

And I knew him so well, and Tuesday and Philip so well, that I was able to sit by the camera, and this drove the crew crazy, and say to the director of photography, "O.K., go in now. Go over to Tuesday. Now open up to a two-shot." I was able to do that because I know Jack so well, and I know when he's going to pull back and when Tuesday's going to go forward. They didn't know why I was doing that, but it worked for me so well that the

whole scene is one long ten-minute take. I've cut away to Orson a couple of times for Tuesday's mind, but that whole scene on the couch with the three of them is one take.

The fluidity of that scene is enhanced by the fact that I had kept Tuesday and Jack away from each other. They had wanted to meet each other for a long time, and I had set them each up by telling them that essentially their whole lives were going to be solved when they finally met, so they were very ready for this romantic moment, and I wanted to have it on screen. And that's what you saw in the movie. You really saw Tuesday and Jack getting it on for the first time in the movie.

I worked on this first as a play in New York, and Karen Black played the part that Tuesday played, and I played the part that Jack played, so I knew really well what I wanted in this character, and Jack was it. He was it in life. One of Jack's greatest abilities is to be who he is on screen, to show his nervousness. If you remember how much he's sweating in that scene, it's really extraordinary. It gives a whole added dimension to it because he's able to go with it. He's not acting that he's hot. He's really turned on, but he's worried about this other guy, but he really doesn't give a shit, and he's worried about what exactly he's doing in the movie. I have some wonderful outtakes of him saying, "What am I doing here? What am I supposed to be doing?" But his willingness to commit was beautiful. He has it in reverse as a director.

I was in Cuzco, Peru, doing Dennis Hopper's movie, *The Last Movie,* and I got a wire from Jack to grow my beard for the part in *Drive, He Said.* He knew exactly who he wanted to look how, and so on. When I got to Oregon, he didn't have a script for me, because he knew me well enough to get the craziness out of me to jump on a cop. I had that happen in life, and he used me to do that. I really think that's a very important part of what we're all trying to do now. Jack's very much in the center of all that, which is using each other creatively to communicate what we get from each other, what we really get from each other, and how

that's relevant to the films we make, rather than imposing some artificial character or some forced dialogue on people.

Question: How did you get Orson Welles to be in your film?

Jaglom: Peter Bogdanovich, who is a friend of mine, gave me an introduction to Orson, and I flew to New York to meet him. And again, Orson Welles is mythical to me. He represents this bigger than life, impressionistic, actor-director, who's mad and who's endlessly making movies that never get finished, that are all quite brilliant and are costing the studios a fortune. He's a danger to every creative director at one level, and at the same time the idol at a certain level, because he's really done his own number somehow. I knew I wanted him for my first movie, that's all I knew, but I didn't want to write a part, because if it wasn't going to be him I wouldn't have used the same part. Now, I knew for him I couldn't count on improvisation, and I would have to write a definite part, which I did, but I only wanted to do that after I got him, which made it difficult to get him. I had to fly to New York, go up to the Plaza, and this huge man in his blue silk pajamas came to the door and said, "Yes, what is it? Oh, it's you, Peter sent you. O.K. you've got five minutes." And I said, "Well, I want you to be in my movie, and I've never directed a movie be-

Jaglom, Nicholson, and Philip Proctor discussing character relationship between scenes in A Safe Place

fore, and I've never written a movie before, and I've written this one, and I'm directing this one, and I can't even tell you what you're going to play, because I haven't written it yet, so I can't show you a script." And he said, "Get the fuck out of here." So I said, "Look, I came all the way out here from California, and I want an hour of your time." So Orson said, "Well, I'll sit down here, but I don't have to listen," and he sort of folded his massive body and looked up at the ceiling. So I started this rap, and I remembered that he was a magician, and I knew that I wanted Noah, the girl in the movie, to meet a magician, a fantasy figure. I didn't know what, but I told him he's got one trick that he can't do. He's got a lot of cheap magic, a lot of small magic, but big magic he just can't do. And he said, "What does he want to do?" And I said, "I can't tell you that." That's because I hadn't thought about it yet; I didn't know what it was. I was developing the character as I was talking to him, out of what I knew about Orson—the magician who disappoints, the parent who tells us stories about what we think movies are going to be like, and they're not. All of those things mixed with my Hassidic thing; I wanted him to tell these Hassidic stories, these parables from Rabbi Nachtmann, who's a rabbi who tells these strange meaningless-meaningful stories about life that I don't understand, but that seem to be full of all that stuff you get told as a kid, but that doesn't mean anything when you examine them.

I told him all this slowly, and he was interested, but he was impassive; he was very unresponsive until finally it occurred to me what it was he tried to do. He kept on saying, "What is it? What is it that he tries to do?" And I said, "You try and make something disappear." He said, "What?" and I said, "I can't tell you that. That's the key to the whole thing. But it's yourself that you succeed in making disappear at the end." And he said, "Can I wear a cape?" and I knew I had him then.

At that time there was a property owned here at BBS that Orson and Jack were both interested in being it, and I wanted to be the first one to have Orson and Jack in a movie together, and even though they never met, I loved the dynamic of the two of them. They never met on the shooting schedule, but I intercut them in such a way that they work off of each other. They represent to me poles of the same thing at different stages of life. If certain things don't happen, Jack could become

Orson, because they're both myths at different stages of development, and that's a danger for Jack, and that's also the potential for Jack.

Question: Do you think that's where he's headed?

Jaglom: No, because he's much better able to take care of himself at a certain level than Orson is. Orson's insistence on purity at certain levels will make him do self-destructive things, and I don't think Jack would. Jack's great power in film, I think, is that he has this incredible reality, this incredible moment to moment reality, mixed with his own charm and communication, that makes you able to believe anything about him, even while you know he's lying to you. You want to believe the lie, and he represents something very powerful that way. You just can't expose the lie as a lie too overtly. I think that's what the problem is when he tries to do something like *Marvin Gardens,* which is a terrific acting job. But they did that with Brando initially, too, who was the last person, I think, that had that kind of impact, except for James Dean, who died. If you remember in the beginning, when Brando got tired of doing that sweatshirt thing and tried to do other things, like *The Young Lions,* jn which he was great, he got put down for it, because they wanted him to be Brando, and what is this thing with the German accent and the blond hair?

Jack is also a very complicated actor with a lot of facets, who wants to do more than just what America loves so much about him. And he's also a very important film-maker who's going to make a lot of very significant films.

Question: What was *A Safe Place* basically trying to communicate to its audience?

Jaglom: It's hard to synthesize. To me it's a film about the loss of innocence; it's a film about how nostalgia kills, about how dwelling on the seemingly beautiful past is really a killer and stops you from being able to live in the present and function for the future. And how our society, and the oppression of our society is a very seductive one, the seduction of the Jack character, the Orson character, of those musical songs from the forties, of the whole society where parents and schools and music, and the movies more than anything else, lie to you about what life is going to be like and prepare you for a life that doesn't exist. So to me, it's a film about disappointment, about isolation that comes from disappointment, about the lack of the ability to accept the reality of the present, when

Jaglom trying to motivate Orson Welles and Tuesday Weld

you have been constantly forced to live up to the dream of the past.

It's a movie, hopefully, that is an anti-myth. It becomes another myth, of course, because that's the problem with movies. By definition they become myths. I tried to replace the myth with an anti-myth. I tried to break down all the barriers that traditionally exist in movies, and what's happening now, which I think is really nice, is that the kids are going to see it now and really responding to it. What happened in New York was that Columbia saw it, and they didn't know what it was, so they tried to sell it as another *Love Story,* aiming it at a middle-aged audience and using the names. Anybody that goes in to see it because of Jack or Orson is going to hate that movie. The kids in New York that would have responded to it didn't get to know about it because of the ads. I wouldn't have gone to my own movie if I had read those ads.

To summarize, I really tried to make a movie about my own fantasies, my own isolation, and the isolation that I perceive women specifically have in society, and how I relate to that as an artist in society, because how a society is oppressive to an artist is very similar to how society oppresses women. They treat women and artists like children, who are humored and seduced at a certain level, but not really respected, or trusted, or given any power or authority. I tried to express through a woman those particular sensibilities and traps. Plus my own concept of time, the danger and destructiveness of perceiving time as a linear form. I don't feel that life is a straight line. We know that it doesn't have a beginning, middle, and end. We know that there's a constant input of fantasies, and memories, and things that seem to be, and while we're talking there are hundreds of things that are going on in our minds, feelings and memories, many of which have, or may have, or we don't

Nicholson and Weld in A Safe Place

know if they're dreams or what. I wanted to create that inner landscape on the screen, in some fashion. I'd never seen that done on the screen— I'd seen attempts at it, but never really a trip through an inner landscape—so I wanted to connect that desire with the conveying of that kind of oppression, and what it leads to.

Now for somebody of my generation and Jack's generation, who were children in the forties, who were at school and at college in the fifties, we grew up in completely diseased societies, full of lies, and we were much more isolated, because now what's happened is that kids know that they're being lied to, and they have identified themselves separately from the lie. There's large numbers now, so you don't feel totally isolated, because you know you're part of a whole alternate culture, and it's creating its own life-style, and it's freer for that reason. It doesn't have the political power that it should have now, but it will take it. It's just a question of a very short time.

When we grew up, the few of us that sensed that we were being oppressed were freaks. We were really isolated, because the majority were Eisenhower quiet, short-haired, really crazy people, it seemed to us, but then we were crazy, it seemed to them. Dennis Hopper grew up in one place, and Jack in another, and I in another, but we shared a very similar kind of feeling, being the isolated one in our areas, the strange one. So when we make our films now, we really try to reflect that sensibility, and we have an audience now for the first time.

I think that all of us, those who grew up in this business together, and who were oppressed at a certain level by the restrictions of this business that wants to make *Love Story,* and at their best want to make *The Last Picture Show,* which is a well-made rehash of an old movie, and at its worst make movies like *The French Connection,* which are, to me, really fascist, oppressive movies. There are a whole group of us—Monte Hellman, and Jack, and myself, and Dennis, and Peter Fonda, and Michael Sarne, and Carol Eastman—that are really trying to reflect different sensibilities, that show more of the environment as we really perceive it. Our job now doesn't stop with the making of the movie, but with finding the way to make the movie, and then finding the way to communicate it to the audience, and then finding the audience, which is what I've been doing with *A Safe Place.*

Drive, He Said is a film that should have had an audience, whether you consider it a successful film or a flawed film, or whatever you may consider it. It's a film that certainly, to me, deserves an audience much more than a *French Connection.* It explores things, it attempts things; it's not just an easy emotional rip-off. Yet because of the nature of studios, and that structure, it has no way of having a life. A way has to be found.

Question: We understand that you were instrumental in reshaping *Easy Rider.*

Jaglom: Yeah, but I'd like to be careful about how I put that. Dennis Hopper shot and directed *Easy Rider,* and I think he did it brilliantly. Bert Schneider produced it, and I think brilliantly, and part of the brilliance of Bert Schneider producing it was that he knew that some of the excesses of Dennis had to be sat on a little bit, which I think we all, as artists, need. That's what a good editor does for a writer, and I think that's what a good producer does. Not sat on in a heavy way, but sat on by giving alternate choices. Bert hired me to help cut *Easy Rider.* I spent ten weeks on it, and I helped cut *Easy Rider,* but it's still Dennis' vision entirely. Jack helped cut *Easy Rider* also. We worked on it in different sections. Dennis worked on the rides. Peter on the graveyard thing at the end. What I did was called editorial consultant, and I think that's the best way to define it. I would work with the editor, and I would tell them what changes to make, and we would run them, and we would discuss them. Jack did that with his editor. Bert would look at what we both did, and Dennis would be doing his thing also, and some synthesis took place, which allowed us all to contribute the best that we had to offer to it. That's the way I would prefer to have my participation in *Easy Rider* described.

Question: Can you tell us specifically which parts you and Jack edited?

Jaglom: Dennis shot some scenes with what, a lot of us felt, had too little of Peter in it. The scene with Jack and Dennis, where Jack is talking about the Venutians, didn't have Peter in it at all, so we had to put Peter in it, which meant that we had to find Peter in a similar setting, and I had to flip it over so we would be facing the right direction, and where he would have a line of dialogue that would make it seem that he was talking to Jack. To create a higher visibility for Peter was very important, I thought; we all thought. I had nothing to do with the New Orleans stuff, and I had nothing to do with the whorehouse stuff. I had

Philip Proctor, Gwen Welles (no relation to Orson), William Tepper, unidentified woman, and director, Henry Jaglom

a lot to do with the acting scenes; the swimming scene with Peter and Luana Anders, and the scene where they walk through the commune, and the campfire scenes, which we felt were really important to establish along the road—what was going down in these peoples' heads. It was really honing what Dennis had presented, putting it together, pulling it together, but I wouldn't call it changing anything. It was helping to convey what Dennis was trying to convey.

Question: Getting back to *A Safe Place,* did you write it the way it appears on the screen or did you conceive of it as a linear story?

Jaglom: No, I never conceived of it as a linear type of thing, but in order to get it done it was, of course, necessary to present them with a script, and a script by definition is linear. It has a page one and it has an end. I presented an outline script, with thoroughly worked-out dialogue in those

scenes where it was possible and indications about what the rest would be. But because of the freedom afforded me by Bert, I was able to do the movie in three stages. That is, first I wrote the script. Then I shot the movie, disregarding what I had written. I didn't look at it once the whole time we were shooting. I brought other people into the movie, like Gwen Welles, who weren't in the script, but whose emotional lives were important to me. Gwen came to me on a one-week job, but she stayed for six weeks and had a very significant part in the movie, it seems to me. I had the freedom to violate the script. Some of it I didn't violate at all, like with Orson. Except that with Orson I had to sometimes let him go a little longer, and let him tell other stories to get him to do the stuff that I wanted. He started out to be very difficult, and turned out to be very easy—once he got relaxed. He since has directed me in a movie called *The*

98

Other Side of the Wind, where he's now using a little improvisational stuff, and he didn't write a script for me. He has me playing a younger director to his older director, and he's trying some new things.

When we initially started on *Safe Place,* we had a very difficult time with him. He was trying to direct the crew, direct Tuesday, direct me. I mean, he was impossible, and when I asked him what was wrong at the end of the day he said, "I've never seen anyone as arrogant as you. You stop me after nine takes." I explained to him that we were working in such a fashion that nobody had more than one take, and if it didn't work we tried something else, rather than covering. I didn't believe in doing that. And he said, "Well, I sometimes give myself eighty-five takes." And I said, "Well, it's not your movie. My problem with you is that you're trying to make it your movie, and it's not." And he says, "Well, what am I going to do? You're the director. You've got the choice finally of what take to use. You'll make the wrong choice anyway, so at least I want to know that I get one good one down there." So I said, "O.K., we'll keep on going until you get exactly what you want down," and he said, "You'll do that? They'll let you do that? They never let me do that." I said, "Absolutely. You can take a line of dialogue, and repeat it as many times as you want until you're perfectly satisfied." He said, "Oh, my God, that's great. What do you want in return?" I said, "In return, you have to let me direct my movie. Don't talk to the actors, don't talk to the crew." After that he was a pussycat; he was sensational. He was helpful. That wonderful day when it rained he said, "God must really love you, Henry. He never did this for me. Let's go back out on the rock and do it again in the rain," which is what I wanted. He gave me good support, and he even gave me a final day free, because he felt that he had messed up the first day. So in the second stage was the flexibility that I had when I shot the movie, and the third stage was taking all the stuff that I had shot back to California and looking through it—hours and hours of film—looking through it almost like a jigsaw puzzle. I forgot the script that I wrote and the shooting script, and just thought, "Now what have I got here, and what do I want?" I want an emotion; I want a feeling, because I had no idea from the beginning how this film should look, but I knew from the beginning how *A Safe Place* should feel. So I just put it together like I would do a painting. I took this tree, and put it there, and then I put that house around it, and when the house got bigger I realized that I wanted some clouds, and I built the film that way, and I don't think that's ever been done before, and Bert let me do that, and that's what's extraordinary. It's certainly never been done that way with a studio. You can imagine what their response was when they saw it.

Question: What was their response?

Jaglom: Leo Jaffe, one of the heads of Columbia, said, "Jesus Christ, I didn't even piss once." And I said, "I don't understand, what does that mean?" And he says, "Well, usually I piss—what?" and he points at some guy, and some guy says, "Twelve, thirteen times." And he says, "Yeah, usually I go the john and piss twelve, thirteen times, and this time I didn't piss once. I haven't not pissed once since—what was it?" And some guy says, *"Anastasia."* And he says, "That's right. *Anastasia.* That's the last time I didn't piss during a movie." And I said, "Oh, does that mean you like the movie?" And he said, "No, no, no, it has nothing to do with that. It just means that this movie was so weird that I couldn't take my eyes off of it. But I'll tell you one thing. After the movie, did I have a good piss." I don't know what their response was. They figured that they had a weird film that was interesting enough that they didn't have to piss, but it was strange to them.

They didn't know, and they tried to aim it wrong, but they've been really nice in giving me the opportunity now, having learned that it's not going to work as a commercial, regular movie; I've told them, and I believe, that it can be a commercial movie if we forget about older audiences. There's twenty-five million young people in this country, a large number of whom would go to see this movie and be open to it. We've gotten extraordinary reviews from all these counter-culture and youth-press publications. The most important thing is that it should have a visibility, an accessibility. The trouble in the studio system is that if it doesn't have the kind of mass audience appeal that makes families go to see it, like a *Godfather* or a *Love Story,* then they'd rather take a tax loss, because it doesn't pay for them to put the same manpower on my movie. But, fortunately, Columbia was really nice, and they turned over the money to me—it was little money—and I handled all the advertising myself.

Question: What was Jack's reaction to your film?

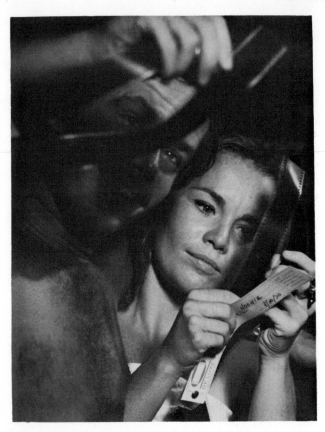

Nicholson and Tuesday Weld looking at clips from
A Safe Place

Jaglom: He liked it very much. He's very positive about it. It was an exploration that he respected very much. I think he liked it a little more in the longer version that I had, which was a three-hour version that I had while I was cutting it, but I couldn't keep all that in.

I think we really respect each other's work, you know, because we respect each other as people. He's an extraordinarily bright person, and incredibly talented in a whole range of areas, both as a writer and as a director, in addition to being an actor.

Question: So first you were directed by him, and then you directed him?

Jaglom: Yeah. First we acted together in a movie called *Psych-Out,* where he got me the part as his sidekick in the movie. That was our first professional involvement together, I think. Then *Easy Rider* came along, and I spent a lot of time with him during that. I went downstairs with him at the old Columbia to the barbershop when he got his hair cut for *Easy Rider,* and he was very annoyed at that, because he didn't want to do the part. He had a lot of other things going, and they had just

gotten through this complicated and devastating thing with *Head*. But he went down there and got his hair cut, and reluctantly went off to Texas, or wherever it was, to do *Easy Rider*. Then, as I said, I got this wire from him when I was in Cuzco to let my beard grow. Actually he said to let my "Scrooge McDuck's" grow. In *Psych-Out* I had worn these terribly pasted-on sideburns that they used then, and he said I looked like Scrooge McDuck, you know, Donald Duck's uncle with the fuzzy sideburns, and I went to do his movie. He was great as a director. He was really easy and confident, and had a really interesting kind of a sense of what he was trying to do. And then he came to New York to be in *Safe Place*.

Question: Can you pinpoint some things that you've learned from Jack?

Jaglom: He communicates very well what I think is most important for an actor who's not playing a character part, and that is how to really be true to using yourself, how to really trust your own instincts and go with your instincts. And as a director he was enormously encouraging of our being who we were, and a lot of people have difficulty with that. I like being who I am; I like playing that, and he just wanted me to be manic with that. He just said, "Be nuts." So I went nuts. Just watching him over the years has given me a great awareness of how to trust my actors, and who to trust, and where to trust them. You can't do that a lot of times, of course.

We've all sort of learned from each other, because we've all developed at similar paces together, and our life-styles are remarkably similar, our involvements, our political beliefs, which I don't think you can separate from. I have the best home movies, the best eight-millimeter movies in the world. I've got movies from *Easy Rider* days with Fonda and Hopper and Nicholson and Bert Schneider and Rafelson all hanging out at Columbia, which is torn down now, which makes it even more interesting, and at different peoples' homes, at Schneider's home, at Rafelson's home, and at Nicholson's home with the daughter and the children and the different girl friends from the different periods of time, and there's this tremendous overlapping which has really become an interesting piece of history. I think all these people are really the closest thing there is to a New Wave like the French had.

Bert Schneider is really responsible for most of the good stuff that's happened. Almost all of it has come from his courage to take on challenges that nobody else would attempt and to commit himself to the artists to let them have the freedom to do their films.

Question: What do you think Jack wants most out of his work in film?

Jaglom: I think he's as much a film-maker as he is an actor, and on some levels I think he's more. And I think he wants to create his own body of film literature, which represents the way he perceives his environment. I think he'll do that.

Question: What do you think has been the high point in his career?

Jaglom: There's no question that *Easy Rider* was the high point simply from the fact that it enabled everything else to happen. It has definitely been the catalyst for his visibility. His visibility makes him economically supportable for the studios and this whole system, and it's inevitably enabled him to direct, and the whole thing. My particular opinion, and he probably wouldn't share it at this point, is that his high point was directing *Drive, He Said,* because of what he learned from that experience and what it was like, including the commercial failure of it. I think that that will turn out to be the high point when you look at his career from the vantage point of ten or twelve years from now. But *Easy Rider* really made it all possible.

He's really such a complicated person, because he operates on so many different kinds of levels, that he's got a lot of high points. He's a very high person. I really think that way beyond the facility he has for being a terrific actor, and how successful he can be at that, he's a really serious artist, who is going to communicate his own vision in a body of film literature.

Question: In talking with Richard Rush, he mentioned that he thought Jack had a great ability to lower his IQ according to the character he's playing at the time. Do you agree with his observation?

Jaglom: I wonder about that. I'm not sure that's right. I never believe Jack when he's playing low intelligence. I always believe that that's a guy playing low intelligence, because there's something else too interesting there for that truck driver. I wonder about the success of that. He has a naturalness in being of the streets, but there's a street intelligence that comes through. I must say I don't agree with that. I always see a thinking, intelligent person. I don't see Jack doing a ninety-five IQ successfully. I think he's best when you can see him thinking.

Jack, obviously, speaks English properly and correctly, but he has elected to communicate with a certain kind of style that sounds almost illiterate at times, and yet is informed by a very high intelligence, which is an interesting duality. I think he has that duality as a person, also. I think he's very attracted to the street thing, to the averageness, and at the same time he is profoundly nonaverage. I've always observed that conflict going on. We've spent a lot of nights out on the streets together over the years. He digs the anonymity of it, even before he was a star. He digs being one of "those guys," but at the same time there's an intelligence coming through it that belies the language, belies the style and the attitudes expressed, and I think it's a role for him. He's an extraordinarily bright person, who grew up in a way that didn't encourage intelligence, as opposed to some of us who grew up where intelligence was commended. One of the things that I think is so attractive about Jack playing these lower guys is that he always makes you realize that these guys have a great deal more than they seem to have.

Question: Getting back to *A Safe Place* again, how much of Susan/Noah's dreams and illusions were your own?

Jaglom: All of them. I would say that the character of Susan/Noah, who's Susan when she's with Orson and Noah when she's grown-up, is one-third Tuesday, one-third Karen Black, and one-third me. Karen had a very strong influence. The speech that Tuesday makes in the closet about lights in the eyes—while I was going with Karen at one point in our relationship as boy and girl friend, she started telling me some story about lights in the eyes, and I remember getting out my pencil and writing it down. She was crying, and I was writing it down, and then I used that in my movie. I didn't realize that until I showed Karen my movie on my cutting machine, and then she flashed and I realized where that had come from.

I had to exorcise a lot of private ghosts from myself for that film. The apartment that Philip Proctor takes Tuesday to is my parents' apartment where I grew up. That's a very personal trip, and I don't usually mention it. I'm really taking the audience through my childhood. That's still where my parents live. That's where I spent the first twenty-three years of my life. Once having done that I can let go of it, and that's what's really important to me. And when Jack is fucking Tuesday, and Philip leaves and goes to his father's office— that's my father's office. And while he's there he sees Tuesday's face, and on her face are childhood images. Those images are thirty-year-old eight-millimeter home movies of my brother and me that my parents had taken when I was a baby. Philip's voice is saying, "I love you from London to Paris," and then there's a shot of my father on Tuesday's face. "I love you from Paris to Geneva," and then there's my mother, "No I don't, no I don't," and then there's my brother and I playing around. All I wanted to evoke was childhood. "I love you from London to Paris. I love you from Paris to Geneva." That's how I learned geography as a kid, from my parents, who were traveling all the time. You know the maid opens the door—that's my maid, that's my parents' maid. My parents always were in Europe. I had a very isolated kind of childhood as a result. There was a kind of post-card love from long distance.

The movie's very personal. It's the most personal thing that a movie could ever be. I'm using images which are very private, personal images to try and trigger the audiences' private images, rather than to try and give a universal, objective reality which we can all hook into, but which we're all removed from. What really excites me is when somebody comes out of the movie and tells me that it stimulated their thoughts or their remembrances of childhood. A lot of younger women have said it was like reading their diaries. They said they didn't know that other people felt that way. Hopefully it conveys emotions but not specific ones.

Question: When do you find Jack the most comfortable offscreen?

Jaglom: He doesn't relax, I think, like a lot of other people. There's been a lot of pressure on him throughout his life, and that hasn't changed. He's easiest in a one-to-one relationship. In the privacy of a one-to-one relationship, with somebody he knows, he knows why they're there, and he feels comfortable with them, and he knows what that's about. He has a certain kind of public ease, which he adopts very successfully. When my movie opened at a film festival, we went on a panel show afterward, and he was terrific on it. On that occasion I was very uneasy, and Dennis was there, and he was uneasy. All of us—we didn't handle ourselves that well, I felt. Jack was just totally in command, and totally at ease, but it was that external kind of ease that he can do very well. The internal, private, quiet ease that he gets most successfully I've only seen when I'm really totally alone with him. Even if there's one other person, no mat-

ter how familiar or friendly with that person, even if he knows them as well as he knows me, the fact that there are two of us creates a different kind of behavioral pattern.

When he was casting *Drive, He Said* and I was writing *A Safe Place,* we had offices next to each other over at Columbia, and there were so many things going on at one time that I remember having to take him in the closet in his office to find out what the fuck was going on, to get some sanity out of him, because there was just too much. It was dark in the closet, and everything was fine. He was totally easy. We sat there for half an hour, and had a terrific time.

He's badgered by a lot of pressure now. He's expected to be a lot of different things to a lot of different kinds of people, to fulfill a lot of roles, and Jack's genuine niceness gets him into more trouble, because he doesn't want to hurt anybody, you know, and some asshole will come up and really lay a bad thing on him and he will be nice with them, and courteous with them, and charming, and he'll go through a whole deal, because he doesn't want to be arrogant, and at the same time he feels really bad. And afterward he's pissed off at himself for having done that. He's annoyed at the fucking guy, but he'll never show that. He'll never say, "Hey, don't bother me." He will give always an extension of himself in such a way that it wipes him out, because he gives the same amount of energy to that person as he does to someone he knows very well. I think the worst thing for Jack would be to be accused of being false, to be accused of being pretentious, to be accused of being arrogant, and I think he goes to such lengths to show that he's not any of those things that he suffers for it a lot, and I don't think he should have to do that. But I think he wants to be President. I mean really at some bottom level would like to be President. He used to carry a bag around that said "Nicholson for President" on it.

He's just really—Oh, I don't know, he's up there at his house next to Brando's house, and to me that really represents something really interesting. The two of them are up there on the top of the mountain, they see each other, they're next-door neighbors, and that symbolizes something to me. They share the top of this mountain, and that's really heavy in terms of film history.

Question: Can you characterize Jack Nicholson in one sentence?

Jaglom: Teeth.

Mitzi McCall

Our interview with comedienne Mitzi McCall came about purely through coincidence when we arrived at the Sahara Tahoe to interview Ann-Margret. We were met in the hotel's posh lounge by Allan Carr and were taken immediately backstage to meet the other people connected with the Ann-Margret Show —among them the comedy team of Mitzi McCall and Charlie Brill. They are a very funny first act for the show. As we got to talking about why we were there, the pixieish Ms. McCall announced that she had once been in a film with Jack Nicholson. On further questioning, we discovered the film to be *The Cry Baby Killer*—Nicholson's first film, and Ms. McCall played Evelyn in the film; one of the teen-age girls. We immediately imposed upon her for an interview, which she was willing to do after the second show—about 1:30 A.M.

In the time between our interview with Ann-Margret and the start of the second show, we managed to form a list of questions for Ms. McCall. After the show we again made our way backstage, and, retreating to a small nook in the dressing room, conducted the following interview.

Mitzi McCall in her dressing room at the Sahara Tahoe

Question: Can you tell us how you got your part in *The Cry Baby Killer*?

Mitzi McCall: Oh, my God, it was so long ago. If I recall, it seems that I had worked for the director before on another movie. It was in the days of those kind of tacky teen-age movies. I had worked for Roger Corman before, and he was one of the innovators of these type movies.

I did a scene with Jack Nicholson. First of all, I found his looks dynamite, even then. I guess I was ahead of my time in knowing what was dynamite. He had an attitude that was reminiscent of, and I'm sorry to do this—I hate when people have to compare—but he had a James Dean quality as far as I was concerned. James Dean was a good friend of mine, and I found a lot of James

Dean in Jack Nicholson. He was very serious about his work. I mean, there wasn't any horsing around on the set, where he was concerned. He was dedicated even in a cockamamie B movie. Being a comedienne, naturally, I would tend to find the people that are sort of laughing and scratching over in a corner, but Jack Nicholson wasn't one of them. He was in deadly earnest about everything he did. I found that very appealing, because opposites attract, and with my being a nut and he being serious—I found it charming.

I ran into Jack several times after *Cry Baby Killer*. He always was friendly and sweet. He's just a very groovy man. I used to see him at unemployment. I used to see him in the B line very Wednesday.

When he hit in *Easy Rider* I wasn't surprised at all. In fact, I thought it would happen a lot sooner, because I really felt that he was that good.

Question: Why do you think it took so long?

McCall: That's the industry. There's really no answer to that, is there? I'm convinced it has nothing to do with talent. It has to do with timing, breaks. It has to do with somebody who is not afraid to take a chance. In the days when I started out you had to be a Sandra Dee to make it, and that's not the case anymore. Jack Nicholson is very lucky, because I think he's got it all going. He's got the looks, and the charm, and definitely the talent.

Question: On the other hand, did you find any qualities in him that were offensive?

McCall: In retrospect, I might have thought that Jack was too moody. That would have been the word that I probably would have used. He was very moody, but then I was a screwball. But it's Jack's talent that counts. It's not a popularity contest of how cute he is off the set—who cares?

Question: Do you think Jack is a male chauvinist?

McCall: Jack Nicholson came from that whole *Playboy* era. Of course they were male chauvinists. The whole concept of the bunny is the most ridiculous thing in the world.

Question: How much of a rapport were you able to build up with him?

McCall: Oh, on a scale from one to one hundred, I'd say about one-half.

Question: Why was that?

McCall: It just didn't happen. I mean, I was such a dumb nut in those days, and it's only in retrospect that I want to kill myself that I really didn't get to know this man. But at the time I was striving for my own survival, and I didn't have it straight in my head to sit down and figure out what Jackson Nicholson was all about. I was too busy trying to figure out what I was all about.

Question: Did you get any idea of what Jack was striving for at that time?

McCall: Just to act, and be good, and to do things that were valuable. Yes, I do remember that.

*Question*s Did you learn anything from working with Jack?

McCall: He taught me everything I know. No, seriously, I can't think of anything that I learned. I do think he's dynamite, and I would like to work with him now.

Question: What kind of role would you like to play opposite Jack?

McCall: His rug. The lady he can step on. I think if I would work with Jack Nicholson I would be that poor soul, vulnerable type that he could just twist around his finger.

Question: Can you characterize Jack Nicholson in one sentence?

McCall: Evil, sexy, crazy, super—oh, God, help me.

William Tepper

Drive, He Said offered filmgoers two "firsts": Jack Nicholson's critically acclaimed directorial debut, and the debut of a promising young actor, William Tepper.

Tepper is truly representative of the 1970's film personality. He is a graduate of a university film school and has written a few unproduced screenplays and written and directed a short. He also proved to be a natural and multifaceted actor in *Drive, He Said,* his only major film role to date. At the time of the interview, Tepper was in the process of getting ready to go to Europe for a film.

After a few phone conversations between Tepper, his agent, and ourselves, the interview was set up at Tepper's apartment in Beverly Hills.

When we arrived, Tepper was knocking out an old-time melody on his upright piano, which takes up most of the space in his one-room flat. The furniture was noticeably used, but very comfortable.

The start of the interview was delayed for a few moments as Tepper talked to his girl friend over the telephone. He then lowered his towering frame into a cushioned, high-backed chair and began to relax.

William Tepper in Drive, He Said

105

Question: How did you get the part of Hector in *Drive, He Said*?

William Tepper: I was a client at Creative Management Associates as a writer and a director, and they wouldn't handle me as an actor because I was unknown. Well, I had heard that they hadn't cast the lead in it yet, and I figured the reason that they hadn't was because they needed an individual that was young enough and that could play basketball, and that was one of the things that I could do. So my agent got on the phone and started giving them all these lies like I was an all-city basketball player, and I was a great actor, and of course they'd never seen me act. I went down, and I read for Jack once and he liked the reading, and we had a good rapport. Then I read again, and the third time I read with Karen Black for the producers, and two days later we were shooting. It happened very quickly.

Question: What were some of Jack's good and bad points as a first time director?

Tepper: The good part of it is that anytime anybody does something for the first time it's a new experience for them, and there's absolutely no complacency about anything. For me it was exciting for obvious reasons; it was a large part in a major film, and I had always wanted to do this, but also observing him directing his first film was an interesting experience for me. Directing is a multifaceted job. Of the things that one has to learn, I learned from watching Jack during the first few weeks where you have to expend your energies. There are certain things that can be taken care of by other people, and as the shooting went on I observed Jack being better able to spend his energies on creative issues and let assistant directors do other things.

Along those lines, after he had done *Carnal Knowledge*, he came back and said it was sort of too bad for us, the actors, that we couldn't have done *Drive, He Said* after he had had the experience with Mike Nichols.

One of the best things about Jack as a director is that he's very sensitive to the problems of the actor, and he is always concerned with getting life happening on the screen. Something that's very close to ninety-eight point six degrees, you know. And he would create an atmosphere where an actor can work, and that's all you can really ask for. It's one thing when you're working on a play, and the director becomes slightly a bit of a director-teacher because you have a lot of rehearsal, but in a film ninety per cent of the director's work in relation to the actors is to create an atmosphere where something can happen. He did that.

Question: Can you pinpoint something that Jack taught you?

Tepper: I would say basically to have a good time. I mean, at that time I had just come out of film school, and to me film-making was very academic, very serious, and I had some very strong ideas about how things should go, and his basic outlook is to have a good time. He does, he does in life, and after awhile I saw that was the best way to do it. You don't have to be serious all the time, because being serious isn't analogous with doing good work. So I would say if there was one major thing I learned while making the film, and there are obviously a myriad of specifics, but the one major thing was to have a good time.

Question: Did Jack have any trouble relating what he wanted to the actors?

Tepper: No, I don't think so. In fact that's probably his strongest point. He even said before we started shooting that we should ask him a million questions, because that's the area that he could handle very well, and to keep him away from the technical people. He didn't want to deal with that. Of course, he was saying that slightly tongue in cheek.

A number of the people in the film were old friends of his, so he had a lot of reference points. I would say that once in awhile he had trouble relating to me, because here I was, a twenty-one-year-old Jewish guy, with a large ego, who has the lead in his film, so, of course, he's going to have a little trouble relating to me. But the accent is really on little. He has a very good understanding. I think we had a good undertsanding of each other. I was in a position that he would identify with so strongly that he had a lot of empathy for my problems.

Question: How honest do you think Jack was to the crew when he needed help?

Tepper: There are an infinite number of ways to go about making a movie. Some film-makers when they begin to make a dramatic film know what they want to see on the screen, the final hour and a half or two hours. The other way to do it is to have some semblance of a script, and to keep working it, keep kneading it, and it continues to change. I would say the only person who had an idea of what he wanted to do was Jack, because of the nature of the film, where some of the scenes were improvised, and others were written in the morning, and then changed during the shooting. And it turns out that that state of flux was an active element in the film, and I think it shows on the screen, too.

He was working with a very professional crew. Guys that are the best in their fields, because we had to expose a lot of film in a short period of time, so they hand-picked the crew. And I think that Jack wanted to show them that he was very professional in that area, which he really was. I mean, even if it was just a simple thing like frontal nudity. I remember one specific. He wanted the basketball sequence not to be perfect, to get out of focus sometimes, because that's how an athletic event is, and of course the camera crew wanted it all perfect and no jiggling, and there was even one or two times in rushes when we saw that something very good was about to happen and the cameraman would put his hand over the lens.

Professionalism is very antiartistic and anti-creative, because it's an agreement to certain norms, and whereas Jack understood the norms, understood the agreements, understood professionalism, when there were the times when he wanted to try something a little bit different the crew figures that this was a wild man, but they were behind him one hundred per cent.

Question: How much of a say did you, as an actor, have' in what the film was saying?

Tepper: I knew what he was trying to do. I made a special effort to not read the book before doing it, because I realized that his adaptation of Larner's novel is quite different. There are certain elements that were borrowed, of course, but it really is Jack's film.

As far as my character was concerned, it was basically my own. We didn't have a whole lot of discussions going into it. He assumed I was the character. When I read for the part I showed him a certain thing. I wasn't about to show him anything different, you know, I was playing it innocent and naive. Understandably, Jack wanted me to be attractive and gallant at certain times, and I wanted to make the guy a little more of a "schli-mazel." When these things would come up we would talk about it, and I would try to please him. I mean, it's his film, his vision. Eventually, after about a week or two, we got it down to a good form of comunication. If we'd do a take, and he wanted one thing or another, he'd say, "Gimme a little less Ronald Colman," or "Gimme a little more foolish boy." I knew that meant a certain thing, it had a certain quality.

Question: What do you think the film was basically trying to say?

Tepper: To me, it probably says a different thing than it does to Jack, because it is the sort of film where there's a lot of room to read in things. It's the periphery things that matter. The glue that holds it together actually becomes the substance of the film.

In Larner's book, the Bloom character is sort of analogous with America. This big sort of thing that could do a lot, but stepped over other people, and was real confused. I think the film asks the question through my character and Margotta's character, "Who am I today?" It's the same thing with the country, because we're in this state of immediate information where things are changing so quickly.

Question: Did Jack have any hassles with BBS over the final product?

Tepper: As far as I know, he had total control. Not that BBS doesn't own final cut, because they do, but they believe in the individual film-maker that they're going behind. That goes for any of the films they've made. You know, Bert Schneider is a very special guy, and he realizes that the only way to go about it is to find a guy you believe in, and a project you believe in, and say, "Go make the film, and bring it back." Any other way is absolute bullshit. It really is.

Question: How did you, as an unknown actor, get along with more established actors such as Bruce Dern and Karen Black?

Tepper: For me it seemed like a logical progression of how things were going. I mean, ever since I was in my mid-teens I decided this was what I was going to do, and I had always assumed that I was going to be, whatever it meant to me at the time, a "movie star," and do put that in quotes. At that point in my life I had just finished my first film, which I had written and directed, and just finished a screenplay, and was really feeling good about things, and I remember the first shot of *Drive, He Said*, and Jack chose to shoot a scene that had no dialogue in it. I had to make a long cross across the street, and we got it on the first take, and it all felt right. What can I tell you?

I must admit, at the time I wasn't a kid out of the woods, like this is New Hollywood. I mean, I recognized the situation, I recognized that if the

After a rape attempt by Michael Margotta (not shown), Karen Black is consoled by William Tepper in Drive, He Said

film were to be a big success I would become very popular, et cetera. There was no reason for me to be up tight. I wasn't playing the king of England. This was a character that was well within my experience, so of course that made it a lot easier.

Question: How long did it take to shoot the film?

Tepper: A little less than two months. Seven, seven and a half weeks.

Question: What kind of a rapport were you able to build up with Jack off-camera during that time?

Tepper: It varied at different times. He represented, at that time, a very secure pillar. I mean, he'd been through it; he could understand me, he could understand my ego, but it would really vary very much depending on how both our lives were going at the time. When you're making a film you're also living your life. I would like to hang out with him while we were shooting the film, because I suppose I was very insecure at the time.

Question: What do you think are the strongest and weakest parts of the film?

Tepper: The weakest parts of the film, as far as I'm concerned, were the scenes that just weren't resolved. They got to the point of dramatic tension and then they would cut away to another scene. Some people might say that feeling is an integral part of the movie. It's hard for me to be ojective about that, because I see myself in a scene, and I want that to be a perfect scene. You have a tendency to look at things out of the whole. It almost goes for me, when I see the movie, from moment to moment. Some moments I'd think, "God, that was really fine," and then other moments I'd say, "I detected bullshit." You always see that in your own work, especially in retrospect.

Question: This is kind of a loaded question, but do you have a favorite performance in the picture aside from yourself?

Tepper: Yeah, Bruce Dern is great, and that's including myself. He's terrific in the movie. My favorite thing in the movie is something that he does. It's just before a scene where he walks into a hotel room where Mike Warren and I are. He's walking down a corridor, and a girl passes in front of him, and he just snaps his fingers twice at her! That's my favorite thing in the film. That's because he's relaxed and susceptible to any stimulus that goes on, and that's a very large part of a man's work, to be as vulnerable as you are now when you're working.

Question: Why do you think *Drive, He Said* failed?

Tepper: A number of reasons, and in no specific order. One reason is that the majority of the film-going public, aside from the film buffs and the people in Hollywood, opened up their newspapers on Friday night and saw *Drive, He Said,* and I think that *Drive, He Said* didn't sound like the kind of picture that they wanted to see. The other thing is that because of the nature of the ending, the way the film resolves itself, leaves a lot of people hanging. If the film has a different ending, and I'm not saying that I would prefer a different ending, the audience word-of-mouth is going to be qualitatively different. That's really what its' about; the word-of-mouth the next day. It's the Ping-Pong ball on mousetraps motif, right? So I think the ending had a lot to do with it.

Also, the nature of the film. There were a few films, namely *R.P.M.*, *Strawberry Statement*, and *Getting Straight*, which were really bullshit, and people had seen those, and the people who had that thing in their experience, the young people, just said that's horseshit. By that time, *Drive, He Said* had come out it was the classic situation of the movie industry crying "wolf" once too often. It doesn't even have to do with the quality of the film, but just the nature of the film. The best thing about the film, as far as I'm concerned, is that it was uncompromised.

Question: Why do you think the film had an X rating?

Tepper: I know why. The way that the censors, nonsensical people that they are, set up their thing it's simple; if you say "fuck" that's an R; if you do fuck, but you don't say it and you don't show it, then it's a PG; and if you don't do it or say it, but show it, it's an X. I don't know, it's ridiculous. They said some bullshit that there was some sodomy involved. I think one thing involved Margotta where they thought he was beating off. But, of course, this is all beside the point; the whole point is that we shouldn't have that.

Depending upon who's billed above the title, and what the title is, and what the rating is, determines what the title means. In other words, if there's a film called "Porky-pine," and its rated G with an unknown name above the title, then that title means a certain thing to you. If it's "Porky-pine," and its rated X with another name above the title, it's a different title. So that little rating thing plays an active part in deciding what film to see.

Question: How was the film received at BBS?

Tepper: Well, while I was up there, they had seen a few different days of rushes, and they came up and the word was "cashbox." Really. I went to sleep with that word on my lips. Cashbox, cashbox. They were all very happy with it. Bert Schneider expressed to me that he thought it would do business somewhere between the business that *Five Easy Pieces* and *Easy Rider* did. They were quite surprised that it didn't do business.

Question: Do you think the comedy of the film puts down the seriousness of it?

Tepper: No, not at all. Comedy is just tragedy in a chicken suit.

Question: Did you have any thoughts about Jack Nicholson before you worked with him?

Tepper: A few days before *Easy Rider* was released I went with someone to see a screening of it. I had never heard of him or Dennis Hopper or the film. I had heard of Peter Fonda because of his father, *Bert* Fonda. And I saw the film, and it didn't totally blow me out, but I was quite impressed with this guy who played the lawyer. Then the movie became well known, and he became well ksown, but I only knew him from *Easy Rider* until I met him and read for the part in *Drive.*

Question: Can you characterize Jack Nicholson in one sentence?

Tepper: He's a guy whose ego is very well suited to his position in life; he has a large ego, and he has a large talent, and it's quite in balance with his position.

He's wanted to be a movie star for a very, very long time, and he was as well prepared for that first-person sociological phenomenon as anyone really can be. Like anyone else, like any healthy, adjusting human being, he went through a year, two years, where, I won't say it was bigger than him, but until you become totally comfortable within it, it's hard on you, and I think now his talent and ego and self-image are pretty much at one with the actual going on. And that's pretty healthy.

Hal Ashby

Looking at gray-bearded Hal Ashby sitting cross-legged on top of his bed on the second floor of his home high atop Laurel Canyon suggests a misplaced guru.

Ashby is, in fact, a film editor turned director. He had a long and successful association with Norman Jewison as a film editor, culminating in winning the Academy Award in 1967 for editing *In the Heat of the Night*. In 1969 Jewison produced Ashby's directorial debut, *The Landlord,* which was critically acclaimed but did only fair business at the box office. In 1971 his second film, *Harold and Maude,* was released to a totally lesser reaction than his debut film.

In the summer of 1972 he was to begin his third film, starring Jack Nicholson for MGM, but after many unresolved differences over script and casting the project was canceled. Nicholson and Ashby wanted to work together, though, and in November of the same year they were to leave for Toronto to begin shooting the Robert Towne screenplay, *The Last Detail*.

Ashby followed the enormously successful *The Last Detail* with *Shampoo,* the story of a Beverly Hills hairdresser and his many adventures, starring Warren Beatty, Julie Christie, and Goldie Hawn, and written by Robert Towne and Warren Beatty.

In the summer of 1974 there was a re-release of *Harold and Maude* for a limited engagement because Paramount realized that there was a growing cult for the film and the work of a major new director, Hal Ashby.

As we began to get ready for the interview, attended by Chuck Mulvehill (Ashby's assistant) and an unidentified woman, we quickly noticed that Ashby is an art lover. The house was sparsely furnished, but in a rich manner specifically suggesting his love for rock music, for example, a colorful painting-montage of the Rolling Stones and Neil Young.

As Mulvehill tried to wake Ashby up with some coffee, we settled in our director-style chairs and were informed that Ashby, Nicholson, cast, and crew would be leaving the following week for Toronto to start production.

Question: How did you fist come into contact with Jack?

Hal Ashby: My first contact with him came when I was doing *Harold and Maude,* and I was at Bob Evans' house discussing the film with Bob, and Jack happened to be visiting there, and he took the time to come over and introduce himself, and sit down, and tell me how he enjoyed my first film, *The Landlord,* and a few things about it. So the first contact I had with him was purely on a social level like that.

Then I was involved in a film over at MGM that I thought Jack would be right for, so I made contact with him, and I took the script up to him, and I sat with him, and sat with him a number of times from the first time on, and about six weeks after that he said he would do the project. But everything ended up in a mess over at MGM, and we didn't do it.

Question: What caused the cancellation of the film?

Ashby: What happened to it was, I was going to do this film, and I finally got it down to where Jack agreed to do it—it was called *Three-Cornered Circle,* and it was taken from *The Postman Always Rings Twice*—and at that point I wanted to cast Michelle Phillips in the girl's role, and another actor in the other role, and it just came to a gigantic dispute with MGM as to how to cast my film. I guess they'd say their film; I say my film. I just couldn't work that way; I'm sure there are some people that can let the studios cast their films. It wasn't the kind of film-making that I was used to, or could actually get involved in. It became very messy at that stage, and I had to say no, and then they said no, and then Jack, in essence, said no, too. I would assume that his reasons for saying no were basically the same as mine. What their ideas on the casting were I really don't one hundred per cent know. It just wasn't the way that I saw it. I'd been involved with it for about three months, but if it had been laid out in front exactly what they wanted I never would have been involved in it in the first place. For myself, I was under the impression that they (MGM) wanted to attract film-makers over there, because they had quite a bad reputation. They got Danny Melnick in, and maybe someday he'll make that thing work, but what they want to do now is to attract guys and still give them the old "yes" and "no." That results in a breakdown in communication. Whenever you have somebody coming in and saying, "You have to do this," or "You have to do that," then something, somewhere, is going to get up tight. In this case it was me.

Question: So MGM owns the project, then?

Nicholson, Randy Quaid, and Otis Young in The Last Detail

(above) Sailors taking their charge on the train to Portsmouth Naval Prison. (below) Arriving at Portsmouth

Ashby: Oh, yes, they've always owned it, because they made the film of *The Postman Always Rings Twice.* Gordon Carroll was going to produce it for them, and he had talked to me about the script, and I read it and I saw some good possibilities in it. I made my deal, and from that point on went after Jack. I was really happy when I got him. I thought it was a big, big plus. I wanted to use Michelle. First of all, on one level she's a much bigger name than they think she is, because those people don't know anything about the music business. They really don't. I mean, besides Michelle, you could mention someone like Leon Russell, and they'd say, "Isn't he some country-folk singer or something?" Or you say Neil Young, and they say, "I don't know him." That's kind of a weird experience in its own right, in that they wouldn't keep up on all the levels of the entertainment business especially on the level that they basically function at, which is a financial level. You'd think they'd look around and see who's making a lot of money, if they just want to go at it at that level.

Also, because of the relationship between Jack and Michelle, I thought that they would be very exciting together on film. I really thought Michelle had it. I was almost locked into Michelle before we got Jack, as a matter of fact.

Question: Why did it take so long to get Jack?

Ashby: I think just because he's very, very thoughtful about what he does do. That was basically what it was. You know, he's had a lot of things come to him, obviously. And he has a lot of things to consider, you know, like how does that role compare to the last one, and to the next one that he thinks he might be doing.

As for myself, I can't remember picking up a script and deciding on it in less time than he did.

Question: What did you think of *The King of Marvin Gardens*?

Ashby: I liked it. I understand there's been a lot of negativism about it, and so forth, but I was pleased for Jack, and I was pleased for Rafelson because I thought they did a remarkable job. Jack's character was certainly different from anything he's ever done before. He sold me; I believed that character. I thought Bruce Dern was marvelous. And certainly, Ellen Burstyn was great. I haven't read any reviews for it, except for a little mention it got in an article about the New York Film Festival in *Newsweek,* but I don't really know what the reviewers are taking out after. I'm not really sure where their heads are, but then I never am, in that sense. I thought it was a very daring thing, because it was out of the mainstream of films, or where they want you to go with films, or what characters they want you to have on the screen. That's why I found it intriguing. I liked the look of the film, the locale where they put it, those two interesting brothers, and making Jack the introverted of the two brothers, which was not the usual casting. I thought he was marvelous.

Question: Can you tell us how all the elements came together in *The Last Detail*?

Ashby: I became involved in it out of the MGM deal; Jack was already involved in it, and they were just at the stage when they were beginning to look for a director. Jack was in it, Gerry Ayres was producing it. We had talked a little bit about it before, but not very much, when we were doing the MGM thing, but I figured it wouldn't happen for me, because since this had to be done in the winter, I'd probably still be in post-production on the MGM thing. Well, when the MGM thing fell apart Jack said, "Why don't we try and move you over and get you to do this?" And I said, "That would be great." It got a little bit messy for awhile, because I was involved in a thing over at Warner Brothers at the same time, but I really wanted to do *Last Detail*.

Question: Can you tell us a little bit about the story?

Ashby: Yeah, I really like the story. It deals with three sailors, but two of them are lifers, one of which is Jack. And Jack and the other sailor, who's black, are in transit, like at Norfolk, and Jack's been in twelve years, and the other guy, Mule, has been in fourteen years—they don't know each other. They're in separate transient barracks, just awaiting orders, and they pull this temporary detail as chasers, as SP's, to take this eighteen-year-old kid up to Portsmouth, New Hampshire. He's rather naive, naive because of a lack of life experiences, and he's a kleptomaniac who just stole money from the wrong fund. It was the commanding officer's favorite charity, and they really gave him a rather hard sentence.

As for the two lifers, they're just going to get him up there, and come back on kind of a paid liberty. They first go by bus to Richmond, and then they take the train, and the relationship starts to build between these three guys. It becomes episodic, with all the things they fall into and get involved in. It also deals a lot with people doing their jobs

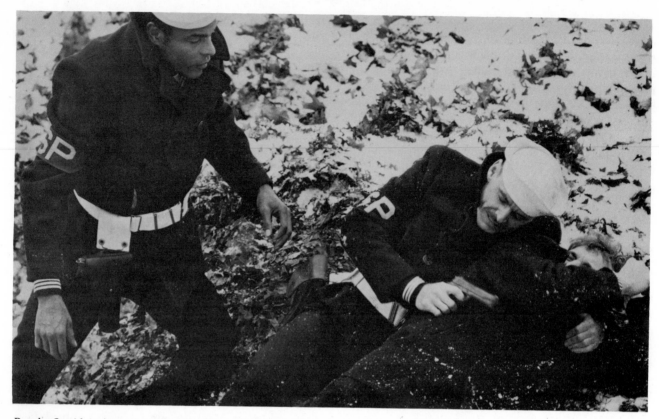

Randy Quaid (prisoner) tries to flee his guardians, Nicholson and Otis Young, in The Last Detail.

and how that fucks everybody up. Of course, when you get two guys like this in situations there's a lot of good humor in it. But on the other level it's a good character study. You've got a couple of lifers that are very complicated characters. It's interesting to see what motivates them and helps them get through life. They've got their ows things going; they couldn't give a shit about this dumb kid when it starts, they're kind of parental towards him; they still don't know how to break out of that other mold. What we'd like them to do is for all of them to go to Canada and blow the whole thing off, but I don't think that would be honest either. We go through that all the time, showing what they are, rather than what we'd like them to do. So by the time we get to the point where the kid, who's not really dumb, but he's not really bright either, decides that he really wants to get away, he can't because he's concerned about what will happen to these two guys. He doesn't want to get away, because he knows it will be their ass. At the same time, they'd like to see him get away, but they know they can't let him. So there's a lot of complexities involved, which I think will be very, very good. I'm very high on it. Bob Towne

did the screenplay, who's a long-time writer, and a very particular writer who doesn't put his name on a lot of things. He's a long-time friend of Jack's.

Question: How is Jack preparing for this role?

Ashby: The way I see it, Jack prepares for a role as well as an actor can. He tries to look at as many different thoughts or sides that the character might have at any given time, and constantly questioning that, especially at this stage. I spent yesterday with him, and I'm going to spend today with him again, just really going through the script and questioning things. That doesn't really mean that we're solidifying the answers right now, but what we're doing is narrowing it down from twenty possibilities to five possibilties in hopes of getting to the one possibility for this complex character that we both want.

Question: Do you believe in rehearsing with the cast as a group, or do you like to work just on a one-to-one basis?

Ashby: On this one, since it's basically a three-character story, I won't really rehearse with the people that they run into along the way. We'll basically do read-through rehearsals about a week before, so we can all talk about each other's characters and so forth. If we can get the relationship of the characters established in the read-throughs, then I think the spontaneity will happen on its own, which is important to a film. We're going to try and shoot as much in continuity, at least the heavy scenes, as we can. Usually continuity doesn't matter; it's all part of film-making, and sometimes it's interesting, it's part of the game, but in this, since it is a character study, I wanted to do it in continuity, especially in respect of the unfolding of the relationship with the boy.

Question: Do you have the actors set for the other two parts?

Ashby: The other sailor isn't set yet. We were going to do it with Rupert Crosse, but there have been some problems which we're still trying to work out, in fact, desperately trying to work out, because we're getting so close. Rupert would have been marvelous. We've set the boy. A boy by the name of Randy Quaid. He's the kid from *The Last Picture Show* who took Cybill Shepherd to the swimming party; kind of a strange looking kid. He's big, too. I like him; I like his quality. I had a feeling we'd have a good start with him,

because he has kind of a naive quality. He doesn't look like he's off the streets of New York. And visually, I think his size is going to work for us. He's not the classic small guy who's always getting picked on.

Question: What makes this film different for you from *The Landlord* and *Harold and Maude*?

Ashby: I think it's the subject matter more than anything else. In essence, it deals with the military and military justice, and what a lot of shit all that is, but it doesn't profess to give any answers, but it lays a lot of it out, and that's something that's always intrigued me. Intrigued me in the sense that the story's worth being told in all those areas, and I liked this one because it doesn't go after the obvious. We're not saying that he did something wrong in Vietnam that he's being called on the floor for, but he did something wrong here, and it's still military justice in the way that they respond. It deals with guys who are lifers in the service, and how they respond. It's about bondage—this is all on an intellectual level, of course, we never get into dialogues about it, but it's stuff that we fight for to come out.

Nicholson takes a naive sailor (Quaid) for his first visit to a whorehouse in The Last Detail

115

Question: What qualities do you think Jack has that attracts filmgoers to his movies?

Ashby: Film is a very personal medium, at least for me it is. I think basically there's an honesty to Jack that comes through. But then again, it's on an ethereal level. People aren't watching the film and saying, "Gee, I like his honesty, and that's why I like to see his films." That's just not the way it happens; people feel a kind of electricity, an attraction to this person to watch him and see what he does, because you're never exactly sure what he is going to do, and I think that's the kind of thing that's fascinating. Like in *Marvin Gardens*, even though Jack is playing a subdued character, it's interesting because it's not what I expected him to do. I'm not four reels ahead of him, saying "This is gonna happen, this is gonna happen, this is gonna happen." An actor in film has to have a real sense of honesty, whereas some actors put up a façade, and you don't feel that you ever get through to them. With Jack there is no façade; it's just right out there. There is just innately a great appeal to a lot of people for that sort of thing. I may be intellectualizing it, but I think that's what a lot of the draw is. We all know that he did quite a few pictures before *Easy Rider*, but when he came on the screen in *Easy Rider*, you went, "Wow, here comes somebody, let's watch this." And it's a great thing because it isn't forced, he isn't pushing like hell to make it happen. Whether he's pushing like hell inside to make the character happen doesn't matter, because again if he is doing it, he's doing it very honestly and you're not put off by it. That's one of the differences between Jack and Steve McQueen. Steve is much

Bad Ass Buddusky (Nicholson) taking charge in The Last Detail

more of a personality actor, and he tends to be less honest. Jack's honesty is his great attraction to the people because they feel like they really know him.

Jack is really a special guy; on all levels, too. I loved his picture, *Drive*, that he directed, and he's written some great things. I thought *Ride in the Whirlwind* was a hell of a picture. He's done a lot of different things on really deep levels.

Question: Can you characterize Jack Nicholson in one sentence?

Ashby: To put it down in the simplest terms I think Jack is just great—a great person and a great talent, and I love him.

Robert Evans

Many people in the film industry may be inclined to say that Robert Evans has almost single-handedly saved Paramount Pictures from dissolution since he became the company's executive vice president in charge of worldwide production. During his tenure, Paramount has produced such landmark hits as *The Godfather, Love Story, Goodbye, Columbus, True Grit, The Odd Couple, Rosemary's Baby, Lady Sings the Blues, Paper Moon, Serpico,* and *Godfather II.*

At the age of twenty Evans was a long way from the motion picture industry as he joined his brother Charles and Joseph Picone as a partner in their rapidly-growing clothes firm, Evan-Picone, Inc. While on a business and pleasure trip to Hollywood, a chance meeting with Norma Shearer established his career as an actor. Universal, which was filming the Lon Chaney biography, *The Man of a Thousand Faces,* had been unable to find an actor to portray the famed producer, Irving Thalberg. Miss Shearer, Thalberg's widow, arranged a screen test for Evans, who was signed almost immediately for the role opposite James Cagney, who played Chaney.

Evans next caught the attention of Darryl

Robert Evans (l.), Roman Polanski, and Faye Dunaway between takes on Chinatown

Faye Dunaway and Nicholson after a love scene from Chinatown

Zanuck, who contracted him to play the bullfighter in the film version of Ernest Hemingway's classic, *The Sun also Rises,* which starred Tyrone Power, Ava Gardner, Errol Flynn, and Mel Ferrer.

In 1958 Evans starred as the villain in *The Fiend Who Walked the West,* and made his last acting appearance as a wealthy playboy in the 1959 film, *The Best of Everything.* Evan-Picone was purchased at that time by Revlon, and Evans was required to spend five years with the merged organization in a full-time working capacity. After fulfilling his commitment, Evans decided to return to motion pictures, but in production instead of acting. He landed a position as an independent producer for Richard Zanuck at 20th Century Fox, and during the first four months of his association with Fox he acquired six story properties for filming, including the widely sought-after novel, *The Detective,* which he purchased after reading the galley proofs. The film version starred Frank Sinatra. In 1966 Evans terminated his producers' agreement with Fox and joined Paramount Pictures.

In addition to overseeing the entire production schedule of Paramount, Evans has been contracted to personally produce five films for Paramount, the first of which is *Chinatown.*

After three weeks of daily conversations with Evans' two secretaries, a date and time for an interview with him was finally set. When we arrived at his plush suite at the executive offices of Paramount in Beverly Hills, Evans was terminating a meeting with the writer of *Chinatown,* Robert Towne, about an upcoming project. As Towne was leaving, Evans asked him to join our interview session, but Towne declined. We settled into antique chairs facing a corner of his suite, the walls lined with 8 x 10 photographs of Evans with acquaintances from the film-making and political worlds, as well as some fine original art including an oil by de Cachard.

Fidgeting with two pairs of dissimilar eyeglasses, Evans appeared relaxed, but cautious, a study of a powerful man ultimately trying to please his audience.

Question: How did *Chinatown* get started?

Evans: It started with Bob Towne and I sitting down for dinner at Dominic's [a Los Angeles restaurant] one night. He told me about an idea he had, and that he wanted to do the project for Jack. I wanted to do it for Ali. We wanted to do a man-woman story, and we started it off with Jack in mind. Totally with Jack in mind, and Jack was almost committed to it from the beginning.

Question: Even before the screenplay was written?

Evans: That's right. He was the only actor it was being written for, and as soon as the screenplay was finished, it was shown to Jack, and he read it, loved it, and committed to it.

Question: And Ali was going to be the female lead?

Evans: It wasn't definite. We wanted to do a good man-woman story, and I had Ali in mind—at that time I was married to her. Well, in the interim she left me, so it wasn't for her. We showed the screenplay to Faye Dunaway. She loved it, and did it, so the casting was very easy.

Question: At what point did Roman Polanski come into the project?

Evans: He came in after the first draft of the screenplay, and then worked very closely with Bob Towne on the second and third drafts. He was

A close-up being lined up in Chinatown

Nicholson as detective J. J. Gittes in Chinatown

very involved in it.

Question: What kind of elements did he bring to it?

Evans: Structural elements. He added his touch because he's a screenwriter as well. He did the screenplay of *Rosemary's Baby.* He was very, very productive as a constructive element in finishing off the screenplay.

Question: Where do you think *Chinatown* fits into Jack Nicholson's overall body of work?

Evans: It's his first romantic lead. The first time he's played really with a woman, and having a man-woman relationship. It's a very important step forward, and I also thinks it puts him in a real stardom category. It projects him into the genre of leading man parts, and it's a very big step forward for him. He's possibly had more startling performances as a character lead, but this establishes him not as a character lead but as a real lead.

Question: With the proliferation of nostalgia movies that were being made at the time weren't you leery about doing another period piece?

Evans: Not at all; because we had a different look on this period film than any film that was being made. Number one—we shot the film in Panavision, vis-à-vis a 1:85, which is wide screen. We wanted to tell a 1937 story through the eye of a 1974 camera. That's number one. Number two— we made sure that our backgrounds were the backgrounds of the times, but we didn't overexpose the backgrounds and say, "Hey look, guys, it's 1937." We just sort of played it like it was. We had a different look in our films, I do believe, and then I have to give Roman credit for it—for his concepts.

Question: At what point did you first become aware of Jack Nicholson?

Evans: We used Jack in *On a Clear Day;* he came up to audition for it and he got the part of Barbra Streisand's brother, and I think I can blackmail him on it. He had a song on which he didn't do too well, and he didn't get along with the director, Vincent Minnelli, that well. He's God-awful in it, and I think he'd offer me a percentage of the picture if I cut him out of it. That was my first exposure, and before I hired him I saw a lot of his bike pictures that were run for me, and I thought that he had a great personality and smile, and that's why we hired him for *Clear Day.*

The part was a lousy part. The picture wasn't too good, and it was really no part for him. It wasn't his fault—nobody else could have played it any better. At that time in his career he needed a big picture to be in.

Question: At what point did you know that *Chinatown* would be a success?

Evans: Not until I saw a rough cut—you can't go by dailies. The old proverb is that dailies are like brides—how come so many beautiful brides and ugly wives?

Question: How much of the final cut was Polanski's?

Evans: The final cut was Roman's. We had mutual approval of final cut. The interesting thing about it was that the first cut ran two hours and thirty-five minutes without music, and it still held your interest.

Question: What elements make *Chinatown* a success as opposed to the failure of *The Great Gatsby*?

Evans: Gatsby is not a failure. I hope *Chinatown* does as well as *Gatsby,* believe it or not. You mean critical success possibly. It's unfair to compare the two; I mean, Jack Nicholson would have made a great *Great Gatsby.* I'm just a much bigger fan of Jack Nicholson as a screen personality than I am of Bob Redford. I think Jack is mesmerizing on the screen, and I also feel that Faye is unique in the film, which is a big surprise because she's done a lot of shit, and it's the best picture she's done since *Bonnie and Clyde.* I have to say that Roman was my first choice for director on *Chinatown.* Ever since *Rosemary's Baby* I'd always wanted to work with him. I think Bob Towne is a unique writer. I think all the elements we have are unique; much more so than any other period piece I can remember.

Question: Was the role of Gatsby offered to Jack?

Evans: We thought of Jack, but we couldn't afford him at the time. Jack wanted a lot of money

(l. to r.) Roy Jensen, Nicholson, Cinematographer John Alonzo, and Polanski, in an afternoon rehearsal of the nose-slitting scene from Chinatown

The actual filming of the nose-slitting scene

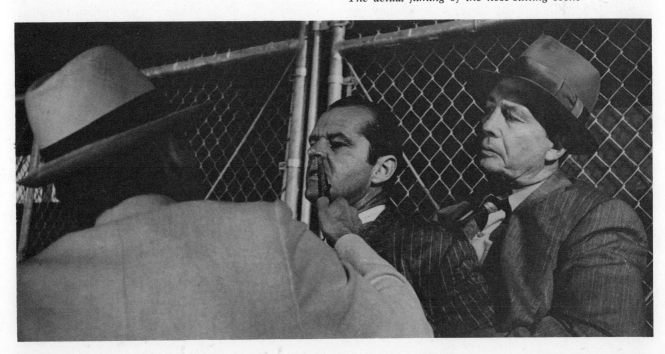

121

Nicholson, who wears a bandage on his nose for most of the movie, receives a tip on a murder case in Chinatown

to play the part, and he wanted to play it badly; we just couldn't afford him.

Question: How important is the success of a film like *Chinatown* to Jack?

Evans: Very important—it establishes him as a major box-office star, which he hadn't been until *Chinatown* came out. He was as important critical star, and he had his coterie of fans, but now *Chinatown* is a breakthrough picture. It's a very important picture to Jack, as evidenced by his being on the cover of *Time* magazine.

Question: And the fact that he put his hand and footprints in front of Grauman's Chinese Theater (now owned by the Mann theater chain).

Evans: That's right.

Question: Looking back on it now, would you make any changes in *Chinatown*?

Evans: I would have liked to have told the story with fifteen minutes out of the picture possibly, but there's no way you can take any time out of it. I wish the story could have been constructed so that it could've been told in a shorter period of time, but it couldn't have. That's the only thing.

Question: Is that because there is a lesser market for a two-hour-and-fifteen-minute film than for a one-hour-and-fifty-minute film?

Evans: No, it's just hard to stay in your seat, but I think the picture would've worked at any length.

Question: But nowadays two-hour movies are the exception, and it seems as though films are getting shorter.

Evans: No, they don't. They don't get shorter, they get longer; look at *The Godfather*. It used to be that films ran eighty-five minutes, and seventy-five minutes, and back in the days of Adolph Zukor pictures ran twenty-two minutes. They didn't think they could hold the audience for an hour. Pictures have been getting longer not shorter, because the market is more sophisticated now than it has ever been. It used to be film-makers looked down at the audience—now they look up to them. There's a difference.

Question: As far as you can tell, do you see any differences between Jack's work in *Chinatown* and his efforts in the lower-budget BBS films?

Evans: *Chinatown* hits more of a mass audience. It establishes him—he's so good as a leading man, as a romantic leading man. He's up there with everybody else who's a romantic leading man. That's very important.

Question: What aspects of the J. J. Gittes character were a challenge to Jack? What things did he have to reach for?

Evans: Nothing that I know of. He had it all down. Jack knew that character very well when he started the picture.

Question: Is it possible for you to see what kind of stimuli Jack picked up from Roman Polanski?

Evans: He has a great respect for Roman, and Roman never got frustrated with Jack's performance. Roman has very definite ideas as a director, but he and Jack got along very well. As far as Roman's concerned Jack is the finest actor he's ever worked with.

Question: Can you see any differences in Jack's work under Polanski than, say, under Mike Nichols?

Evans: I thought Jack was terrific in *Carnal Knowledge;* I loved him in it. Mike is a great director. It was just a different kind of part. I would have liked to have seen possibly a little more humor in *Chinatown*. There was humor, but it wasn't that much, and Jack is so good with humor.

Question: Whose idea was it for Jack to wear the bandage on his nose for so long?

Evans: Roman's. Jack's the only actor who could wear it for three-quarters of a movie and get away with it. It's a marvelous prop. Penelope Gilliat's review started, "A private nose . . ."

Question: We feel that Jack's recent career has had two major peaks—the first one being *Easy Rider* and *Five Easy Pieces,* and now a second one with *Chinatown*. Most stars peak once and then it's all downhill from there. Can you explain the resurgence of Jack's popularity?

Evans: He was never down, per se, he was just out. I think now with *Chinatown* Jack is as important an actor as there is today. I don't know of another actor that I'd rather do a picture with than Jack. Not one.

John Alonzo, Roman Polanski, and Nicholson prepare a scene for Chinatown

Question: Do you have any projects in the works?

Evans: Yes, we do, but I can't talk about it.

Question: What characteristics of Jack's screen personality do you think audiences most relate to?

Evans: Humor. Smile. Naturalness. Vulnerability. I'd say those.

Question: On the other hand, which characteristics do audiences have trouble with, *Marvin Gardens,* for instance?

Evans: The trouble with *Marvin Gardens* was the subject matter. Jack, like many actors, has very special tastes in subject matter. That's why I say it's taken him this long to play a leading part.

Question: Do you think the public will now expect to see Jack in this Bogart or Clark Gable type leading role?

Evans: No, I don't think so. I think they'd like to see him again in the leading role, but Jack is that versatile an actor that he can do just about anything. Now he has to pick the right thing to do. He now has the opportunity to go down in the years to come as the Bogart of our era, and I think he will, more than any other actor. He's memorable, you see. A lot of actors are not. They do a lot of parts where you can't tell one from the other. Jack's memorable—everything he does is special—that's what makes him so goddamn good. He's a lot more sure of himself than he used to be. He's the easiest actor of any star I've ever worked with. Easiest actor. Best temperament. Most cooperative, and maybe the brightest. His instincts are so good, and he's so terribly bright. There were a lot of arguments on this picture, and more often than not he was right and I was wrong.

Question: Any major areas?

Evans: Major areas, but I'd rather not get into it.

Question: How much of Jack's life is consumed by being a movie star?

Evans: A lot of it. I think he grooves on it; nicely, not adversely. He's amongst the nicest men I know. He's easy to get along with; he's wonderful with kids; he's just a terrific guy—sensational guy.

Question: What kinds of things make him nervous?

Evans: I don't know. He's as cool a cat as I know.

Question: Can you characterize Jack Nicholson in one sentence?

Evans: He's Mr. Cool.

Jack Nicholson

On the spur of the moment we arranged to do a second interview with Nicholson. He was leaving the next day for a month's vacation in Colorado.

Sunning herself on the front porch as we drove up was Helena Kallianiotes (the talkative hitchhiker from *Five Easy Pieces*). She escorted us into the living room where we set up our equipment while waiting for Jack to come downstairs. As always,

Jack was comfortably dressed. He was wearing a terry-cloth wraparound and an open shirt, but this time he was sporting a full beard.

Whereas the first interview was more film-oriented, we tried, this time, in the two hours that the tape recorder ran, to cover a broader range of topics, and hopefully to capture a little bit more insight into Jack Nicholson's private self.

Question: Did you always have aspirations to get into the film-making business?

Nicholson: No, not really. I always thought it was a nice occupation, but I didn't really identify myself with it until I was out here working in a movie studio. It's appealing; it was appealing to me then, and it's appealing to me now.

Question: Are there any kinds of roles that you haven't played that you would like to play?

Nicholson: Yeah, lots. I could never play all the roles that I would like to play. I'm lucky, in that I can play just about anything. There are certain limitations that I'm still working on. Obviously, I'm not ideally set up to do costume drama at this point, because of certain regional characteristics that I have. I've been asked to do things in every area; people believe that I can do things in all kinds of areas, and even if I can't I'll get the opportunity to try them. That's the situation I would like to try and maintain as an actor.

Question: What kind of an educational background did you have?

Nicholson: Just high school.

Question: Was it worthwhile?

Nicholson: I went to a fairly good high school —it was definitely worthwhile to me. The main problem with American education is a lack of correlation. The system is so designed to fragment that they don't put what you learn in history together with what you learn in French or some other area. There's no real attempt to give anybody a comprehensive view of their education. That's the main problem that I see with it. I'm not an expert on education, I mean, I skipped grades when I was

in high school, and then I was too young, by my standards too young, to go to college; I wanted to wait a year. Well, by the time I had waited a year I didn't want to go at all.

A guy from my high school called me up the other day, and asked me if I wanted to come down and address the national convention of high school principals. They wanted me to give them my view on education. Well, the main reason why I didn't do it was because the lecture was scheduled for eight o'clock in the morning in Anaheim. Also, when someone says, "What do you think of education?" I say that I really liked school, but I liked it simply for the social event. I had a couple of good teachers, and in areas like mathematics you had the feeling that you were really learning something, but in all the other areas I always had the odd feeling that I had just learned that last year, and sometimes just the opposite way to the way it was now being taught. English was like that. You were given all the rules as to how this was diagrammed, and this is the subject, and so on, and the next year someone else had a whole new theory.

Question: How much of an influence did your parents have on you?

Nicholson: Well, I never really had a father around the house, because my mother and father were separated before I was born. My mother and my sisters and my brother-in-law were in the house, so I guess he was kind of like my father figure. It's hard to say. I always had a very adult dialogue with all of my family, because I think I established an early communication on a person-to-person level. They analyzed my character pretty well. The problems that they had with me turned out to be the problems that I had with other people later in life. I had a very sort of nonpuritanical, non-Kiwanis, middle-class upbringing. I mean, no organizations in the house, my mother was an independent businesswoman. She didn't have tremendous scope in her thinking; she didn't want to run the town or the area. My family was always big into honesty—not too much punishment. So, I suppose my sort of easy view toward things, discipline and all that, is a result of my family's approach to living, rather than their approach to me.

Question: What caused your divorce?

Nicholson: My divorce was good like the marriage was. It was a clear, nonviolent, nontumultuous decision. My wife, Sandra [Knight], and I had just come to a very real separating of the ways. It was obviously the only thing to do, and we did it very simply. The probable cause was that she became stimulated in a mystical area, and I couldn't get with that. I didn't want to get caught in a situation where I was in competition with God, or something like that, and I felt I would be and that I would do it myself, because I felt the strength of this new flow into my ex-wife's life.

Question: Would you ever get married again?

Nicholson: I don't really know about that. I don't have anything specific against it. I don't envision myself being stimulated to stand up and take a major oath before God, or something like that, because I don't imagine myself ever creating that kind of a God image. I don't feel that ritualistic need to announce my social position before a community, because I am before the community a lot anyway. I've probably offered to marry someone a couple of times since my marriage in some half-assed way. No one took me up on it; I don't know whether that's fortunate or not.

Question: Doesn't being in the same business put strains on a relationship more so than if only one person is in show business?

Nicholson: It doesn't have to be in marriage —it can be with a friend. I'll tell you this; you can walk around with someone who's a bigger star than you in a different region, say with Muhammad Ali, and if you walk around a fight arena with him, you can very easily begin to identify with the problems between men and women, which aren't really men-women problems, but problems which are simply indigenous to the craft that your practice. It makes you think.

Question: What kind of a relationship do you have with your daughter?

Nicholson: I see her every week; we're going to Colorado for a month. I have a great relationship with her. There are some very true dues that are paid in a relationship where you don't get to continue to live with your children. If the original breach was a difference in feeling about God and purity, the realities of the relationship are that my daughter is a little bit whiter were she to have the mutual influence of both her parents. It's a very subtle thing, but I think it's fair to say that there is a difference; it might be better for her, I don't know, but not by my way of thinking. That's the area where you can feel the failure of a marriage that isn't classically successful. It's my fault that she has to pay the dues for that, if there are any. I watch her very closely, and I don't see any emotional discrepancies in her character, because we are very close. It's one of those fortunate family things where you have an extraordinary child, who's very sure of herself. She's been a very strong individual for a long time. I've been able to talk with her, and grow with her for a very long time. We get along very well. She's not overly strung out on her relationship with me. She's impressed, as I would be, having a father who's a movie star, I mean everyone in her class knows, and all that.

Having the experience myself, I always felt that I did fairly well coming from a so-called broken home, emotionally and every other way, and now I feel that Jennifer is equally as able to survive emotionally and have her own very sure universe and essential living position that she maintains. I don't worry as much about other people in that situation as I would have had I not had the experience. You hear how grim it is to be starving in India, or something like that, and it probably is, but sometimes when you go there you find that the people don't know it is, and it's not as grim as it would be if you hadn't been there.

Question: What kinds of things excite you?

Nicholson: I'm still very excited by almost everything I have been; I still like to travel; I like people. I have a lot of good friends, and I'm excited by their and my mutual growth. This is a very pivotal period of history to be living in, and that's exciting. My work really gets and keeps me going pretty good.

Question: Why don't you appear on talk shows?

Nicholson: I don't appear on talk shows for a lot of different reasons. I have done radio interviews and stuff like that. Well, like this interview here; even though you transcribe the words I say and someone reads it, the process is removed enough so that I don't feel like the person has this total, definitive, picture of me. They have some idea of my thoughts, and can agree or disagree with them, but on a television show you're sort of captured in there. I don't really understand the format, emotionally. Why am I having this conversation with a stranger in front of the nation? That's one reason.

The feeling that I wouldn't be particularly interesting on a talk show, because in that kind of situation I tend to get very laid back. I've always hated acting interviews, like every actor does, so I've completely broken down my anecdotal style, you know what I mean? Someone doesn't say something, and then I say, "Hey, that reminds me of the time I was with so and so." I don't do that; you know how you break your own habits.

Also, I felt it wouldn't be good for my work. I felt it would be good for my career. In terms of movies, I probably am in a weird position, in that I'm a fairly popular film actor, but I'm not so widely known as anyone else who's ever held that position simply because I don't do television, and they don't know me. A lot of people never go to the movies, it's as simple as that.

What I do is to create false people. It's very hard for you to believe Cary Grant as Louis XIV once you've known him that long. Well, I'm trying to maintain a certain level of anonymity regarding my work. Sometimes you have to be more defined in public than that. It's that, and also I don't like television. It's at the throat of my livelihood.

Question: So you can't ever see yourself doing a television series?

Nicholson: I'm sure I'll have to wind up making my living in that way. All old actors do. I mean, you have to go on making a living. Do you know any completely retired film stars? Cary Grant's maybe the only one; he doesn't have to do a television series. John Wayne probably never will either. These are all people that have had twenty-five-year film careers, which is not too usual, and most of them have been broke at some time during it. I mean I will do everything I can to avoid doing a television series, you can bet on that.

Question: What is the hardest thing you've had to adjust to with your success?

Nicholson: Entering and exiting rooms. There's a lot of people to say hello and good-by to.

Question: Do you feel that you have many hangers-on?

Nicholson: No, I don't know that I have any.

Question: Do you ever find yourself lonely?

Nicholson: No.

Question: Getting back to films, then, where do you think films are going?

Nicholson: Into more figurative films, less prosaic.

Question: Such as?

Nicholson: Anything in Cocteau's area, or *King of Hearts* if you saw that French film, or Godard. These kinds of films are what I'm talking about.

Question: What did you think of *The Last Movie*?

Nicholson: I thought more of it than most of the people who saw it. I thought it was a very fair expression of Dennis', the film-maker's, work. Like anyone involved in the editing process, or seeing the film in other stages, I thought some good things were lost in the editing, but essentially I think the editing followed what Dennis wanted to say at the time. I personally enjoyed seeing the movie; saw it a couple of times, in fact.

My honest feeling while I was watching it was that others were not going to enjoy it, but that doesn't destroy for me the validity of Dennis' having made it. Dennis always tries to make a classic. He said what he wanted to say; if there's anything really wrong with the film, it's that he said it too many times within the context of the film. It was a difficult film, a difficult film-making experience, and a difficult time for Dennis. I think it's a very pure kind of confessional movie of some kind of depth. What the film essentially says is that the industry of movies was created in America, and the magic of movies was released through America. The germ of movies was picked up most strongly in the American psyche at the time when America was at the perimeter of civilization. The motivation for films, and what they're about, is superficial related to what they are in actuality, and what they do create—not only the action of making them, but the action of having viewed them; the fantasy and values created by them. All these things Dennis feels guilty about, the victim of first, and involved with second, as a kind of ultimate expression of movie neurosis. This is sort of what he's saying, and what I feel he says very well in the film, and for me, very movingly.

For others it may seem to be too esoteric a

theme. In other words I think it's the kind of work that if it is to be appreciated now, or at some later time, it will not be for that central idea, which is the most important thing to Dennis. The film is very rich in incidents; his performance is very good —there are a lot of good performances, and it's visually beautiful. There's a lot going on to make it worth your while to see it.

Question: How important were your early films to the advancement of your career?

Nicholson: Very important. Any work that you do as an actor is important to you as an actor in learning it. This is how you develop; you have to work. Very few factors have been any good in movies before they've done a few. What's happened in the commercial marketplace is that only the young people are pulling the people into the theatres right now. John Wayne, or any of these guys, aren't really pulling people. This has caused the young actor to be more prominent than he would be normally. I always felt that I was lucky to be doing all those movies, even though I felt that at least half of them were really stinky. A lot of actors are having to learn—like I was having a conversation with Warren Beatty, and it's hard for someone like Warren to have to learn the acting while doing it at a very important commercial level. It's a painful and difficult experience—one that I'm glad I didn't really have to go through. Warren did it very well, I think. He did mostly good, interesting films.

Question: How much of your life is a put-on?

Nicholson: Very little; I'm not attracted to that style. Sometimes, conversationally, I don't like to be serious every single minute, but I prefer non-put-on situations really. I suppose there are mild forms of put-ons that everyone indulges in—that's just a part of them, but basically I'm not attracted to that.

Question: What do you think of gossip columnists?

Nicholson: I'll tell you, I'm very protective of myself in this area. I don't read them, so I don't have to have an opinion of them. It's the same thing with talk shows. It's fine with me, I don't care what they say about me, because I won't read them. I honestly don't read them. Every once in a while someone will bring me an article. I talk to a few of them—they're nice to me person to person. I've had a couple of things come in the paper that were embarrassing to me, and I was embarrassed. I don't take any of it seriously, so my assumption is that

no one else does, and if they do that's not really my problem.

I like anyone who's doing something to help the entertainment industry and its vitality. If these people are helping to create audience, then hallelujah.

Question: Is there anyone that you hate in Hollywood?

Nicholson: If there is, I don't want them to know about it until I want them to know about it.

Question: Would you teach Sunday school if someone asked you to?

Nicholson: If I had the time. It would have to be in the afternoon. I'd get intrigued by that particular proposition to teach Sunday school to children. I'd try and open 'em up fast before they got rid of me.

Question: What kind of a philosophy would you try and open them up to?

Nicholson: It sounds so oversimplified to say "get with what is," but that's the only real philosophy that I have.

Question: Is there anything that particularly impresses you about females?

Nicholson: First of all, that they are females particularly impresses me. I'm very democratic; I've got about the same number of female friends as I do male friends. They'll change any group of men that they walk into. There is an amazing change in the atmosphere—that impresses me. I'm totally intrigued by females actually. Now that there's a feminist movement, I'm even more intrigued. I feel that the dialogue that's coming from that area is very interesting.

Question: Do you ever think you'll be able to get down to a one-to-one relationship and not feel the need to "cruise around"?

Nicholson: Well, I don't know. I'm sort of away from the need to cruise around right now. Whether I would ever be free from that set of impulses, I don't know. Honestly, I can't say that I am. Sometimes I would like to be, actually. It's very distracting and very time-consuming for one thing.

Question: How competitive are you?

Nicholson: I'm not real competitive for parts anymore, just as long as I'm going along, getting work. I think someone would say I'm a competitive personality. Outwardly I try and minimize that, because I don't think that's always the best way to deal with a situation, unless it is a competitive one.

You know I've been nominated for Academy

Awards a couple of times—I don't take ads, I don't do anything toward that end. In that area I'm not competitive. I like to make a competitive product; I like to be involved in the making of a good film. In that way I am competitive.

Question: Have you ever had a secret ambition to be a rock 'n' roll star?

Nicholson: No. I'm developing one now, but I didn't before. What I like about it is that the music business makes a lot more money than the movie business.

Question: Do you remember your performance in *Flight to Fury*?

Nicholson: I remember all my performances.

Question: How do you think it compares with your other performances?

Nicholson: Well, as compared to any other performance, I would say that it's slightly above the middle. It's probably in the top half of my tremendous body of work. I liked a lot about it; I thought it was very scary, and I liked the idea of the character. I wrote the script for the film. I thought it was in the area that we were talking about earlier —figurative art. In other words, if that film were viewed as it's written, it's not a completely realistic film, it's a very figurative film. That's one of the

best characters that I've gotten to play, and certainly one of the best ones that I've written. You know, it's a hundred-thousand-dollar movie, so there are certain limitations on the final product, but I liked the character, I felt it was very strong, I thought it said interesting stuff. I thought it was entertaining, and I thought the performance helped the film. It was in those couple of films there that I really started to get into my own sense of style about things. From having written, and so on, I felt a little freer than if I had been hired to play the part, because having written the part, no one had to punch home the things that they wanted the character to say; I had the confidence that they were in there. I had a feeling for how they should appear in the overall film through conversations with Monte [Hellman].

Monte got me over the line of being exclusively an actor. He got me into writing and producing, and just thinking about films in general. We were both, out of context, probably overserious about things. I learned a lot about the interior makings of films while I was working with Monte, because essentially on all the films we did together, he did most of the film-making and I helped him with whatever else there was to do, so between us

After a brawl, Nicholson watches a friend being carted off to jail in Five Easy Pieces

we actually made all the films from inception and financing all the way up to the brick wall of distribution. So I learned a lot, and Monte was the first person who was really interested in me as an actor. I mean really interested in me, not just to see me, but he felt a real rapport with whatever he felt my abilities were, and we worked very well together. I think I was as good for Monte. When we were together we made four or five or six movies in a short period of time, and in a similar period of time he's only made one, and it's easier for him now than it was then, so I think you can see what we've done for one another.

I, also, haven't done a lot of film-making over the same period of time myself. I was working to a position to where I could direct, and in the middle of it, I became a movie star.

Question: If *Flight To Fury* was slightly above the middle, what do you think are on the top and bottom as far as your performances are concerned?

Nicholson: Probably *Five Easy Pieces* would be the top. I mean, *Easy Rider* was as good as it could have been—it was a realized part, but to me it's not as good a part as *Five Easy Pieces*. And yet, I don't think the part in *Five Easy Pieces* is as totally realized as it could have been. I liked both of those.

The Terror embarrasses me as much as anything. The television stuff I did was all shit. You know, I don't think I was ever worse than the basic material of the film. I don't think that's ever happened to me. I've been involved in some of the most horrendously insane projects of anybody who ever survived them. A lot of people do these movies, but they're so bad that they can't get work anywhere else usually. You know, when I was with William Morris, aside from my own agent there, everybody thought that all I did was bike movies. That's the way it was. In fact, yesterday someone was telling me a story about Sandy Bresler [Nicholson's agent then and now]. He was always writing memos saying, "What about Nicholson," and all this, and everybody in the agency was saying, "Oh, there goes Bresler with his Nicholson memos again."

Question: Knowing that you've attended many of the film festivals, can you tell us about some of your impressions of them?

Nicholson: Yeah, man, but this question's a novel.

Question: Can you tell us briefly, then?

Nicholson: Briefly's ridiculous. O.K., I have

these: lady running in a red dress after the opening; Keith Richards screaming and yelling, "perverts"; standing on the roof with Dennis; flags flapping; religious award—Huguenot cross; scene over here; hookers on the strip; seven o'clock in the morning; Communists; lecture—Posalini—what is the unit of film? the shot, or the content of the shot?; opera house full of critics; Godard and Corneau arguing balcony to floor. I mean, do you have impressions? There's millions of them.

Question: Can you ever see yourself directing yourself?

Nicholson: Yeah, I'm going to do that soon, I think.

Question: Do you have a project that you're working on?

Nicholson: No. Right now, I'm in a very interesting state of mind about work. I don't have anything in my mind, and I've been hung-up because I don't, because I really want to direct. I don't feel anything within what's happening that really turns me on to want to go beyond it, and I don't feel a fully strong impression from just within myself.

What I'm trying to learn is that transition where I allow that to be the rhythm of my output, rather than forcing work all the time. In other words, the reason why I've done more work than most people my own age is because I insist it of myself that I do it. I think people create their own work rhythm. I'm trying now to see if something comes in in a different way that really impels me to work, that makes me want to do whatever this might be.

Question: Is there something in particular that you want to say?

Nicholson: Well, for acting purposes and performing purposes, very often it's important that you reduce the concept down to a very small, skeletal, germinal idea that's really an oversimplification, and then the process opens it up. At this level, and we're discussing "what is it that you would like to say," and so on and so forth, if I just wanted to say something, I wouldn't make a film. You know what I mean? I'd just go around and say it. I'd say, "Be nice to black people," you know, or "Try and share the bounty of the world with one another." The movies that I make I hope would say a lot of things. I think in my movies all the characters have something to say, and that's how you give a larger picture. I think we've discussed this before—I believe in the positive philosophy of all my charac-

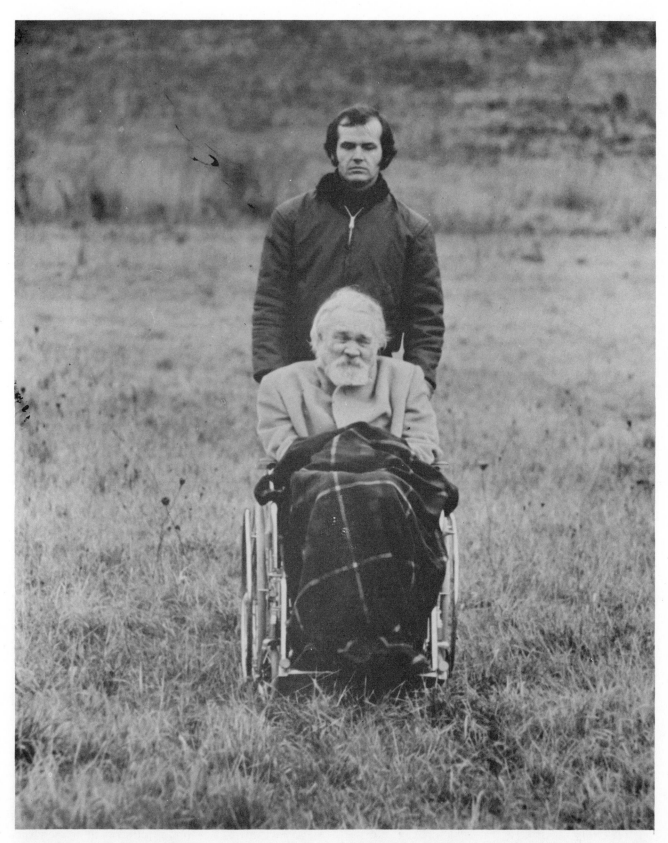

A touching scene between Nicholson and his paralyzed father (William Challee) in Five Easy Pieces

131

ters. If my work is nontotal, it's because my work doesn't include a character who's totally negative or totally negatively motivated. Like this killer in *Flight To Fury,* who's totally positively motivated, and he's ready to discuss it with anybody. His rationale is, "There will be murders." It's as simple as that. Everyone will agree with that at this point in society. There will be arranged murders; everyone will agree with that. His point of view is that that's not his problem. He's just filling a job category, because he happens, through no fault of his own, through an accident of birth, to be attracted to that kind of work and to do it well—better than other people—and it's a function that will be done, so it should be done well.

I think, for instance, right now the most positive function in film is literally for people to have something to do outside their homes that they can relate to. I mean, sociologically speaking, it's nothing more complicated than that. Forget about the inner content of ideas, or what is effective, it's really, more and more because of television, the entire world is no longer contacting one another. We're getting further and further apart, as people, which may be good because they tell us it's getting more and more crowded.

Question: Are there any gaps in your life right now?

Nicholson: Oh, God. Yeah, I suppose.

Question: Anything that you can pinpoint?

Nicholson: Well, I don't feel that I'm on quite solid enough ground personally to pick one out. There aren't any particular gaps, and besides I don't really think in those terms, because basically I think everything is so good right now. I have very few dissatisfactions which aren't extremely momentary, and I'm capable of overreacting to them, but the reality of it is that, because I've had experience with this kind of a cycle, I can overcome it.

Question: Can you characterize Jack Nicholson in one sentence?

Nicholson: He just wanted to make it nice.

Nicholson directing Drive, He Said

two

COMMENTARY

with
CHRISTOPHER FRYER &
ROBERT DAVID CRANE

Fryer: Why do you think that *Easy Rider* was the most successful film for Jack Nicholson?

Crane: It was the biggest film for him, and Fonda and Hopper and BBS and Columbia, because of the time it came out. Back in 1969 when it came out the generation gap was a most serious and important topic, and certainly *Easy Rider* deals with that problem—youth versus the hierarchy. Protesting was more fashionable then among youth, and certainly *Easy Rider* is a protest film. Besides the important topics relating to what was going on in America at that time that the film dealt with, it also possessed a few elements within the framework of the film that made it successful—such as the heavy use of rock music throughout the film, which had never really been done before, and the "on-the-road" theme where two fairly young men had no responsibilities at all and were totally free. And the fact that the two main characters were fashioned after Western folk heroes, exemplified by the fact that one of them had the title of Captain America. It's like Billy the Kid or some other folk hero like that. All these elements had something to do with the film's success.

It wasn't a film done by fifty-seven-year-old executives who thought that that was the way a film for young people should look. It was done by relatively young people who conceived it and filmed it and acted in it. I think if *Easy Rider* came out today it wouldn't have the impact it had in 1969.

Fryer: But you can't really say that, because *Easy Rider* pretty much changed the course of film. Everybody else then went out and tried to make an *Easy Rider,* and from those films it went into something else. Now whether or not we would have ever gotten to the something else without *Easy Rider* is hard to say, but it was instrumental in starting a whole new genre of film.

Crane: What genre was that?

Fryer: The relatively low-budget, youth-oriented protest movie.

Crane: And you'll notice that all the subsequent campus movies and pseudo-hip movies, with the exception of *Getting Straight,* bombed.

Fryer: Exactly. That's why I think that it's not so much the timing as it is the content of *Easy Rider* that's important. But it's interesting that only Nicholson has gone upward as far as career is concerned. Both Hopper and Fonda have done very little since *Easy Rider.* Why do you think that is?

Crane: I think it's all a matter of timing. Nicholson happened to be playing the right part as far as the audience was concerned in the most important film of 1969—box office and publicity-wise. The audience tends to like you sometimes depending on whether or not you're playing the good guy, and Nicholson was definitely the good guy in *Easy Rider* because he was the most up-front with the audience. On one hand, you had the relatively quiet, well-traveled wise man, Fonda, and his naive, edgy companion, Hopper, and it was hard to get behind either of them, because they didn't let you in on all of the facts. Nicholson did. If you have a choice between going with the guy that thumbs his nose at the audience and the guy who appreciates the audience and lets them know it, you'll go for the latter.

Fryer: But it seems to me that there isn't one dynamic element in the film—one clear-cut thing that really makes *Easy Rider* a successful film.

Crane: It's like a thing I read in *Cinema* magazine, where it said that the whole of *Easy Rider* is greater than the sum of its parts. If you took each segment by itself, it's nothing; there's no great direction, there's no great script, if there was a script to work from, but when you put the whole thing together, it's like the Watts Towers—it's a bunch of junk that makes a successful film.

Crane: What's your feeling about what Jack Nicholson represents to the filmgoing audience as well as to his peers in the business?

Fryer: First of all, as far as the filmgoing audience is concerned, I think there's a lot of people that don't even know who he is. That's a curious situation in itself, in that a guy that's done as many films, and as many successful films as he has, should retain so much anonymity as far as his star personality is concerned. Certainly the *Time* magazine article has eliminated a lot of that.

Crane: Yet some people still think he's a golfer.

Fryer: Right. But I think Nicholson represents an alternative character to a lot of people. They go to see a Jack Nicholson movie because, since *Easy Rider*, he has pretty much portrayed a character in a state of flux. He isn't satisfied with his current position in life, but he doesn't really know where he wants to get to. He showed a lot of those characteristics in some of his early films as well, from *Psych-Out* to *Hell's Angels on Wheels*. He represents a kind of freedom to the people that go to see him. It's a freedom that they don't have—the freedom to leave their present situations in life to go and look for the greener grass on the other side of the fence. I think the negative identification with his character in *Carnal Knowledge* is very strong. I think people don't necessarily recognize those characteristics in themselves, but they see them in people that they know, and it makes them feel good because they don't think they themselves are like that.

It's hard to say what the impact of *The King of Marvin Gardens* was because not a lot of people saw it. But judging by the mixed reactions that it did get, people didn't like him in that, because he wasn't what he had been in previous films, but his character was still searching for something new in life.

Crane: I think that worked against him in *Carnal*, too. It's a downer movie; so is *Marvin Gardens*. I don't think people want to pay three dollars to go and get depressed. I think there's too much to be depressed about in everyday life.

Fryer: I disagree. If you look at the successful films today, you'll find that people love to go and get depressed. That's the basis for their entertainment. Look at the big recent films. *The Exorcist* had people throwing up in the theaters. *The Godfather* certainly didn't make you come out of the theater singing, either. And even the musicals—*Cabaret* has to do with the occupation of Europe by the Nazis and *Fiddler on the Roof* is about the exile of the Jews from Russia. And these are the films that are winning awards in the comedy-musical categories. Maybe that's what made *Carnal* as big a hit as it was, in that it was such a strong negative statement. All you have to do is look at the successful films today to see that people love depression.

Nicholson is obviously revered by the people in the industry, and I think for a couple of reasons. One, they recognize his fine acting talent, but two, I think everybody is just a little bit jealous of the way that Jack keeps himself hidden from the public eye. Though they're undoubtedly in show business for the recognition, I think there is a part of them that says, "Gee, I wish I didn't have to do public appearances," and "I wish I didn't have to do Johnny Carson's show," and in Nicholson they see a guy who's successful and that doesn't do any of those things, and when he's not working, he's not working. I think it's important to remember who he works with, too. The people at BBS don't say he has to do so many *Tonight Show* appearances for one of their movies.

Crane: But that can work against him, too.

Fryer: Well, BBS has gotten by with "small but intimate," and I don't know how long that will last.

But, like you said, it can work against him. That's why he can be famous and not famous at the same time. It all stems from the fact that he doesn't do talk shows. More people would see his face in one night on Johnny Carson than would ever go to one of his movies. There's no doubt about the fact that television will make you famous, but it will also destroy any kind of mystique that you may have. When you go into the theater it's very important that you believe that Jack Nicholson is David Staebler or George Hanson, or J. J. Gittes, and if you saw him on TV last night that makes it very hard. All actors try to create an illusion, and yet many of them destroy their own efforts by overexposure.

In Nicholson's case, if you don't know anything about the man, then you have to accept what you see on the screen. If you go to see a Steve McQueen movie or a Robert Redford movie, you're watching Steve McQueen or Robert Redford, but I don't think the same is true with Jack Nicholson.

Crane: That's probably because of all the peripheral nonsense that has been created around Redford and McQueen throughout the years, and has not, as yet, affected Nicholson. Though none of them does talk shows, the amount of press for McQueen and Redford makes up for it. McQueen has always had his motorcycle interests explored in the media, and of late, his romance with Ali MacGraw. And, of course, Redford has had his preserve-wildlife-Utah-skier image created by the press. Nicholson is not really a sportsman to speak of, except maybe for women, and therefore displays no public image that the press can exploit. So, when you go to *The Getaway*, you're going to see who this guy is that Ali MacGraw busted up her marriage for, and you're going for the Steve McQueen action movie, and you're going because of the Sam Peckinpah image, too. Even directors have images now.

I would guess that Redford got a lot of scripts that had McQueen's fingerprints on them. You know, all these pictures that involve motorcycling and skiing. It's all the peripheral stuff around these actors. Nicholson doesn't have any of that. He doesn't have a press campaign going on like these other two guys. Nicholson is the only true actor of those three in my opinion. He doesn't rely on the formula picture. There is no one formula for him, no one method. Whatever works. Look at his versatility: the small, public servant in the thirties in *Chinatown* to a self-investigating reporter in the seventies in *The Passenger*, back to the twenties and thirties in *The Fortune* to a singing doctor in *Tommy* to the only sane person in an insane asylum in *One Flew Over The Cuckoo's Nest*. I mean how can you possible have one formula for all of that. If you had *only* one, you'd turn into Clint Eastwood, who's now trying to be a formula director. Nicholson is too restless, too eclectic to be in one place all of the time. I guess one can wear himself thin in that manner after awhile, but I feel that Nicholson is too sure of his instincts to allow that to happen.

Fryer: Do you think that by not having the press that that hurts him?

Crane: It depends. If he wants to be known just for his acting, then I think he's succeeded; but if he wants to be a celebrity in the true sense of the word, then I think he's got to have all the peripheral stuff, too. I think George C. Scott is a lot like Jack. They go act, and that's it—that's their job.

Fryer: On the other hand, after having interviewed all the people that we have, we do find that Jack has an image, but it's not the kind of image that has totally enveloped him. With Redford or McQueen you can't really differentiate between the person, the image, and the actor. They're always the same no matter what the movie is. The image you have of Nicholson changes from film to film depending upon what character you last saw him as.

Crane: I agree, but I think that hurt him in

two of his films, *Carnal* and *Marvin Gardens*. Because he is an actor, and I think that he really believes that first and utmost he is an actor, he will try all of these new things. That's what an actor does.

But the American public is so geared to putting a stamp on everything and everybody that they are confused by Nicholson's never being the same way twice. Because he is different in each film, Nicholson fucks the audience, as Henry Jaglom would say. He doesn't mean to. He just does it, because he is an actor.

* * *

Crane: What do you look forward to from Jack as far as films are concerned?

Fryer: I think that *Marvin Gardens* was disappointing to Jack, and to all those involved, as far as the box-office receipts were concerned, and also because I don't think it had any kind of social impact. *Marvin Gardens* is a myth destroyer. The whole idea of the West, and the sense of escaping to Hawaii, is juxtaposed against the desolate, stagnating environment of Atlantic City in the winter, and in that way it takes the idea of the American dream and explodes it. This is all intellectualized, of course, but these ideas are in the film, and I don't think that they came across to the general public. Everyone wants to escape to a never-never land, and that's what *Marvin Gardens* was all about.

Last Detail, which was very different from *Marvin Gardens*, re-establishing Jack as a major box-office draw, as well as being a brilliant acting talent, and *Chinatown* goes even further. As far as the future goes, the Mike Nichols' film *Fortune* should be a very interesting departure for Jack inasmuch as it's a comedy, and he's never really showed his comedic side before, except maybe in *The Little Shop of Horrors*. Ken Kesey's book, *One Flew Over the Cuckoo's Nest*, which Jack is going to do with Milos Forman, should give him a character in McMurphy that will be very complex. He'll be drawing on experiences that maybe haven't been used before. Napoleon with Stanley Kubrick —that would be really interesting to see those two work together. It would be interesting to see what would come from him directing himself; we'd see what kind of stimuli he needs from outside sources.

It's hard to say. The thing that might destroy Jack as an actor is that people don't have one distinct image of him; he's always different, and consequently, they don't know who to believe. They get confused, and then they don't want to see him, because they don't know who he is.

Crane: You lose interest because you don't have a firm hand on his image.

Fryer: In the end I think he'll have to form some kind of congruent image throughout his work, because people just cannot accept a different character all the time if they admire the man. They have to have some base from which they can start in order to identify with him as a character, but on the other hand, perhaps all this that we've been discussing forms an image. *Time* called Jack "the star with the killer smile." Maybe that's all the public needs to know about Jack. His image is one of obscurities, and clouded meanings, and shadowy figures in the doorway, and we never know what he'll be next. Even his picture that hangs in the lobby at Paramount Picture's main office shows him in a shot from *Chinatown* where half his face is hidden by shadows. You never get the whole picture. I like it like that. Obviously the public does, too.

*   *   *

Crane: Do you have a favorite film of Jack's, and why?

Fryer: Probably *Carnal Knowledge*. The finest moment that I've ever seen on film was the argument scene between Jack and Ann-Margret. It was every frustrated emotion that you've ever had, and he just let it fly. For that scene alone, that film stands out in my mind. He had the same kind of scene in *Five Easy Pieces*, but I don't think it had the same kind of impact. I think the attitudes expressed in *Carnal* were good; not that they were good, positive attitudes, but the way that they were presented was good. I think the way that Nichols structured the film, a kind of sequential character study, with a very strong sense of perspective—meaning Jonathan's point of view—was great. The only time the point of view falls apart is in the beginning when we see Garfunkel and Candice Bergen together alone, but other than that Jack is in almost every scene in the film. *Five Easy Pieces* had a very strong point of view, too. I think those two films would be at the top of his body of work.

Carnal is a very literate movie, obviously because of Feiffer's writing, but I think that Feiffer got through the caricature stage and really wrote characters.

Crane: I think my favorite performance of his was *Five Easy Pieces*. I agree with you that *Carnal Knowledge* and *Five Easy Pieces* are two of his major films to date. To me, the greatest scene that he's ever done was the crying scene with his father in *Five Easy Pieces*, althought the scene that you mentioned from *Carnal* was great, too. It was great to me because of his acting, and because of similar feelings that I have toward my father. It's a very personal scene, and, of course, it's a very personal movie. Also because of Bob Rafelson's style, which I really admire. It's a very eclectic style, using only relevant actors and moods. Also because of his perfect use of the camera—it's always at the right place at the right time. I'd have to call Rafelson one of the foremost directors in film at this time. Much of the success of the film is based on Carol Eastman's script. It's as easy-going and naturalistic as Jack Nicholson himself. It's brilliant the way Rafelson can get this ensemble feeling out of his films. The actors down to the littlest bit player are all perfect. You know you're seeing a Jack Nicholson film, but it's not just a Jack Nicholson film—it's a Karen Black film or a Bruce Dern film. You feel like the people have been together before and after the film.

Fyer: What do you think keeps *Marvin Gardens* from being Jack's greatest film, seeing as we've both overlooked it?

Crane: We're probably succumbing to the image thing, too, though we probably won't admit it. *Marvin Gardens*, for me, was not even a Jack Nicholson movie, because Rafelson's ensemble approach to film totally dominates any one single actor. There was no Nicholson stamp on *Marvin Gardens* as far as I'm concerned. Not that anyone could have played the part better.

Fryer: Is that because the character is low-key rather than high-key? Is the Nicholson stamp the blow-up scene, or the crying scene where you go, "God, that was great"? There wasn't one blockbuster of a scene in *Marvin Gardens*—it's the consummate feeling you get from the film.

Crane: It even gets down to his monologue scenes in the film. During the one at the end where he's crying, I couldn't help but compare it to his crying scene in *Five Easy Pieces*, which was a far more powerful scene. When I think of *Marvin Gardens*, I think of Nicholson/Dern/Burstyn/Robinson/Scatman. The question here is do you have to be the out and out star of a film in order to be remembered for it, or can you be in a film for five minutes and still be the star of it?

Fryer: He did it in *Easy Rider.*

Crane: That's a perfect example. He was in it twenty minutes, and stole the show.

* * *

Fryer: It's a curious situation that most of Nicholson's characters in his films are always greatly alienated from whatever family they have in the film. It's true in *Marvin Gardens, Five Easy Pieces, Easy Rider,* and a lot of his earlier films. There's no strong sense of family in any of his works. That fact that these roles appeal to him, and that he chooses these kinds of roles, I wonder if that's indicative of his own feelings about his family. What do you think about that?

Crane: From what we know of his family, and what he's told us, it seems to be a very sensitive area, an area that he would not like to relate to much, or talk about, and that comes through in his films. He's a loner. The old anti-hero figure.

It's a good point, but no one will ever really know, and even if Jack tells you, it may just be something to get by that question so he doesn't have to talk about his family. It's just a very sensitive area to him for reasons that we can't know.

Fryer: Even in *The Last Detail* he plays a guy who's a lifer in the Navy, so again there is no sense of family, and there's no family at all in *Chinatown.*

Crane: Well, that's true of his personal life, too, from what we've seen. Both of his parents are dead, and he's got only one sister.

Fryer: Then there was his divorce, and his only child doesn't live with him. All these things constitute a kind of . . .

Crane: Open wound. And I think any film where there is a strong sense of family, or strong bonds between a mother and son or a father and son, would be like pouring salt on the wound.

Fryer: Or possibly, having never had a large intimate family, Jack would have trouble relating to that situation. But then again, he didn't come from a family where there was no love, as far as we know, so it's impossible to say.

* * *

Crane: What were your impressions of Jack after our first interview?

Fryer: I felt that he was honest and open with us as far as answering the questions, but he still had total control over the interview even though we were asking the questions. I didn't feel that we were always getting the total picture. Maybe that's because he doesn't like to do interviews. It might have to do with his mystique, in that even though the reasons that we were there was to get information he didn't want to totally let us in on what goes on. I don't think he gave us any hype—I think he told us the truth.

Crane: He treated us like old friends. It's a shame that more people can't meet him and talk with him. Karen Black described him as a Will Rogers type figure—he really is deep-down Americana. He's really a straightforward, honest, and simple guy actually. It's all the outside stimuli and the situation that he's in that makes him a complex man.

three

FILMOGRAPHY

The Cry Baby Killer

1958

Allied Artists

Cast and Credits

Porter Harry Lauter
Jimmy Jack Nicholson
Carole Carolyn Mitchell
Manny Brett Halsey
Julie Lynn Cartwright
Joey Ralph Reed
Gannon John Shay
Mrs. Maxton Barbara Knudson
Sam Jordan Whitfield
Werner Claude Stroud
Mrs. Wallace Ruth Swanson
Mr. Maxton William A. Forester
Reed John Weed
Gambelli Frank Richards
Mr. Wallace Bill Ervin
Al James Fillmore
Rick Ed Nelson
Evelyn Mitzi McCall

Executive Producer Roger Corman
Co-producers David Kramarsky and David March
Director Jus Addiss
Screenplay Leo Gordon and Melvin Levy
From a story by Leo Gordon
Director of Photography Floyd Crosby, A.S.C.
Film Editor Irene Morra, A.C.E.
Sound Phil Mitchell
Assistant to the Producers Stanley Bickman
Assistant Director Robert Agnew
Music Gerald Fried

Synopsis

Jimmy Walker (Jack Nicholson), seventeen, is brutally beaten by Manny Cole (Brett Halsey) and two of his teen-age punks, Joey (Ralph Reed) and Al (James Fillmore), because Manny wants to move in on Jimmy's girl, Carole Fields (Carolyn Mitchell). Later Jimmy shows up at The Hut, a drive-in hangout of the teen-age crowd, to take Carole away from Manny. He challenges Manny to a fight in the rear of the drive-in, but Manny's two buddies move in on Jimmy with brass knuckles. Al pulls a pistol which drops to the ground. Jimmy picks it up and shoots Manny and Al. A police officer, Gannon (John Shay), orders Jimmy to surrender, but the youth, thinking he has killed the pair, panics and dives into a small storeroom. Also in the storeroom is a black drive-in employee, Sam (Jordan Whitfield), and a mother, Mrs. Maxton (Barbara Knudson), and her infant child. The siege starts as Jimmy holes out in the storeroom with his hostages and a police lieutenant, Porter (Harry Lauter), sets up the police cordon. Tension mounts through the next few hours as Porter and others plead with Jimmy to either surrender or release the hostages. Jimmy, however, is terrified and threatens Sam and Mrs. Maxton with death if they try a breakout. The scene takes on a Roman carnival aspect as TV crews arrive; vendors sell hot dogs and drinks. A large crowd gathers and at one point almost breaks through the police lines to storm the storeroom. Finally, Porter decides to use tear gas, with a rescue unit standing by to help Mrs. Maxton and the baby. Jimmy is captured, but because he shot in self-defense he looks forward to leniency in the future.

Too Soon to Love

1960

A Universal-International Release

Cast and Credits

Cathy Taylor   Jennifer West

Jim Mills   Richard Evans

Mr. Taylor   Warren Parker

Hughie Wineman   Ralph Manza

with Jack Nicholson, Jacqueline Schwab, Billie Bird, William Keen

Producer/Director   Richard Rush

Executive Producer   Mark Lipsky

Story and screenplay   Lazlo Gorog and Richard Rush

Director of Photography   William Thompson

Film Editor   Stefan Arnsten

Music   Ronald Stein

Art Director   Victor Ramos

Sound   Larry Aicholtz

Assistant Director   Bruce Bilson

Synopsis

Jim Mills (Richard Evans) and his girl friend, Cathy (Jennifer West), find out that she's pregnant. She hides the truth from her parents; her father wouldn't understand, and her mother is close to a nonentity. The young couple arrange a makeshift abortion. But Cathy is repulsed by the sight of another girl upon whom the operation is performed, and the pair go off in search of a physician to do the illegal work skillfully.

They find a doctor who wants $500 for the job. Jim can't raise the fee so he steals the money from his employer. That sets the police on his trail. When Cathy learns that Jim has stolen in order to pay for the operation, she drives off to the ocean—only a short ride from her home—intending to drown herself. Jim reaches her in time to reassure her that life is still worth living.

Studs Lonigan

1960

A Longridge Enterprises Inc. Production
A United Artists Corporation Release

Cast and Credits

Studs Lonigan	Christopher Knight
Kenny Killarney	Frank Gorshin
Lucy Scanlon	Venetia Stevenson
Catherine Banahan	Carolyn Craig
Weary Reilly	Jack Nicholson
Paulie Haggerty	Robert Casper
Patrick Lonigan	Dick Foran
Mrs. Lonigan	Katherine Squire
Father Gilhooey	Jay C. Flippen
Miss Julia Miller	Helen Westcott
Frances Lonigan	Kathy Johnson
Charlie the Greek	Jack Kruschen
Eileen	Suzi Carnell
Mother Josephine	Mme. Spivy
Jim Doyle	James Drum

Written and produced by	Philip Yordan
Based on the novel by	James T. Farrell
Associate Producer	Leon Chooluck
Director	Irving Lerner
Music	Gerrald Goldsmith
Producer's Assistant and Special Photographic Consultant	Haskell P. Wexler
Art Director	Jack Poplin
Assistant Directors	Louis Brand and Eugene Anderson, Jr.
Director of Photography	Arthur H. Feindell
Film Editor	Verna Fields
Associate Editor	Melvin Shapiro

Synopsis

In Chicago, on New Year's Eve of 1919, eighteen-year-old Studs Lonigan (Christopher Knight) looks to 1920 with mingled feelings of fear and uncertainty. He is torn between two things—his love for Lucy Scanlon (Venetia Stevenson), and his gang of fellow teen-age jobless idlers, Kenny Killarney (Frank Gorshin), Weary Reilly (Jack Nicholson), and Paulie Haggerty (Robert Casper). Studs is frustrated by his prudish girl friend at a party, so he goes off with his gang to get drunk. He later seeks the comfort of a friendly spinster schoolteacher in whom he confides his fears and uncertainties. Later, at home, he argues with his father. The senior Lonigan wants Studs to settle down and join him in his painting firm. Mrs. Lonigan sticks up for Studs, but she wants him to become a priest.

Studs spends the next two years with his cronies under constant pressure from his parents. His father finally orders him out of the house, and Studs goes to a bar to get drunk. There he makes an unsuccessful attempt at joining up with some gangsters. Realizing his failure, Studs vows to his father that he will find a job, but his animal desires get the best of him after seeing a strip-tease show and he goes back to see his teacher and unsuccessfully tries to rape her. Studs finally goes to work for his father, but he still keeps seeing his buddies. He learns, however, that drinking can cause great harm after his friend Paulie dies suddenly and leaves a widow and child.

After some time, his friend Weary is arrested for rape. Studs seeks guidance from the spinster teacher with whom he has kept in touch, and he meets her niece, with whom he has an affair. But Studs is still in love with Lucy, even though by this time she has moved away from Chicago.

The depression ruins father Lonigan's business, and Studs is left to face some harsh realities. Lucy is gone. His gang is no more. Studs is given guidance by a priest, who also tells him that the teacher's niece is pregnant. Studs rushes to her and tells her that he loves her. As she looks pityingly at him, he pleadingly asks her to marry him.

The Wild Ride

1960

A Roger Corman Production/A Filmgroup Release

Cast and Credits

Johnny   Jack Nicholson
Nancy   Georgianna Carter
Dave   Robert Bean

Producer/Director   Harvey Berman
Executive Producer   Kinta Zertuche
Screenplay   Ann Porter and Marion Rothman
Film Editor   William Mayer
Camera Operator   Taylor Sloan

Synopsis

While driving his hot car, gang idol Johnny Varron (Jack Nicholson) causes the death of several policemen by forcing them off the road. Jealous of anyone who receives attention and praise, Johnny tries to persuade his friend Dave (Robert Bean) to give up his monopolizing and clinging girl friend. Dave is considered "chicken" by the gang for his lack of adventurousness and recklessness.

Resentment builds as Dave's fidelity to Nancy (Georgianna Carter) increases. Johnny is torn between his friendship with Dave and his overpowering conceit. Johnny wants Dave to share his exploits and not divide his time between himself and Nancy. Tricked into believing that Dave will meet her, Nancy comes to the big race and sees Johnny win by causing the death of another driver.

Taking Nancy away on the pretext of finding Dave, Johnny and the girl leave for the local hangout. In his frustration, Dave inadvertently proves Johnny is no hero and that the big-time car can destroy power as well as build it.

The Little Shop of Horrors

1961

A Roger Corman Production/A Filmgroup Release

Cast and Credits

Seymour — Jonathan Haze
Audrey — Jackie Joseph
Mushnik — Mel Welles
Winifred — Myrtle Vail
Mrs. Shiva — Leola Wendorff
Fouch — Dick Miller
Masochist in dentist's office — Jack Nicholson

Producer/Director — Roger Corman
Screenplay — Charles B. Griffith
Director of Photography — Archie Dalzell
Film Editor — Marshall Neilan, Jr.
Art Director — Daniel Haller
Music — Fred Katz
Assistant Director — Richard Dixon

Synopsis

The simple-minded Skid Row character of Seymour (Jonathan Haze) is unaware of the strange appetite of his invention, a carnivorous hunk of chlorophyll, which he sentimentally names after his girl friend (Jackie Joseph). The timid Seymour, who works in a flower shop, finally attains notoriety as word of his fast-growing plant spreads. The Audrey Jr. success, however, becomes a burden as the inventor lamentably learns that his plant requires human victims in order to grow. The invention eventually devours the inventor.

The Broken Land

1962

A Lippert Production/A 20th Century-Fox Release

Cast and Credits

Deputy	Jody McCrea
Marshall	Kent Taylor
Waitress	Dianna Darrin

with Jack Nicholson, Gary Snead, Robert Sampson

Producer	Leonard A. Schwartz
Director	John Bushelman
Screenplay	Russ Bender & Edith Pearl and Edward Lakso

Synopsis

The marshal (Kent Taylor), a sadistic officer dominating a small Western town, imprisons Jack Nicholson, harmless son of a famous gunfighter, and also arrests Gary Snead and Robert Sampson when they attempt to help Nicholson. Taylor tells the waitress (Dianna Darrin) to leave town. Dianna, going to the jail and giving the three men the cell key, is seen leaving the building by Taylor's deputy (Jody McCrea). The three men break jail and head for the mountains, intercepting the stagecoach carrying Dianna, and although they don't demand it, the frightened driver throws down the money box. Taking Dianna and the money, they continue their escape. Taylor, McCrea, and two posse men find the escaped men's hideout, but Nicholson and Sampson get the drop on them and force Taylor to take the money and leave. Taylor decides to double back and capture the men, but McCrea objects. Taylor kills him. Taylor sneaks back, kills Snead, disarms the others, and hauls them off to town. When the town's population learns of McCrea's death, Taylor is stripped of his badge.

The Terror

1963

A Filmgroup/American International Pictures Release

Cast and Credits

Baron Von Lepp   Boris Karloff
Andre Duvillard   Jack Nicholson
Helene   Sandra Knight
Stefan   Richard Miller
Old Woman   Dorothy Neumann
Gustaf   Jonathan Haze

Producer/Director   Roger Corman
Screenplay   Leo Gordon and Jack Hill
Director of Photography   John Nickolaus, Jr.
Executive Producer   Harvey Jacobson
Associate Producer   Francis Coppola
Film Editor   Stuart O'Brien
Music   Ronald Stein
Sound   John Bury

Synopsis

Jack Nicholson plays an officer in Napoleon's army who has been separated from his regiment on the Baltic coast. He meets a strange girl (Sandra Knight) who gives him water, but then disappears. His search for the girl leads him to the Baron Von Lepp's (Boris Karloff) castle, where he sees a painting of the same girl who helped him, and learns that she is the long-dead wife of the Baron. Nicholson engages in a search of the complex castle, and learns from the baron's servant that the real Baron Von Lepp was killed two decades ago and that the man who killed him has assumed his identity. The girl appears and beckons the murderer-turned-baron to the crypt, where he finds that she is really a decaying corpse. Nicholson tries to free the girl from the power that possesses her, but he is unsuccessful and she turns to dust at his touch. The baron is drowned in the crypt when the sea roars through the castle walls.

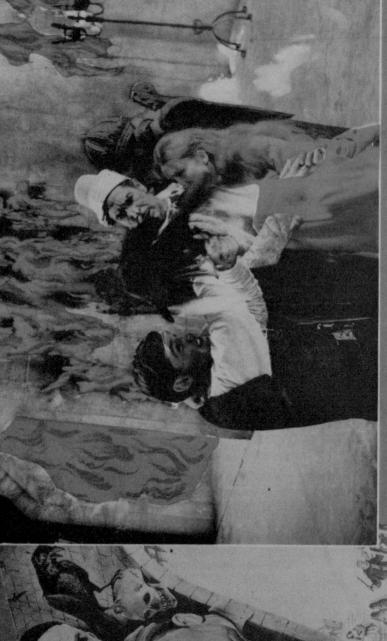

THE TERROR BEGAN AT MIDNIGHT!

American International presents

EDGAR ALLAN POE'S 'THE RAVEN'

FILMED IN PANAVISION AND PATHECOLOR

STARRING VINCENT PRICE · PETER LORRE · BORIS KARLOFF

Executive Producers JAMES H. NICHOLSON · SAMUEL Z. ARKOFF · Music by LES BAXTER

Screenplay by RICHARD MATHESON

Produced and Directed by ROGER CORMAN

HAZEL COURT · OLIVE STURGESS · JACK NICHOLSON

The Raven

1963

A Roger Corman Production
An American International Pictures Release

Cast and Credits

Dr. Erasmus Craven   Vincent Price

Dr. Bedlo   Peter Lorre

Dr. Scarabus   Boris Karloff

Lenore Craven   Hazel Court

Estelle Craven   Olive Sturgess

Rexford Bedlo   Jack Nicholson

Maidservant   Connie Wallace

Grimes   William Baskin

Gort   Aaron Saxon

Producer/Director   Roger Corman

Screenplay   Richard Matheson

Based on the poem "The Raven" by
    Edgar Allan Poe

Director of Photography   Floyd Crosby, A.S.C.

Film Editor   Ronald Sinclair

Music   Les Baxter

Sound   John Bury

Production Designer   Daniel Haller

Assistant Director   Jack Bohrer

Synopsis

Vincent Price plays a sixteenth-century magician, who allows a raven into his study one night only to find that the raven is Peter Lorre, another sorcerer, who has been transformed into a bird by the wicked magician (Boris Karloff). Dr. Craven (Price) returns Lorre to his human form, and Lorre tells the doctor that he has seen his dead wife at Karloff's castle. Lorre, Price, his daughter, and Lorre's son (Jack Nicholson) go to the castle where Karloff is a gracious host, but the meeting becomes a battle for supremacy in magic. Dr. Craven learns that his wife is not dead but has joined Karloff, because of his wealth. Karloff tries everything he can to gain the knowledge of Dr. Craven's magical powers, but he cannot; he and Dr. Craven's wife die in a fire in the castle. The others get away.

Thunder Island

1963

An Associated Producers, Inc. Production
A 20th Century-Fox Release

Cast and Credits

Gene Nelson

Fay Spain

Brian Kelly

Miriam Colon

Art Bedard

Antonio Torres Martino

Esther Sandoval

Jose De San Anton

Evelyn Kaufman

Stephanie Rifkinson

Producer/Director   Jack Leewood
Screenplay   Jack Nicholson and Don Devlin
Director of Photography   John Nickolaus, Jr.
Film Editor   Jodie Copelan
Music   Paul Sawtell and Bert Shefter
Sound   Jack Solomon and Harry Leonard
Assistant Director   Frank Parmenter

Synopsis

A group from an unnamed Latin American country hires an American killer to assassinate a deposed dictator, who has taken refuge on a well-guarded private island. The plane bringing in the killer also carries the wife and child of a charter-boat operator, a refugee from Madison Avenue. As part of the assassination plan, the kidnapping of the wife is arranged to force the charter-boat captain to carry the killer to the secluded island. After the assassination attempt fails, the captain goes after the killer. The killer escapes in the charter boat and meets his employer, a woman agent of the government in power, at El Morro Castle. He becomes infuriated when he learns that her associates left with her car, and he kills her when the police and the boat captain show up, thinking she notified them. After a chase through El Morro Castle, the boat captain kills the killer.

Ensign Pulver

1964

A Warner Brothers Release

Cast and Credits

Ensign Pulver   Robert Walker

Captain   Burl Ives

Doc   Walter Matthau

Bruno   Tommy Sands

Scotty   Millie Perkins

Head Nurse   Kay Medford

Billings   Larry Hagman

LaSueur   Gerald O'Laughlin

Gabrowski   Sal Papa

Taru   Al Freeman, Jr.

Insigna   James Farentino

Skouras   James Coco

Mila   Diana Sands

Dolan   Jack Nicholson

Producer   Joshua Logan

Associate Producer   Ben Kadish

Director   Joshua Logan

Screenplay   Joshua Logan and
     Peter S. Feibleman

Based on a play by   Thomas Heggen and
     Joshua Logan

From a novel by   Thomas Heggen

Directory of Photography   Charles Lawton

Film Editor   William Reynolds

Music   George Duning

Sound   M. A. Merrick

Art Director   Leo K. Kuter

Assistant Director   Daniel McCauley

Synopsis

In this sequel to *Mister Roberts*, the setting is a cargo ship of the U.S. Navy where the morale is very low. The reason for this depressed state is the captain (Burl Ives), who believes in all work and no play. When the infant daughter of a radio operator (Tommy Sands) dies, the captain denies him a leave to attend the funeral. Anger among the crew ferments. Two main sources of opposition are channeled against the captain. One is from Ensign Pulver (Robert Walker), and the other is from the sarcastic ship's doctor (Walter Matthau).

As the story proceeds, the captain topples overboard during a storm, with Pulver reluctantly going to his rescue. The crew doesn't discover their absence until the next day. Faced with a dim future, Pulver and the captain are afloat in a little raft at the mercy of the ocean. When they finally land on a native island, the captain gets appendicitis. As a ceremonial rite of the natives begins, Pulver performs the operation via radio communication with the doctor back on ship.

Back Door to Hell

1964

A Lippert-Medallion Film
A 20th Century-Fox Release

Cast and Credits

Soldiers   Jimmie Rodgers, Jack Nicholson,
              John Hackett

with Annabelle Huggins, Conrad Maga, Johnny
Monteiro, Joe Sison, Henry Duval

Producer   Fred Roos
Director   Monte Hellman
Screenplay   Richard A. Guttman and
              John Hackett
Director of Photography   Mars Rasca
Music   Mike Velarde

Synopsis

A few days before the United States launches its attack on the Philippines, three American soldiers (Jimmie Rodgers, John Hackett, and Jack Nicholson) are sent ashore to determine the strength and disposition of the Japanese forces. The three make contact with the leader of the local guerrillas (Conrad Maga), and he agrees to help them. They capture a small village, and gain some vital information for the American forces.

Unfortunately, their radio has been destroyed, and they set out to capture a Japanese group that has one. Nicholson is killed in the battle, but Rodgers and Hackett survive, and the attack that follows is a success.

Flight to Fury

1964

A Lippert-Medallion Production
A 20th Century-Fox Release

Cast and Credits

Joe Gaines   Dewey Martin

Destiny Cooper   Fay Spain

Jay Wickam   Jack Nicholson

Gloria Walsh   Jacqueline Hellman

Lorgren   Vic Diaz

Garuda   Joseph Estrada

Al Ross   John Hackett

Lei Ling   Juliet Prado

Bearded Man   Jennings Sturgeon

Police Inspector   Lucien Pan

Producer   Fred Roos

Director   Monte Hellman

Screenplay   Jack Nicholson

Based on a story by   Monte Hellman and
Fred Roos

Director of Photography   Mike Accion

Synopsis

At a gambling casino in Southeast Asia, adventurer Joe Gaines (Dewey Martin) first meets Jay Wickam (Jack Nicholson), an American who claims to be a tourist. While Gaines is momentarily absent, Wickam accompanies a beautiful Oriental girl named Lei Ling (Juliet Prado) to her room. After forcibly searching Lei Ling's room for a cache of smuggled diamonds, Wickam murders her. Soon after, Gaines boards a nonscheduled third-class airliner being piloted by an old friend. Among the other passengers are Al Ross (John Hackett), Lei Ling's associate; Lorgren (Vic Diaz), an obese Oriental; Destiny Cooper (Fay Spain), Lorgren's American mistress; and Wickam, who says he wants to share Gaines' adventurous life. During the flight, engine trouble develops and the plane is forced to crash-land in the jungle. Several passengers are killed, and Ross, who is carrying the cache of diamonds, is critically wounded. Before dying, he secretly passes the gems to Gaines, unaware that the real owner is Lorgren. (Ross and Lei Ling, it seems, had unknowingly been working as go-betweens for Lorgren.) After Lorgren has taken the diamonds from Gaines at gun point, native bandits capture the group and imprison them in a shack. Although they escape, Wickam seizes the diamonds, kills Lorgren, and then also shoots Destiny when she intervenes. As Wickham flees into the jungle, Gaines wounds him with a pistol shot. During the chase that follows, Wickam, knowing that he is doomed, throws the diamonds into a river and then puts a bullet through his head. Gaines, the last survivor, is left to wait an almost certain death at the hands of the bandits.

Jack H. Harris presents

Jack Nicholson
Millie Perkins
Cameron Mitchell
Rupert Crosse

Ride in the Whirlwind

Color by De Luxe

produced by MONTE HELLMAN & JACK NICHOLSON
written by JACK NICHOLSON / directed by MONTE HELLMAN

G ALL AGES ADMITTED
General Audiences

Jack H. Harris
Enterprises, Inc.

Ride in the Whirlwind

1965

A Favorite Films/Jack H. Harris Release

Cast and Credits

Vern   Cameron Mitchell

Wes   Jack Nicholson

Otis   Tom Filer

Abby   Millie Perkins

Catherine   Katherine Squire

Evan   George Mitchell

Sheriff   Brandon Carroll

Indian Joe   Rupert Crosse

Blind Dick   Dean Stanton

Hagerman   Peter Cannon

Sheriff's aide   John Hackett

Outlaw   B. J. Herholz

Producers   Jack Nicholson and Monte Hellman

Director   Monte Hellman

Screenplay   Jack Nicholson

Director of Photography   Gregory Sandor

Film Editor   Monte Hellman

Music   Robert Drasnin

Synopsis

Wes (Jack Nicholson, Vern (Cameron Mitchell), and Otis (Tom Filer) are cowboys on their way to a job in a cattle roundup. They come upon a Western truism—you're either quick, or you're dead. Swaying in the breeze are the victims of a vigilante lynching. The cowboys ride on, sobered but still not imagining that all too soon they may be fleeing a similar fate.

They take shelter in a cabin where outlaws who had held up a stagecoach and killed the driver are holed up. A posse closes in, burns the cabin, hangs the outlaws, and takes off in hot pursuit of Nicholson and Mitchell after killing the third cowboy. In a rancher's cabin which seems to offer a temporary refuge, Nicholson grabs and holds Abby (Millie Perkins) as a hostage. Later, in the rancher's barn, they come to a brief understanding before Nicholson again is forced to ride off—this time as a killer, having shot the rancher in self-defense.

The Shooting

1965

A Favorite Films/Jack H. Harris Release

Cast and Credits

Billy Spear   Jack Nicholson

Woman   Millie Perkins

Gashade   Warren Oates

Coley   Will Hutchins

Leland Drum   B. J. Merholz

Indian   Cuy El Tsosie

Bearded Man   Charles Eastman

Producers   Jack Nicholson and Monte Hellman

Director   Monte Hellman

Screenplay   Adrien Joyce

Director of Photography   Gregory Sandor

Film Editor   Monte Hellman

Music   Richard Markowitz

Synopsis

A man has been killed and one of his companions has escaped. Their other two associates (Warren Oates and Will Hutchins) understand nothing of this mystery. A woman (Millie Perkins) arrives who asks them to help her cross the desert, offering them a large sum of money. She doesn't offer her first or last name. From time to time she fires her revolver without apparent reason. But after a few hours of travel both men realize that they are being followed. An enigmatic stranger (Jack Nicholson) joins them. There is no apparent relationship between the stranger and the woman. But they are now all participants in a chase. Why the chase and after whom is not known until the end of the film when Warren Oates meets up with his exact look-alike. Is he chasing his brother, or is he chasing himself?

Hell's Angels on Wheels

1967

A Fanfare Film Productions Release

Cast and Credits

Buddy   Adam Roarke

Poet   Jack Nicholson

Shill   Sabrina Scharf

Abigale   Jana Taylor

Jock   John Garwood

Bull   Richard Anders

Pearl   Mimi Machu

Gypsy   James Oliver

Bingham   Jack Starrett

Moley   Gary Littlejohn

Justice of Peace   Bruno Vesota

Artist   Robert Kelljan

Lori   Kathryn Harrow

Producer   Joe Solomon

Director   Richard Rush

Screenplay   R. Wright Campbell

Director of Photography   Leslie Kovacs

Film Editor   William Martin

Music   Stu Phillips

First Assistant Director   Willard Kirkham

Set Director   Wally Moon

Technical Advisors   Sonny Barger and
Tommy Thomas

Synopsis

In this film Jack Nicholson plays a gas-station attendant who is trying to find something else than gas pumps in his life. He joins up with a gang of motorcycle toughs, but finds that he really doesn't fit in with their brawling, women-swapping lifestyle. We follow the gang through a series of escapades which include killing a sailor and an old man, having quite a few parties, and brawling in a bar. Poet (Nicholson) is attracted to the gang leader's girl friend (Sabrina Scharf), but she just strings him along. It finally comes down to a showdown between Buddy (Adam Roarke) and Nicholson. Buddy tries to run him down with a motorcycle, but crashes the bike and is burned to death. The girl still does not want to go away with Nicholson, and he is left alone once again.

THE SHATTERING TRUE STORY OF THE HELLS ANGELS OF NORTHERN CALIFORNIA

The Violence.... The Hate.... The Way-out Parties.... Exactly as it happens!

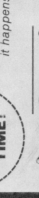

NOW! FOR THE FIRST TIME!

In Exciting COLOR By Movielab

HELLS ANGELS ON WHEELS

A FANFARE FILMS PRODUCTION · A U.S. FILMS RELEASE · © U.S. FILMS

FOR MATURE ADULTS ONLY

The St. Valentine's Day Massacre

1967

A 20th Century-Fox Release

Cast and Credits

Al Capone   Jason Robards

Peter Gusenberg   George Segal

Bugs Moran   Ralph Meeker

Myrtle   Jean Hale

Jack McGurn   Clint Ritchie

Sorello   Frank Silvera

Wienshank   Joseph Campanella

Scalisi   Richard Bakalyan

Frank Gusenberg   David Canary

92—Jack Nicholoson   (166)

May   Bruce Dern

Frank Nitti   Harold J. Stone

James Clark   Kurt Kreuger

Charles Fischetti   Paul Richards

Guzik   Joseph Turkel

Adam Heyer   Milton Frome

Schwimmer   Mickey Deems

Dion O'Banion   John Agar

Josephine Schwimmer   Celia Lovsky

Newberry   Tom Reese

Willie Marks   Jan Merlin

Aiello   Alex D'Arcy

Hymie Weiss   Reed Hadley

Rio   Gus Trikonis

Salvanti   Charles Dierkop

Bobo Boretto   Tom Signorelli

Albert Anselmi   Rico Cattani

Diamond   Alex Rocco

Heitler   Leo Gordon

Gino   Jack Nicholson

Producer/Director   Roger Corman

Screenplay   Howard Browne

Music   Lionel Newman

Director of Photography   Milton Krasner, A.S.C.

Art Direction   Jack Martin Smith and
        Philip Jefferies

Associate Producer   Paul Rapp

Film Editor   William B. Murphy, A.C.E.

Unit Production Manager   David Silver

Assistant Director   Wes Barry

Sound   Herman Lewis and David Dockendorf

Synopsis

This story takes place in Chicago in 1928 during the war between Al Capone (Jason Robards) and Bugs Moran (Ralph Meeker). The two leaders are struggling for control of the syndicate, and each is plotting to kill off the vital men in the other's organization. Capone is the first to succeed. On St. Valentine's Day, 1929, Capone's men, dressed like policemen, corner Bugs and all his top men, and create the bloodiest day in the history of crime. Moran escapes the ambush, but is virtually powerless against the Capone mob.

Rebel Rousers

1967
A Paragon International Picture
A Four Star-Excelsior Release

Cast and Credits

Mr. Collier   Cameron Mitchell

J.J.   Bruce Dern

Karen   Diane Ladd

Bunny   Jack Nicholson

The Rebels   Dean Stanton

    Neil Burstyn

    Lou Procopio

    Earl Finn

    Phil Carey

Producer/Director   Martin B. Cohen

Screenplay   Abe Polsky, Michael Kars, and Martin B. Cohen

Director of Photography   Lazslo Kovacs and Glen Smith

Production Manager   John Gardes

Synopsis

The film chronicles the hedonistic rampages of a motorcycle gang in Chloride, Arizona. By chance, a sedate architect, Mr. Collier (Cameron Mitchell), is in town as a motorcycle pack arrives, and he recognizes the leader J.J. (Bruce Dern) as a friend from high school days in Los Angeles. The gang goes on into town to a bar where they engage in a swinging party until the local sheriff arrives to drive them away. The gang heads for the sanctity of the beach.

Meanwhile, the architect meets with his girl friend, Karen (Diane Ladd), who tells him that she is going to bear his child but refuses to marry him despite his sincere offer.

On a drive to the beach to further discuss their problems, the car is attacked by members of the gang, and the woman is taken to the beach where she becomes the object of an attack. The gang leader attempts to head off the violence and proposes a contest to stall for time. Whoever wins a drag race along the beach will get the woman for the night.

The architect, after taking a fierce beating, manages to break away and attempts to find help. He is finally aided by a young boy who leads him to the home of a Mexican family related to the sheriff.

During this time one of the gang members, Bunny (Jack Nicholson), wins the bike contest and begins molesting the helpless, pregnant woman.

Later, at night, the Mexican family, armed with pitchforks, confront the outlaw motorcyclists and free the woman, and the "Rebel Rousers" move on in their search for thrills.

Psych-Out

1967
A Dick Clark Production
An American International Pictures Release

Cast and Credits

Jennie	Susan Strasberg
Dave	Dean Stockwell
Stoney	Jack Nicholson
Steve	Bruce Dern
Ben	Adam Roarke
Elwood	Max Julien
Arthur	Robert Kelljan
Warren	Henry Jaglom
Sadie	Barbara London
Wesley	Tommy Flanders
Pandora	I. J. Jefferson
Greg	Geoffrey Stevens
Plainclothesman	Gary Marshall
Landlady	Beatriz Monteil
Preacher	Ken Scott
Lynn	Linda Gaye Scott

Producer	Dick Clark
Director	Richard Rush
Production Manager	Paul Lewis
Screenplay	Betty Tusher and Betty Ulius
Story	Betty Tusher
Director of Photography	Leslie Kovacs
Assistant Director	Elliot Schick
Sound	Leroy Robbins
Film Editor	Ken Reynolds
Art Director	Leon Ericksen

Synopsis

Psych-Out is the story of the tuned-in, dropped-out world of the flower children, who took up residence in the Haight-Ashbury district of San Francisco.

Jennie David (Susan Strasberg) plays a deaf runaway who has found her way into a commune in the area. She is searching for her brother (Bruce Dern) and is helped along by those in the commune, among them Stoney (Jack Nicholson), who's an aspiring rock star. The story becomes a chase, with both the hippies and the "squares" looking for Jennie's brother. Stoney runs into Steve (Dern) and sets up a meeting for him and Jennie. At the nightclub where they're supposed to meet, the squares see Steve and take off after him. Jennie becomes hysterical, and is given a depressant to calm down. Not knowing what she has swallowed, Jennie wanders out in the street in search of her brother. Steve, meanwhile, has barricaded himself in his house, and tries to burn himself alive. Jennie comes upon the blaze while totally under the effects of the drug, and she then wanders off onto a heavily trafficked street. Stoney and Dave (Dean Stockwell) come to her rescue, but Dave, who is also doped up, is killed by a car. Stoney and Jennie leave together, bitter about the world that they are trapped in.

The Trip

1967
An American International Pictures Release

Cast and Credits

Paul	Peter Fonda
Sally	Susan Strasberg
John	Bruce Dern
Max	Dennis Hopper
Glenn	Salli Sachse
Lulu	Katherine Walsh
Flo	Barboura Morris
Alexandra	Caren Bernsen
Cash	Dick Miller
Waitress	Luana Anders
Al	Tommy Signorelli
Wife	Mitzi Hoag
Nadine	Judy Lang
Helena	Barbara Renson
Go-Go Girls	Susan Walters
	Frankie Smith

Producer/Director	Roger Corman
Screenplay	Jack Nicholson
Director of Photography	Archie Dalzell
Film Editor	Ronald Sinclair
Production Manager	Jack Bohrer
Assistant Director	Paul Rapp
Musical Score	The American Music Band
Sound	Phil Mitchell
Camera Operator	Bill Mendenhall

Synopsis

Paul Groves (Peter Fonda) is a director of TV commercials. He is just finishing an assignment at the beach when his wife, Sally (Susan Strasberg), arrives to chide him about missing an appointment to sign separate-maintenance papers. All of a sudden the tremendous pressures of his personal and professional worlds are closing in on him. Later, Paul meets his friend John (Bruce Dern), who will act as the guide when Paul takes a dosage of LSD in order to better understand himself and perhaps those who surround and depend on him.

At first, Paul's trip is cool, soothing. Brilliant colors, soft meadows, the sea. Everything is alive. The trip is getting complicated. Paul dies in his hallucination. It should be the breakthrough for him. He can see the mourners. He attends his own funeral. He is called to the Judgment Room where Max (Dennis Hopper) is the judge. Paul is asked to defend against his sins.

John realizes Paul is in trouble. He tries to slow the trip down, but Paul explodes running from the room. John has lost him. Paul flees to Max's in search of Glenn (Salli Sachse), a friend. When Max hears that the police are after Paul, he sends him away to meet Glenn elsewhere. Paul eventually finds her. He knows that his trip is about over. She tells him not to be afraid. She takes him through the final moments of his experience.

He knows now he is capable of love. The trip is over. He has died and been reborn. He is starting a new life. But Glenn warns, "It's easy now. Wait until tomorrow." And Paul knows he can't turn back.

A
LOVELY
SORTof
DEATH

Suggested For Mature Audiences

STARRING
SUSAN
PETER
FONDA · STRASBERG
ALSO STARRING
DENNIS HOPPER · BRUCE DERN · SALLI SACHSE

THE TRIP
IN PSYCHEDELIC COLOR

FROM AMERICAN INTERNATIONAL

WRITTEN BY JACK NICHOLSON

PRODUCED and DIRECTED BY ROGER CORMAN

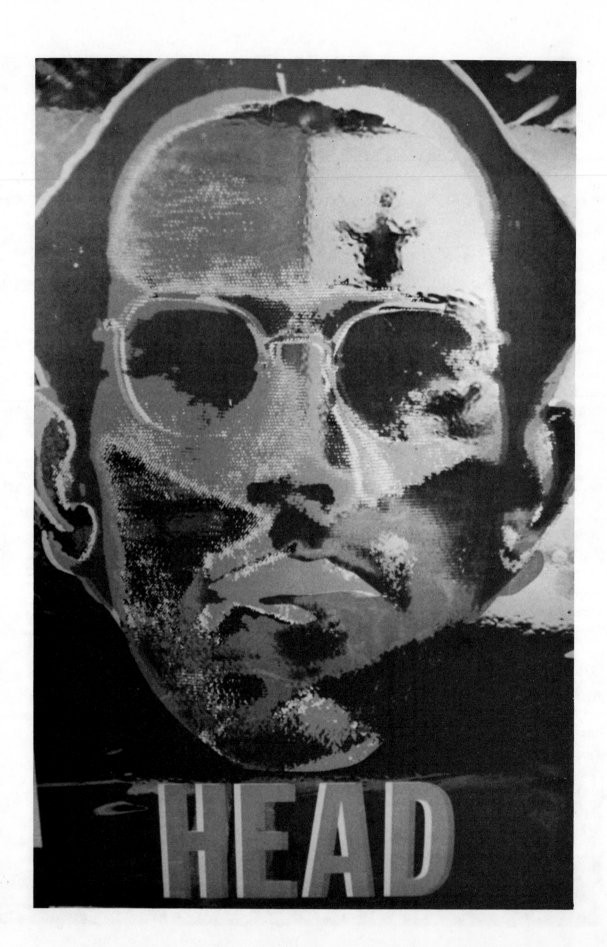

Head

1968
A Raybert Production
Columbia Pictures Release

Cast and Credits

The Monkees   Peter Tork, David Jones,
Micky Dolenz, Michael Nesmith

Minnie   Annette Funicello

Lord High 'n Low   Timothy Carey

Officer Faye Lapid   Logan Ramsey

Swami   Abraham Sofaer

I. Vitteloni   Vito Scotti

Inspector Shrink   Charles Macaulay

Mr. and Mrs. Ace   T. C. Jones

Mayor Feedback   Charles Irving

Black Sheik   William Bagdad

Heraldic Messenger   Percy Helton

Extra   Sonny Liston

Private One   Ray Nitschke

Sally Silicone   Carol Doda

The Critic   Frank Zappa

The Jumper   June Fairchild

Testy True   Terry Garr

Lady Pleasure   I. J. Jefferson

The Big Victor   Victor Mature

Produced and Written by   Bob Rafelson and
Jack Nicholson

Director   Bob Rafelson

Director of Photography   Michel Hugo

Film Editor   Mike Pozen

Sound   Les Fresholtz

Assistant Director   Jon Andersen

Photographic Effects   Butler-Glouner

Art Direction   Sidney Z. Litwack

Set Decorations   Ned Parsons

Production Manager   Harold Schneider

Executive Producer   Bert Schneider

Assistant to the Producers   Marilyn Schlossberg

*Incidental Music Composed
and Conducted by*   Ken Thorne

Choreography   Toni Basil

Songs

"Porpoise Song"   Gerry Goffin, Carole King

"Circle Sky"   Michael Nesmith

"Can You Dig It"   Peter Tork

"As We Go Along"   Carole King, Toni Stern

"Daddy's Song"   Nilsson

*"Long Title: Do I Have To
Do This All Over Again"*   Peter Tork

Synopsis

Head is a free-form series of escapades involving the Monkees. They travel all over the world encountering various types of insanity wherever they go. There is no real plot line to the hip, psychedelic musical, but the film does begin and end with the Monkees doing a free-fall off the Golden Gate Bridge. Some of their antics include attacking an out-of-order Coca-Cola machine, pursuing the Black Sheik and his crazy horsemen, and watching a World War II Italian regiment surrender to a single Allied soldier.

Easy Rider

1969

A Pando Company Production

In Association With Raybert Productions/A Columbia Pictures Release

Cast and Credits

Wyatt   Peter Fonda

Billy   Dennis Hopper

George Hanson   Jack Nicholson

Stranger on Highway   Luke Askew

Lisa   Luana Anders

Sarah   Sabrina Scharf

Jack   Robert Walker

Mary   Toni Basil

Karen   Karen Black

Connection   Phil Spector

Rancher   Warren Finnerty

Jesus   Antonio Mendoza

Guard   George Fowler, Jr.

Cat Man   Hayward Robillard

Pickup Truck   David C. Billodeau

Johnny David

Producer   Peter Fonda

Director   Dennis Hopper

Screenplay   Peter Fonda, Dennis Hopper, and
Terry Southern

Associate Producer   William Hayward

Director of Photography   Laszlo Kovacs

Film Editor   Donn Cambern

Production Manager   Paul Lewis

Consultant   Henry Jaglom

Sound   Ryder Sound Service, Inc.

Post-production   Marilyn Schlossberg

Executive Producer   Bert Schneider

Synopsis

Two devotees of the motorcycle life-style, Captain America/Wyatt (Peter Fonda) and Billy (Dennis Hopper), make a score delivering cocaine to a connection (Phil Spector). They leave Los Angeles with their new-found wealth and make their way for the New Orleans Mardi Gras. On the way they smoke grass, encounter a member of a commune (Luke Askew) and sample the life there, smoke grass, share a meal with a farmer (Warren Finnerty) and his large family, smoke grass, get thrown in jail, liberate an alcoholic young lawyer (Jack Nicholson) from his crippling middle-class life and values, smoke grass, take a beating (fatal to the lawyer) from a group of Louisiana rednecks who resent their appearances and life-styles, go on an acid trip with a pair of New Orleans hookers (Karen Black, Toni Basil), and are casually shotgunned to death by a Bayou truck driver and his sporting friend.

A man went looking for America.
And couldn't find it anywhere...

Cannes Film
Festival
WINNER
"Best Film
By a New
Director"

PANDO COMPANY in association with
RAYBERT PRODUCTIONS presents **easy rider**

starring

PETER FONDA · DENNIS HOPPER · JACK NICHOLSON

Written by	Directed by	Produced by	Associate Producer	Executive Producer
PETER FONDA	DENNIS HOPPER	PETER FONDA	WILLIAM HAYWARD	BERT SCHNEIDER · COLOR
DENNIS HOPPER				
TERRY SOUTHERN				

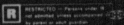

RESTRICTED — Persons under 18
not admitted unless accompanied
by parent or adult guardian

Released by COLUMBIA PICTURES

Paramount Pictures
Presents
A Howard W. Koch
- Alan Jay Lerner
Production
Starring

Barbra Streisand

Yves Montand

LOOK INTO MY EYES

On A Clear Day You Can See Forever

Based upon the Musical Play On A Clear Day You Can See Forever

Co-starring
Bob Newhart / Larry Blyden / Simon Oakland / Jack Nicholson and John Richardson
Music by Burton Lane   Screenplay and Lyrics by Alan Jay Lerner   Produced by Howard W. Koch
Directed by Vincente Minnelli   Music Arranged and Conducted by Nelson Riddle
Panavision® Technicolor® A Paramount Picture "G"—All Ages Admitted General Audiences

Sound track album available on Columbia Records

Paramount
A Gulf + Western Company ®

On a Clear Day You Can See Forever

1969

A Paramount Picture

Cast and Credits

Daisy Gamble	Barbra Streisand
Dr. Marc Chabot	Yves Montand
Dr. Mason Hume	Bob Newhart
Warren Pratt	Larry Blyden
Dr. Conrad Fuller	Simon Oakland
Tad Pringle	Jack Nicholson
Robert Tentrees	John Richardson
Mrs. Fitzherbert	Pamela Brown
Winnie Wainwhistle	Irene Handl
Prince Regent	Roy Kinnear
Divorce Attorney	Peter Crowcroft
Prosecuting Attorney	Byron Webster
Mrs. Hatch	Mabel Albertson
Lord Percy	Laurie Main
Hoyt III	Kermit Murdock
Muriel	Elaine Giftos
Pelham	John LeMesurier
Diana Smallwood	Angela Pringle
Clews	Leon Ames
Millard	Paul Camen
Wytelipt	George Neise
Preston	Tony Colti

Producer	Howard W. Koch
Director	Vincent Minnelli
Screenplay	Alan Jay Lerner
Music	Burton Lane
Director of Photography	Harry Stradling, A.S.C.
Production Design	John De Cuir
Unit Production Managers	Sergei Petschnikoff and Howard Roessel
Film Editor	David Bretherton, A.C.E.
Assistant Director	William McGarry
Music Supervised, Arranged, and Conducted by	Nelson Riddle

Synopsis

Daisy Gamble (Barbra Streisand), seeking a means of curbing her chain smoking, is accidentally hypnotized in Dr. Marc Chabot's (Yves Montand) psychiatry class. Under hypnosis to cure her addiction, Streisand reveals another personality, that of a noblewoman who lived in England in the 1800's. Montand becomes aware that she possesses ESP, but won't believe she's been reincarnated. He becomes fascinated by her alter ego, while Streisand doesn't realize what's going on. Her straight-laced fiance, Warren Pratt (Larry Blyden), proves to be incompatible, while ex-stepbrother Tad Pringle (Jack Nicholson) really cares for her. Montand tells Streisand he wants her other self, not her. Montand insists that she's a remarkable girl and asks if she ever knew him in another life. She replies, "Yes, in 2038."

Five Easy Pieces

1970

A BBS Production/A Columbia Pictures Release

Cast and Credits

Robert Eroica Dupea   Jack Nicholson

Rayette Dipesto   Karen Black

Catherine Van Ost   Susan Anspach

Elton   Billy "Green" Bush

Partita Dupea   Lois Smith

Carl Fidelio Dupea   Ralph Waite

Stoney   Fannie Flagg

Spicer   John Ryan

Betty   Sally Struthers

Palm Apodaca   Helena Kallianiotes

Terry Grouse   Toni Basil

Twinky   Marlena MacGuire

Nicholas Dupea   William Challee

Producers   Bob Rafelson and Richard Wechsler

Director   Bob Rafelson

Screenplay   Adrien Joyce

Story   Bob Rafelson and Adrien Joyce

Director of Photography   Laszlo Kovacs

Film Editors   Christopher Holmes and
Gerald Shepard

Assistant Director   Sheldon Schrager

Sound   Audio Tran

Production Coordinator   Marilyn Schlossberg

Executive Producer   Bert Schneider

Synopsis

Bobby Dupea (Jack Nicholson) works in a southern California oil field with his buddy Elton (Billy "Green" Bush). Bobby's life-style is unmistakably lower-middle class, not in the least bit enhanced by the presence of his childlike girl friend, Rayette (Karen Black), who works as a waitress.

His life is a series of poker games, arguments with Rayette and Elton, one-night pickups, bowling matches, and eating out of lunch pails. On a moment's notice, he travels up to Los Angeles to visit his pianist sister Partita (Lois Smith) at a recording studio. She informs him of the worsening physical condition of their father who lives at the family home on an island off the coast of Washington. Bobby, who hasn't been home in three years, reluctantly brings Rayette on the long drive up to Washington.

Along the way, they encounter two young women of questionable sexuality, whose car has overturned en route to Alaska. One of them, Palm Apodaca (Helena Kallianiotes), spews out hostility disguised as ecological anger. After dropping off Palm and her friend, Bobby leaves Rayette off at a motel and promises to call her in a few days.

Upon reaching home, he finds it more oppressive than he did three years ago. His father (William Challee) is a near-vegetable, attended to by Spicer (John Ryan), a male nurse, whom Partita admires. Bobby's brother, Carl (Ralph Waite), an accomplished pianist, is a teacher to Catherine Van Ost (Susan Anspach), his fiancee and student.

Bobby fascinates and is fascinated by Catherine, a cool and beautiful divorcee. He fastens upon her as the means to change his life. But she is committed to a life of music and Carl.

After she runs out of motel money, Rayette shows up at the Dupea home. Bobby is totally embarrassed by her presence. Early one morning out in a meadow, Bobby is faced with conducting a one-way conversation with his father. He desperately explains his failures and apologizes for his nonmusical existence.

At this point, he leaves the Dupea home with Rayette. At a gas station down the highway. Bobby impulsively abandons Rayette, his car, and his wallet. He must search for yet another beginning.

COLUMBIA PICTURES Presents
a BBS Production

JACK
NICHOLSON

Official Selection
New York
Film Festival and
Edinburgh
Film Festival
1970

*FIVE
EASY
PIECES*

KAREN BLACK
and SUSAN ANSPACH

Screenplay by ADRIEN JOYCE

COLUMBIA PICTURES
Presents
A BBS PRODUCTION

DRIVE, HE SAID

Directed by
JACK NICHOLSON

AN OFFICIAL
UNITED STATES ENTRY
CANNES
FILM FESTIVAL

starring

WILLIAM TEPPER · KAREN BLACK · MICHAEL MARGOTTA · BRUCE DERN
ROBERT TOWNE · HENRY JAGLOM · MIKE WARREN Screenplay by Jeremy Larner
and Jack Nicholson · Produced by Steve Blauner and Jack Nicholson
Executive Producer Bert Schneider

Drive, He Said

1971

A BBS Production/A Columbia Pictures Release

Cast and Credits

Hector	William Tepper
Olive	Karen Black
Gabriel	Michael Margotta
Bullian	Bruce Dern
Richard	Robert Towne
Conrad	Henry Jaglom
Easly	Mike Warren
Sylvie	June Fairchild

Producers	Steve Blauner and Jack Nicholson
Director	Jack Nicholson
Screenplay	Jack Nicholson and Jeremy Larner
From a book by	Jeremy Larner
Director of Photography	Bill Butler
Editors	Pat Somerset, Donn Cambern, Christopher Holmes, and Robert I. Wolfe
Art Director	Harry Gittes
Music	David Shire

Synopsis

The story revolves around an Ohio college basketball star, who is caught between his desire to play professional sports and the pressure to join the radical student forces on campus. Hector Bloom (William Tepper) is in a state of limbo as far as his future is concerned. He is engaged in an affair with a professor's wife (Karen Black), and he feels helpless with regard to his revolutionary friend (Michael Margotta) who is about to be drafted.

Margotta feigns insanity at his draft board, and he does get out of the draft, but the pressure has driven him insane. He attacks Miss Black in her home, but his unsuccessful rape is broken up by the arrival of Tepper and Robert Towne (Karen Black's husband). Margotta escapes and proceeds to the college's science building where he sets all the experimental insects and animals free. An ambulance arrives and takes him away, as Tepper arrives once again in an unsuccessful attempt to aid his friend.

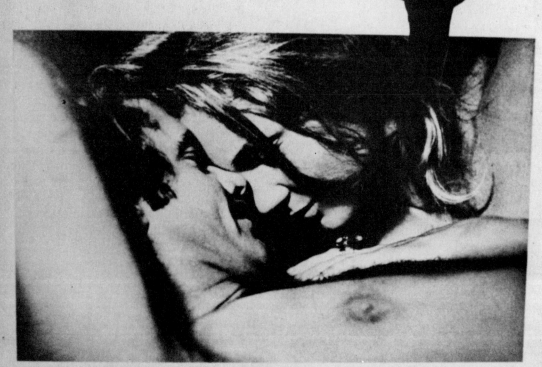

A new dimension
in filmmaking.
A rare and unique
experience.

COLUMBIA PICTURES presents A BBS Production Tuesday Weld · Orson Welles

A Safe Place

Jack Nicholson

Official
Selection
New York
Film
Festival

A Film by Henry Jaglom
introducing Philip Proctor · Gwen Welles
Executive Producer Bert Schneider Written and Directed by Henry Jaglom

GP

A Safe Place

1971

A BBS Production/A Columbia Pictures Presentation

Cast and Credits

Susan/Noah   Tuesday Weld

The Magician   Orson Welles

Mitch   Jack Nicholson

Fred   Philip Proctor

Bari   Gwen Welles

Dov   Dov Lawrence

The Maid   Fanny Birkenmaier

Little Girl in Rowboat   Rhonda Alfaro

Five-year-old Susan   Sylvia Zapp

Friends   Richard Finnochio

      Barbara Flood

      Roger Garrett

      Jordan Hahn

      Francesca Hilton

      Julie Robinson

      Jennifer Walker

Executive Producer   Bert Schneider

Director   Henry Jaglom

Screenplay   Henry Jaglom

Director of Photography   Dick Kratina

Film Editor   Pieter Bergema

Assistant Director   Steve Kesten

Production Manager   Harold Schneider

Costumes   Barbara Flood

Synopsis

Henry Jaglom's *A Safe Place* is an attempt at redefining the emotion of time, a fantasy about reality, a film dealing in the pain and isolation of a girl (Tuesday Weld) who is trapped between her inability to let go of the past, which is personified by Orson Welles, and her unwillingness to accept the inevitability of the present, represented by Jack Nicholson and Philip Proctor.

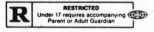
THEATRE

Carnal Knowledge

1971

An Avco Embassy Release

Cast and Credits

Jonathan	Jack Nicholson
Susan	Candice Bergen
Sandy	Arthur Garfunkel
Bobbie	Ann-Margret
Louise	Rita Moreno
Cindy	Cynthia O'Neal
Jennifer	Carol Kane

Producer/Director	Mike Nichols
Screenplay	Jules Feiffer
Executive Producer	Joseph E. Levine
Associate Producer	Clive Reed
Director of Photography	Giuseppe Rotunno, A.S.C.
Film Editor	Sam O'Steen
Production Designer	Richard Sylbert
Sound	Lawrence O. Jost
Assistant Director	Tim Zinnemann

Synopsis

This film is a sequential character study of two men from the time they enter college together until middle age has engulfed them. The focus is on their sexual immaturity or maturity. Jonathan (Jack Nicholson) is the main character that we follow throughout the film as he searches for the perfect girl. It is a search that leads him to frustration, disappointment, alienation, and a growing impotence. Sandy (Arthur Garfunkel) is his best friend caught up in his profession (medicine) and his marriage. He finally escapes both through his sixteen-year-old "love teacher" (Carol Kane). It is a film about unfulfilled dreams and the harsh realities of life.

The King of Marvin Gardens

1972

A BBS Production/A Columbia Pictures Release

Cast and Credits

David Staebler	Jack Nicholson
Jason Staebler	Bruce Dern
Sally	Ellen Burstyn
Jessica	Julia Anne Robinson
Lewis	Benjamin "Scatman" Crothers
Grandfather	Charles Lavine
Rosko	Arnold Williams
Surtees	John Ryan
Lebowitz	Sully Boyar
Frank	Josh Mostel
Bidlack	William Pabst
Nervous Man	Gary Goodrow
Magda	Imogene Bliss
Bambi	Ann Thomas
Spot Operator	Tom Overton
Sonny	Maxwell "Sonny" Goldberg

Producer/Director	Bob Rafelson
Story	Bob Rafelson and Jacob Brackman
Screenplay	Jacob Brackman
Executive Producer	Steve Blauner
Director of Photography	Laszlo Kovacs
Art Director	Toby Carr Rafelson
Associate Producer	Harold Schneider
Assistant Director	Tim Zinnemann
Film Editor	John F. Link II

Synopsis

David Staebler (Jack Nicholson) is an intensely private monologist who, for his late-night FM broadcasts, mingles the facts and feelings of his own life with imagination. At the center of his imagination stands "The King of Marvin Gardens" —his charismatic older brother, Jason (Bruce Dern), front man for a black syndicate run by Lewis ("Scatman" Crothers).

After years of separation, David allows himself to be summoned down to the Jersey shore for a visit. Atlantic City, once a playground for the Eastern Establishment, now decays by the ocean like some vulgar, long-deserted funhouse. There, during the bleak off-season, he is drawn into Jason's life with two women: Sally (Ellen Burstyn), a former beauty fading fast, yet clinging to her *toujours gai* façade, and her stepdaughter, Jessica (Julia Anne Robinson), a pretty young girl just beginning to develop an identity of her own.

Self-assured and energetic, Jason struggles to maintain his fragile domestic scene and his shaky position within Lewis' organization. At the same time, he tries to woo David back into a close fraternal partnership. But time is running out for Sally. Her torment about her future and about her threatened status with Jason boils over in a succession of disruptive incidents. Lewis won't let fatherly feelings interfere with business: he means to indulge Jason no longer. As a warning, he has Jason framed on a felony charge—which he just may let stick. These crises race against Jason's negotiations to take over and retire to an island in the South Pacific. For a time it looks as if his dream for a happy foursome may be realized. But each of them remains locked in his own needs and delusions. A fish out of water in his brother's madcap milieu, David retreats from intimacy. Jason grows desperate. Their timing is off. The wished-for paradise collapses into a nightmare.

Columbia Pictures presents a BBS Production

The King of Marvin Gardens

Jack Nicholson · Bruce Dern · Ellen Burstyn

with Julia Anne Robinson · Benjamin (Scatman) Crothers
Screenplay by Jacob Brackman · Story by Bob Rafelson and Jacob Brackman
Executive Producer Steve Blauner · Produced and Directed by Bob Rafelson

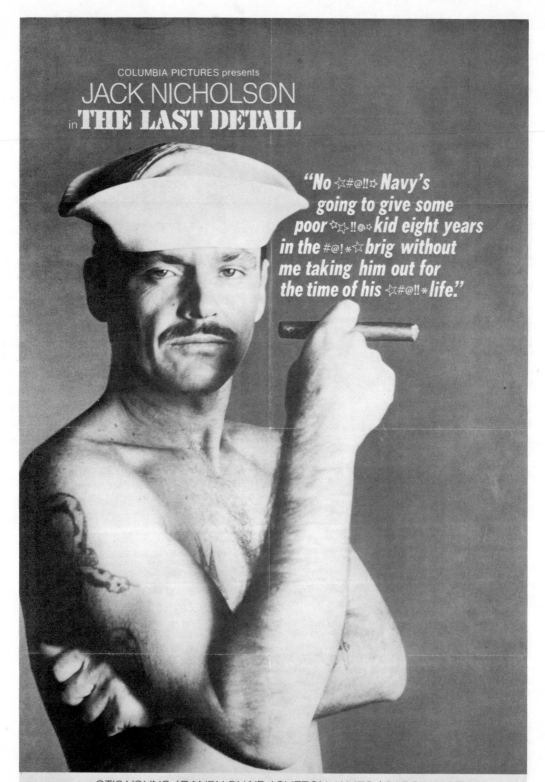

COLUMBIA PICTURES presents

JACK NICHOLSON
in THE LAST DETAIL

"No ☆#@!!☆ Navy's
going to give some
poor ☆☆!!@☆ kid eight years
in the #@!*☆ brig without
me taking him out for
the time of his ☆#@!!*life."

WITH OTIS YOUNG / RANDY QUAID / CLIFTON JAMES / CAROL KANE
Screenplay by ROBERT TOWNE · Based on the novel by DARRYL PONICSAN · Music by JOHNNY MANDEL · Produced by GERALD AYRES
Directed by HAL ASHBY · FROM COLUMBIA PICTURES /A DIVISION OF COLUMBIA PICTURES INDUSTRIES, INC.
AN ACROBAT FILM · A B-P Associates Feature   R

The Last Detail

1973

A Columbia Pictures Release

Cast and Credits

Buddusky	Jack Nicholson
Mulhall	Otis Young
Meadows	Randy Quaid
M.A.A.	Clifton James
Young Whore	Carol Kane
Marine O.D.	Michael Moriarty
Donna	Luana Anders
Kathleen	Kathleen Miller
Nancy	Nancy Allen
Henry	Gerry Salsberg

Producer	Gerald Ayres
Director	Hal Ashby
Screenplay	Robert Towne
Based on the novel by	Darryl Ponicsan
Director of Photography	Michael Chapman
Film Editor	Robert C. Jones
Music	Johnny Mandel
Sound	Tom Overton
Associate Producer	Charles Mulvehill
Production Designer	Michael Haller
Unit Production Managers	Marvin Miller and Dan McCauley
Assistant Director	Wes McAfee

Synopsis

The Last Detail is a salty, bawdy, and very touching story about two career sailors escorting to a naval prison a dumb boot sentenced for petty thievery. The leads are played by Nicholson as Buddusky and Otis Young as Mulhall, the lifers, and Randy Quaid as the awkward, kleptomanic, and trouble-prone kid they take north. The film is a series of episodes in which Buddusky and Mulhall, becoming more and more attached to the young Meadows, as well as feeling sorry for him, try to show the young sailor a good time before he starts his eight-year sentence. From booze to brawls and finally to a whorehouse in Boston, they escort their charge, but ultimately must take Meadows to Portsmouth prison or risk their own careers. After a final picnic in bitter cold and snow, Buddusky and Mulhall reluctantly turn over their friend to prison authorities.

Chinatown

1974

A Paramount Pictures Release

Cast and Credits

J. J. Gittes	Jack Nicholson
Evelyn Mulwray	Faye Dunaway
Noah Cross	John Huston
Escobar	Perry Lopez
Yelburton	John Hillerman
Hollis Mulwray	Darrell Zwerling
Ida Sessions	Diane Ladd
Mulvihill	Roy Jenson
Man with Knife	Roman Polanski
Loach	Dick Bakalyan
Walsh	Joe Mantell
Duffy	Bruce Glover
Curly	Burt Young

Producer	Robert Evans
Director	Roman Polanski
Screenplay	Robert Towne
Director of Photography	John A. Alonzo, A.S.C.
Film Editor	Sam O'Steen
Music	Jerry Goldsmith
Associate Producer and Unit Production Manager	C. O. Erickson
Production Designer	Richard Sylbert
Costume Designer	Anthea Sylbert
Assistant Director	Howard W. Koch, Jr.
Art Director	W. Stewart Campbell

Synopsis

Chinatown, set in Los Angeles in 1937, follows the investigation of high-level city government corruption and its residual effects (cover-ups and murder) by a private investigator, J. J. Gittes (Jack Nicholson). At first, it appears that Gittes is on another routine extramarital affair investigation until the husband, Hollis Mulwray (Darrell Zwerling), Commissioner of Los Angeles Water and Power, is found murdered in a reservoir.

While following Mulwray, Gittes has noticed that water is being "skimmed" from the city's low water supply and diverted to the valleys outside of Los Angeles. Mulwray was married to Evelyn Cross Mulwray (Faye Dunaway), whose father, Noah Cross (John Huston), former head of L.A. Water and Power, owns most of the valley property. Through various cover-up schemes (putting deeds to the valley land in the names of residents of his senior citizens resthome) and the murder of Hollis Mulwray, who opposed his long-range plan, Noah Cross is in the process of taking over total control of the rich valley, the "future" of Los Angeles. When Gittes finally detects Cross' plan, and Evelyn Mulwray attempts to flee Los Angeles with the only object of her dissipated need to love, her illegitimate daughter by her father, Noah Cross, the action shifts to Chinatown for a final showdown between Gittes, Cross, Mulwray, and the Los Angeles police.

Evelyn Mulwray is killed, Noah Cross seems to elude accusations concerning his corrupt activities, and J. J. Gittes is consoled by his detective associates who tell him not to worry, to forget what's happened because it's only another series of confusing and unresolved events "down in Chinatown."

a Robert Evans production of a
Roman Polanski film

Jack Nicholson · Faye Dunaway

"Chinatown"

co-starring
JOHN HILLERMAN · PERRY LOPEZ · BURT YOUNG and JOHN HUSTON
production designer   associate producer   music scored by
RICHARD SYLBERT · C.O. ERICKSON · JERRY GOLDSMITH
written by   produced by   directed by
Robert Towne · Robert Evans · Roman Polanski

TECHNICOLOR® PANAVISION®
A PARAMOUNT PRESENTATION

 RESTRICTED

four

ACKNOWLEDGMENTS

Naturally, this book would not have been possible without the cooperation of the artists we have interviewed. But, we would also like to thank the following people and companies for their generous help:

ACROBAT FILMS; Gerald Ayres, Velda Reimer

AVCO EMBASSY PICTURES CORP.; William E. Chaikin, President; Ted Spiegel, Director of Publicity

BBS PRODUCTIONS; Steve Blauner, Suzanna Schiff

COLUMBIA PICTURES CORP.; Dennis Fine, Publicity Dept.

LARRY EDMUND'S CINEMA BOOK SHOP

JACK H. HARRIS ENTERPRISES, INC.

THE MARGARET HERRICK LIBRARY, Academy of Motion Picture Arts and Sciences

MCFADDEN, STRAUSS & IRWIN, Public Relations; John Strauss

PARAMOUNT PICTURES, CORP.; Carol Pokuta, Publicity Dept.; Linda Agin, Barbara Kalish, Secretaries to Robert Evans

ROGALLAN PRODUCTIONS; Allan Carr and Roger Smith

ROGERS, COWAN & BRENNER; Paul Block

Ed Gaultney
Don Kopoloff, IFA
Chuck Mulvehill
Gordon Molson
Henry Morrison
Rose Pichinson
Peter Rachtman
Fred Spector, William Morris Agency
Carole Steller
David Wardlow, William Morris Agency
Willie Welch

With Special Appreciation To

SANDY BRESLER

Bresler, Wolff, Cota, and Livingston
Representatives for Jack Nicholson

and

BOB RAFELSON

BBS Productions

And Our Deepest Thanks To

JACK NICHOLSON

(above) Before Grauman's ceremony, (l. to r.) Sandy Bresler (Nicolson's agent), daughter Jennifer, Robert Towne (partially hidden), Nicholson, Lou Adler (record producer), Kathryn Holt (Los Angeles artist), and Anjelica Huston (Jack's lady).

Nicholson placing his hands and feet along with his autograph in cement at Grauman's Chinese Theatre in Hollywood

index

Italicized numbers refer to illustrations.